AMERICAN PHOTOJOURNALISM COMES OF AGE

EXTRA
MISSION OF TWO
NO NEW
Is Convoying
Relayed Message Which
ngton Post.
EXTRA
STATES CRUISERS FAILS;
BUTT OR CLARENCE MOORE
York Tomorrow
With Survivors
and Increases Dead to
Probably Error
Relayed Message

# AMERICAN PHOTOJOURNALISM

# COMES OF AGE

MICHAEL L. CARLEBACH

Smithsonian Institution Press
Washington and London

ACQUIRING EDITOR: AMY PASTAN
EDITOR: JACK KIRSHBAUM
PRODUCTION MANAGER: KEN SABOL

LIBRARY OF CONGRESS CATALOGING-IN-PUBLICATION DATA

CARLEBACH, MICHAEL L.
AMERICAN PHOTOJOURNALISM COMES OF AGE / MICHAEL L. CARLEBACH.
P. CM.
INCLUDES BIBLIOGRAPHICAL REFERENCES AND INDEX.
ISBN 1-56098-786-3 (ALK. PAPER)
1. PHOTOJOURNALISM—UNITED STATES—HISTORY. I. TITLE
TR820.C356 1997
070.4'9'0973—DC21

97-17446

BRITISH LIBRARY CATALOGING-IN-PUBLICATION DATA AVAILABLE

02 01 00 99 98 97
5 4 3 2 1

∞ THE PAPER USED IN THIS PUBLICATION MEETS THE MINIMUM REQUIREMENTS OF THE AMERICAN NATIONAL STANDARD FOR PERMANENCE OF PAPER FOR PRINTED LIBRARY MATERIALS Z39.48-1984.


CREDITS FOR THE PHOTOGRAPHS USED IN THE FRONT MATTER CAN BE FOUND IN THE TEXT. FOR P. I, SEE P. 157; FOR PP. II–III, SEE P. 129; AND FOR P. VI, SEE P. 159. CREDITS FOR THE PHOTOGRAPHS USED ON THE FRONT COVER CAN ALSO BE FOUND IN THE TEXT. CLOCKWISE FROM TOP RIGHT, SEE PP. 129, 160, 190, 1, 159, AND 147.

FOR MARGOT AMMIDOWN

# CONTENTS

# ACKNOWLEDGMENTS

In the years spent working on this book, sifting slowly through the work of photojournalists and tracking down a variety of mostly obscure textual sources, I was sustained and encouraged by many persons. I am especially grateful to the archivists and librarians who not only made their collections available, but who clearly appreciate the significance of those materials in the first place—rare qualities. Without their fierce commitment to preserve published images, the historical record would certainly be considerably diminished.

Beverly Brannan, curator of photography, and archivists Barbara Natanson and Sarah Rouse in the Prints and Photographs Division of the Library of Congress, were particularly helpful. The library's collection is best known for images made by Mathew Brady and his talented staff before and during the Civil War and for the Farm Security Administration photographs made during the Great Depression. Less heralded perhaps but no less important are news photographs compiled for the National Photo Company, the George Bain News Service, and the Harris and Ewing syndicate. With the imminent addition of the photo morgues of *Look* magazine and the *New York World-Telegram and Sun*, the library's collection of historic American photojournalism will be unparalleled.

I wish to thank as well Nick Natanson and Jonathan Heller in the Still Pictures Branch of the National Archives; Marianne Fulton, chief curator at George Eastman House; Becky Smith and Dawn Hawn in the Charlton W. Tebeau Library of Florida History at the Historical Museum of Southern Florida; Sally Pierce, print curator, and Catharina Slautterback, associate curator, at the Boston Athenaeum; Debbie Jackson in the Prints and Photographs Library of the Metropolitan Museum of Art; Linda Zeimer at the Chicago Historical Society; Kathy Erwin, curator of the Warren and Margot Coville Photographic Collection; Marguerite Lavin at the Museum of the City of New York; and Mario Vasquez, collections assistant at the California Museum of Photography at the University of California, Riverside.

I received valuable assistance from Rachel Colker, project archivist at the Historical Society of Western Pennsylvania; Thomas Kennedy and April Howard at *National Geographic*; Kathy Ryan, Barbara Mancuso, and Phyllis Collozo at the *New York Times;* Gary Fong at the *San Francisco Chronicle;* Sally Leach and the staff of the Harry Ransom Humanities Research Center at the University of Texas at Austin; Richard Engman in the Special Collections and Preservation Division of the Allen Library of the University of Washington; Susan Knoer of the University of Louisville Photographic Archives; Carol Sullivan at *Newsweek;* Debra Cohen of Time Life Syndication; Ginger Davis at BBDO New York; Robert Moers of Gateway Books; and Maria Zini of the Carnegie Library of Pittsburgh.

Several persons at the Otto Richter Library at the University of Miami helped me gather materials. I wish to thank William E. Brown and staff members Gladys Ramos and Esperanza Varona in Archives and Special Collections, reference librarians Bryan Cooper and Joseph Cardone, and Assistant Director Thomas Rogero. Others at the University of Miami supported this work. A Max Orovitz Summer Research Award in 1994 enabled me to spend valuable time perusing the photography collections at the Harry Ransom Humanties Research Center at the University of Texas in Austin and at the Library of Congress. Later, a Short-Term Visitor Fellowship from the Smithsonian Institution and a grant from the University of Miami's School of Communication made it possible to work with Mary Panzer, curator of prints and photographs at the National Portrait Gallery.

As I began to translate research into narrative, I relied heavily on the advice and expertise of friends and colleagues. I am thus indebted to Margot Ammidown; David Kent; William Rothman; John Loengard; my fellow workers in the Photography Shack, Lelen Bourgoignie and Christine Breslin; Jerry Taksier, Bill and Fred Karenberg, and Tom Stepp at Pyramid Photographics; Arnold Drapkin; Ken Heyman; Elin Elisofon; Reeve Lindbergh; Nathaniel Tripp; Alison Nordstrom, chief curator at the Southeast Museum of Photography in Daytona Beach; Zoe Smith from the University of Missouri School of Journalism; Keith Kenney from the University of South Carolina; Ken Kobre from San Francisco State University; Rochelle Pienn; Michael O'Brien; and Elizabeth Owen.

During my all too brief sojourn at the National Portrait Gallery, I had the good fortune to meet Jeanna Foley, who agreed to work as my research assistant upon my return to Florida. Her enthusiasm, diligence, and enterprise contributed substantially to this book.

I close with a few words of admiration and gratitude for the editors of the Smithsonian Institution Press. Amy Pastan guided the entire project, providing regular doses of encouragement, support, and unerring advice. And happily for me, Jack Kirshbaum, with whom I worked on my first book, agreed to serve as copy editor this time. I also wish to thank Ken Sabol, the production manager, and Lisa Buck Vann, who designed the book. I am deeply appreciative for their help and friendship.

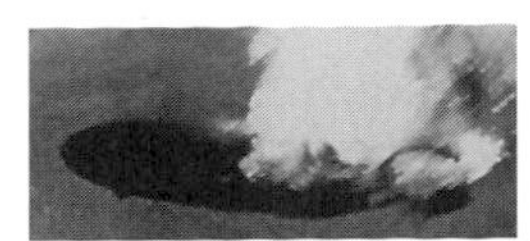

# INTRODUCTION

Through the rain and snow, through the cold and the heat, long hours and the constant ringing into his ears of "Speed, speed," the staff photographer's life on a daily paper is not one of eternal bliss, and yet he is very much human, in spite of the fact that he has been called "the swashbuckler of the camera" and various other names, very few of which have been complimentary.

—Charles D. Miller, *Camera,* 1915[1]

UNCREDITED PHOTOGRAPH MADE FOR THE NATIONAL PHOTO COMPANY, A SYNDICATE BASED IN WASHINGTON, D.C. THE CAPTION ON THE BACK OF THE IMAGE READS, "DIFFICULTIES OF THE NEWS CAMERAMAN—IN THIS POSITION THE PHOTOGRAPHER IS TIED IN BECAUSE A FALL WOULD MEAN THE BREAKING OF A DOZEN PLATES." (LIBRARY OF CONGRESS)

Photojournalism originated tentatively in the era of the daguerreotype; by 1900 it was ubiquitous. From 1880, when the halftone process was first used to reproduce photographs at the *New York Daily Graphic,* to the introduction of large-format picture magazines in the 1930s, a growing number of professional photographers joined the staffs of magazines and newspapers. Their work fundamentally changed American journalism and is the subject of this book.

That printed photographs could furnish news and information to a mass audience was not a new concept in 1880. From the earliest days of the medium, photographs and hand-drawn copies of photographs adorned the pages of books, magazines, and newspapers. However, several factors make the period between 1880 and 1936 significant. First and most important, the explosive growth of illustrated journalism at the turn of the century helped to popularize the news and made the printed photograph an indispensable part of the final product. Second, spurred by developments

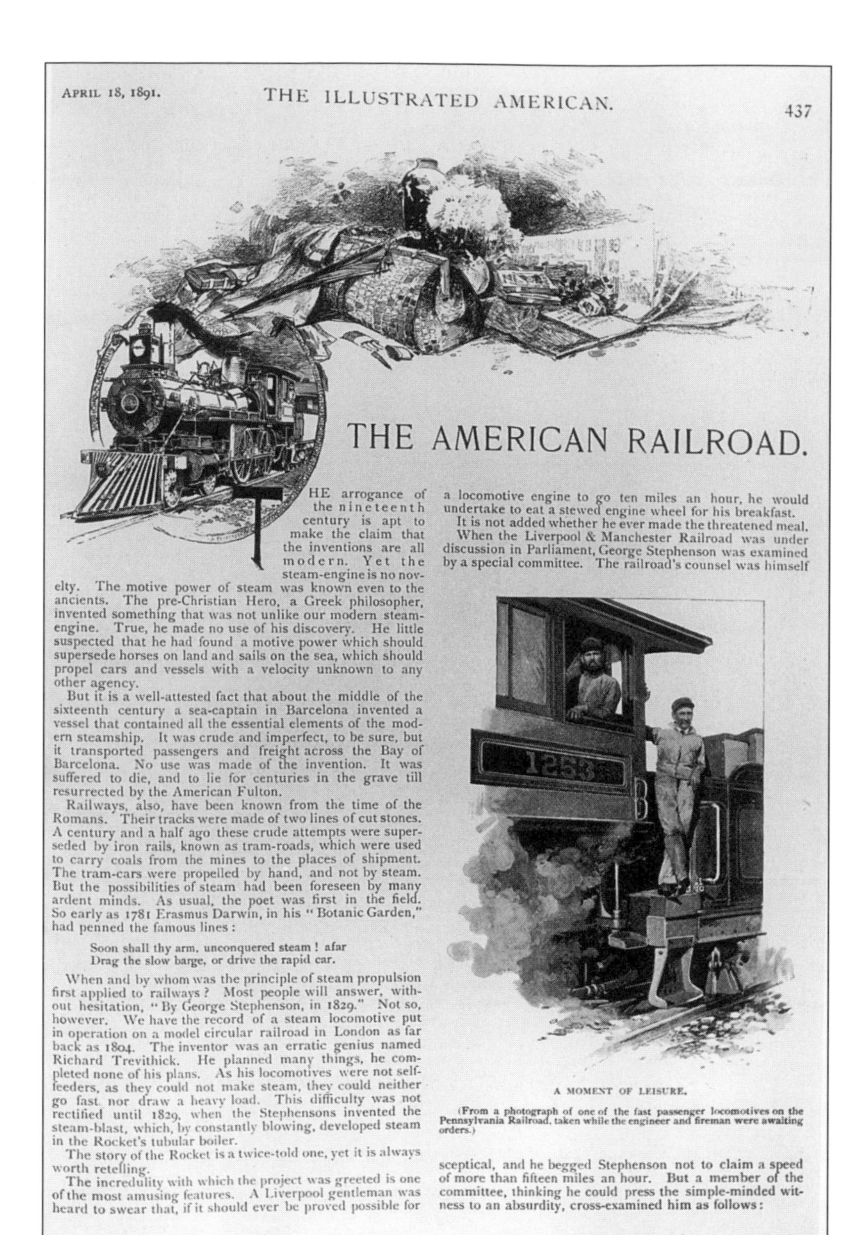

APRIL 18, 1891. THE ILLUSTRATED AMERICAN. 437

THE AMERICAN RAILROAD.

THE arrogance of the nineteenth century is apt to make the claim that the inventions are all modern. Yet the steam-engine is no novelty. The motive power of steam was known even to the ancients. The pre-Christian Hero, a Greek philosopher, invented something that was not unlike our modern steam-engine. True, he made no use of his discovery. He little suspected that he had found a motive power which should supersede horses on land and sails on the sea, which should propel cars and vessels with a velocity unknown to any other agency.

But it is a well-attested fact that about the middle of the sixteenth century a sea-captain in Barcelona invented a vessel that contained all the essential elements of the modern steamship. It was crude and imperfect, to be sure, but it transported passengers and freight across the Bay of Barcelona. No use was made of the invention. It was suffered to die, and to lie for centuries in the grave till resurrected by the American Fulton.

Railways, also, have been known from the time of the Romans. Their tracks were made of two lines of cut stones. A century and a half ago these crude attempts were superseded by iron rails, known as tram-roads, which were used to carry coals from the mines to the places of shipment. The tram-cars were propelled by hand, and not by steam. But the possibilities of steam had been foreseen by many ardent minds. As usual, the poet was first in the field. So early as 1781 Erasmus Darwin, in his "Botanic Garden," had penned the famous lines:

Soon shall thy arm, unconquered steam! afar
Drag the slow barge, or drive the rapid car.

When and by whom was the principle of steam propulsion first applied to railways? Most people will answer, without hesitation, "By George Stephenson, in 1829." Not so, however. We have the record of a steam locomotive put in operation on a model circular railroad in London as far back as 1804. The inventor was an erratic genius named Richard Trevithick. He planned many things, he completed none of his plans. As his locomotives were not self-feeders, as they could not make steam, they could neither go fast nor draw a heavy load. This difficulty was not rectified until 1829, when the Stephensons invented the steam-blast, which, by constantly blowing, developed steam in the Rocket's tubular boiler.

The story of the Rocket is a twice-told one, yet it is always worth retelling.

The incredulity with which the project was greeted is one of the most amusing features. A Liverpool gentleman was heard to swear that, if it should ever be proved possible for a locomotive engine to go ten miles an hour, he would undertake to eat a stewed engine wheel for his breakfast.

It is not added whether he ever made the threatened meal.

When the Liverpool & Manchester Railroad was under discussion in Parliament, George Stephenson was examined by a special committee. The railroad's counsel was himself sceptical, and he begged Stephenson not to claim a speed of more than fifteen miles an hour. But a member of the committee, thinking he could press the simple-minded witness to an absurdity, cross-examined him as follows:

A MOMENT OF LEISURE.

(From a photograph of one of the fast passenger locomotives on the Pennsylvania Railroad, taken while the engineer and fireman were awaiting orders.)

A PAGE FROM AN 1891 ISSUE OF THE *ILLUSTRATED AMERICAN* SHOWING HOW DESIGNERS AND GRAPHIC ARTISTS COMBINED ARTWORK WITH HALFTONES OF PHOTOGRAPHS. (LIBRARY OF CONGRESS)

in camera and printing technology, coverage of news events became more sophisticated and far more effective.

J. Fortune Nott, a Canadian photographer whose images and articles were regularly published in American photographic magazines and journals late in the nineteenth century, described the changes wrought by press photography. "One of the most noticeable characteristics of the past decade," he wrote in 1891, "has been the constantly increasing demand for illustrations that pictorially record events that have a social of historical importance." In place of page after page of "unadorned, lengthy descriptive articles," new combinations of words and pictures made the news at once more accessible and realistic.[2] A decade later, the editors of

*Anthony's Photographic Magazine* noted the emergence of the modern photojournalist. "A chapter on the journalistic instinct is not out of place in the pages of a professional magazine, for scores of people are altogether or in part earning a living as journalist-photographers." The camera, which for many years was but "an adjunct to the journalist," was now rightly considered a necessity.[3]

Curiously, the names and histories of most of those who supplied the pictures, the men and women who lugged heavy cameras and tripods around the country, who cajoled or pestered the famous and infamous for "just one more," are now practically unknown. They produced a great sea of pictures that describe American culture, yet they left few clues about themselves, about how and why they chose to make pictures for the press. During the formative years of American photojournalism, the people behind the camera were usually unsung. Attribution was not a new problem, of course. Mathew Brady, for one, routinely took credit for the work produced by his talented staff photographers during the Civil War. Thirty years later, in the new age of pictorial journalism, most photographers still worked anonymously. Although their pictures were an increasingly significant element in daily and weekly journalism, photographers rarely received either credit or acclaim.

Most professional photographers early in the twentieth century wore their anonymity proudly, like badges. In a six-part series published in the *Photographic Times* magazine in 1905, a news photographer carefully avoided giving the reader any clue to his or her identity; the author of the series was simply "one of them." References to newspapers were similarly oblique. It was the profession and the images that ran on the printed page that counted, not the identity or character of the person behind the camera.[4] "The newspaper photographer is not looking for publicity," wrote Charles Miller of the *Toledo Blade* in 1915. For many of those wielding cameras, lack of formal recognition may have offered some protection as well; after all, nameless individuals were less likely to be singled out for criticism or vituperation. In any event, press photographers, especially those working for illustrated newspapers, kept to themselves, apparently not overly concerned with credit lines and renown. "A good one-minute plate developer and the ability to deliver a wet print on the city editor's desk in record time is more to his liking," concluded Miller.[5]

Early press photographers were often the butt of jokes, the newsroom's most laughable citizens. Loaded down with the cumbersone and mysterious tools of their trade, and smelling of the darkroom, news photographers seemed more akin to common laborers than to the more educated men and women who fashioned stories with words. The first press photographers, according to historian and photographer Gisele Freund, were considered to be inferior to those who wrote for a living and were treated as servants with little initiative but plenty of brawn.[6] Wilson Hicks, the formidable executive editor of *Life* magazine, observed that the professional press photographer is often easily dismissed as "a comic's comic relief—in a word, a clown." Many people "are inclined to believe that the pho-

UNIDENTIFIED STAFF PHOTOGRAPHERS AT THE *NEW YORK WORLD*, 1909. ALONG THE REAR WALL ARE CASES HOLDING THOUSANDS OF NEGATIVES; ALL ARE NOW LOST. (GEORGE GRANTHAM BAIN COLLECTION, LIBRARY OF CONGRESS)

tographer comes of a peculiar breed," Hicks wrote in 1952, because of the necessity to be something of an exhibitionist, forever close to or even amid the tumult of events.[7] Hicks was a stalwart supporter of photojournalists, but not everyone at Time-Life was similarly disposed. In an article on the retirement of Art "Happy" French from the staff of the Hearst Corporation's *Seattle Post Intelligencer* in 1946, one *Time* writer characterized photojournalism as "a trade given to wackiness and jeering illiteracy."[8] However snide and unkind, it is a description some would find apt even today.

It is not my intention here to defend or rehabilitate the sullied reputation of photojournalists, though I admit to a definite bias in their favor. Rather, I seek to examine a significant period in photographic and journalistic history. Although the evolution of the medium as a fine art has been meticulously described, many early photojournalists and the pictures they produced are little known today. There is irony in this, for the images produced for magazines and newspapers made the world visible if not also comprehensible to millions of Americans. To some extent the early professionals were overshadowed by the towering figure of Alfred Stieglitz, who worked tirelessly on behalf of artistic photography in the late nineteenth and early twentieth centuries. The photographs run in mass-market newspapers and magazines were clearly nothing like the pristine works of art displayed tastefully on the walls of Stieglitz's galleries in New York. "Popularization inevitably means low standards," Stieglitz decreed in 1942, and the message was not lost on the cognoscenti: however shocking or revealing or riveting, pictures in the morning newspaper and weekly magazine were not—could not be—the equal of those made by artists.[9]

The low reputation of press photographers and their work was exacerbated by the practice of publishing photographs without credit, and by attitudes prevalent in newsrooms around the country. Press photos were considered by many reporters, editors, and publishers to be merely information or entertainment with but momentary significance and value. Images viewed and perhaps even appreciated on one day were replaced on the next with a whole new set of uncredited pictures. Prints and negatives were rarely archived; many were simply thrown out when ownership of the paper changed hands or the photographer retired or died. Thus was the work of most professional news photographers abandoned with hardly a thought about its historical or aesthetic significance.

In 1928 Louis Wiley, business manager of the *New York Times*, optimistically assured the readers of a popular magazine that the images produced by news photographers would surely be appreciated by future generations. "Whoever, two hundred years from now, writes the history of 1928, will have a valuable aid in the pictorial presentation of today's news, customs, fashions, and personalities available in the files supplementing the written word," he wrote in *Photo-Era Magazine*. Wiley suggested that great news photographs be "selected by a well-qualified board of editors and scholars, suitably catalogued," and preserved at some institution.[10] It never happened. Though some of the work produced by early photojournalists survives, thanks to the efforts of a small number of archivists, librarians, and those who care for old newspaper and magazine picture morgues, a great many images have been lost.

Compounding problems caused by lack of credit and low public esteem is confusion about what constitutes photojournalism. Often it is defined narrowly as photographic coverage of dramatic news events. Thomas Moorhead, director of the permanent photojournalism collection of the Photographic Society of America, argues for a much broader and more inclusive definition. "Some PSA clubs, councils, and chapters have considered PJ to be undesirable," he writes, "suggesting that photojournalism represents only blood and gore, subjects that offend the largely pictorial and nature-oriented members." Moorhead concludes that the actual work of photojournalists is and always has been varied.[11]

"Photojournalism isn't just a spot news picture made in a war in an exotic location," writes Brian Horton, a photographer and enterprise editor for the Associated Press. "Datelines don't change the quality of the picture." In fact, as Horton rightly notes, photojournalists are more likely to cover a "local council meeting where members are arguing about a tax increase."[12] Pictures of accidents, wars, natural disasters, and celebrities are memorable, but they constitute only a small portion of the work of press photographers. It is a mistake, then, to define the profession according to subject matter. The principal unit of photojournalism is the noncommercial combination of text and photograph on the printed page, not the single hard-news image.

In photojournalism words are vital, for they offer the reader essential information that is not always easily gleaned from the image. In short, words supply context. Whether photographs are run with the briefest of captions across two slick pages in a magazine, or as postage stamp–sized images in a thick sea of printed text, the gist of photojournalism remains the same: words *and* pictures. As the novelist and art critic John Berger

214 THE ILLUSTRATED AMERICAN. AUGUST 14, 1897.

## Whisky Morgues and Some of Their Work.

BY W. S. DAVIS.

"DO men often get as low as that?" inquired the camera man of a young hoodlum as he aimed his "snap-shot" at a wretched specimen of humanity who was eating some stale food out of a dirty piece of paper in a dilapidated and deserted store doorway.

"Why, dat's nothin'," responded the hoodlum. "You just lay 'round one of de Bowery morgues for a couple of hours and you'll see de rankest lot of jays you ever looked at. Some of 'em will walk out on dere feet and some of 'em will come out on dere heads."

"What's a Bowery morgue, and what are jays, and why do they come out on their heads?" asked the camera man.

"Hi, Sloppy," shouted the hoodlum, and with that a rather tough young customer, with two companions, came upon the scene, and the hoodlum continued. "Hi, Sloppy, dis fellow don't know what morgue and jays is, and he don't know what jays is chucked out on dere faces for."

"When a bum gets so nutty dat his own family won't live with him," said Sloppy, "dey trows him out into de street. Den he has to beg and steal and sleep in ash barrels. When he is broke he works stale beer kegs wid a tomato can, and when he has got coin he drinks tree-cent whisky at de morgue. When he blows in all de coin dat he's got, de bartender says for him to take a sneak, and if he doesn't moosey out de bouncer takes hold of him by de back of de neck and chucks him out on his face."

"Won't you take me around and show me where I can get some pictures of these sights?" asked the camera man.

"Sure, I can," replied Sloppy, and the party proceeded through Chatham street to the Bowery.

"Do you earn much money blacking shoes?" asked the camera man.

"Nix. I'm goin' to quit de biz. I raked off $50 at de Manhattan Athletic Club show last Tuesday night, and dat's de kind of pie for me. I'm open to any 109-pound kid in

SLOPPY M'GONNIGAN AND HIS CHUMS.

dis state, outside of two or tree fellows dat's way up and only scraps for big money, and yer can bet yer life dat—. Holy Moses! What is dis?" and the next moment we were gazing at Beef Steak John's.

The cashier of the restaurant and a "bum" were rolling around in the doorway in tight embrace. The camera man worked fast to get ready for an exposure, while Sloppy pushed his way through the crowd into the restaurant, where he acted as referee.

After a policeman had carted off a bleary-eyed fellow, with a very red nose, and after business had resumed its normal character at the beanery, Sloppy said:

"Dat's an old gag. Every once in a while some bum puts on a bold front and walks into a beanery just as if he owned de whole earth. Den he fills himself wid beef stews and pies; den he goes up to de cashier's desk and makes a bluff at pulling money out of his pocket. But he aint got no money, and, after a while, de cashier says for him to put de price of de meal on de desk or he will jump on his neck; and den de bum starts to run for de door, but de cashier is too flip for him, and den dere is a fight. But bums can't fight. No man dat drinks much tree-cent whisky can scrap, because it makes 'em buggy—looney—see?"

Just at this point of the conversation we were in front of a "three cent morgue," and, as the camera was being pointed at the

A LITTLE SCRAP WITH THE CASHIER.

wretched den, a Salvation Army girl stopped and said:

"If you are a newspaper man I hope that you will say that such places are a disgrace to civilization, and that a city that will license such places will call down upon itself the wrath of God. You ought to see the poor, human wrecks that these places turn out. Why, lots of the ragged, half-starved, half-crazy, diseased, foul and filthy men that patronize these places have come from goo families. I have talked with them, and know that some of them have possessed extraordinary gifts. Yet how hard it is to reform them after they have got down to the level of swine! We get them fixed up and on the right track, and then the first thing we know they are rolling around in the gutter again! But we do rescue some of them, however."

Waiving her arm in a circle, she continued: "Why, just look at these little children. You can depend upon it that they will give the police plenty of work in a few years. They are born and brought up in this vileness and depravity, where they hear nothing but profanity and foulness from morning until night. What chance is there for them?"

When men begin to patronize these dives they usually last about two years and then they land in Bellevue Hospital or are fished up out of the river. It isn't the character of the rum that is entirely responsible for the quick finish of their lives. Lack of sleep, exposure to the cold and wet weather, and unwholesome food also play their part.

WHERE MEN ARE THROWN OUT ON THEIR FACES BY A "BOUNCER."

If you go into one of these morgues, the first thing that you will notice will be a very large sign notifying customers that they cannot loaf there.

If any great attempt is made at conversation, the bartender immediately makes some such remark as "You are talking through your hat," or "Don't get fresh because you happen to have the price of a drink," or "Shut up, and take a sneak," etc.

A most singular characteristic of the "bums" who patronize these "morgues" is that they are generally looking forward to some stroke of luck that will better their fortunes. They frequently assume most marvelous dignity. They discuss social and religious problems as if their opinions amounted to something, and they build tremendous air castles. They generally attribute their "temporary misfortune" to family persecution, ill-health, an unlucky business venture, but they will show the world that they are still good, intellectual men!

When the weather is moderate professional bums sleep in wagons, coal boxes, large packing cases, under stoops, etc., but are shuffled about from place to place by the police. When the weather is cold and wet the bums are given shelter in the station

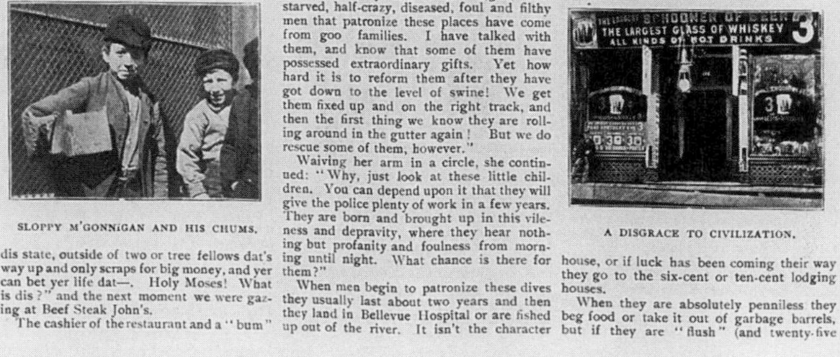


A DISGRACE TO CIVILIZATION.

house, or if luck has been coming their way they go to the six-cent or ten-cent lodging houses.

When they are absolutely penniless they beg food or take it out of garbage barrels, but if they are "flush" (and twenty-five

SMALL, UNCREDITED PHOTOGRAPHS ILLUSTRATING AN ARTICLE ON THE SOCIAL COSTS OF BARS AND SALOONS IN THE POOREST NEIGHBORHOODS OF NEW YORK CITY. RUN IN THE *AMERICAN ILLUSTRATED*, AUGUST 14, 1897. (LIBRARY OF CONGRESS)

JOURNALIST-PHOTOGRAPHERS HELEN JOHNS KIRTLAND AND HER HUSBAND, LUCIEN KIRTLAND, SOMEWHERE IN EUROPE DURING WORLD WAR I. (LIBRARY OF CONGRESS)

writes, "In the relation between a photograph and words, the photograph begs for interpretation, and the words usually supply it."[13] It is a symbiotic and enormously powerful relationship.

Leo Solomon, who worked at Wide World Photos and the Associated Press before becoming chief of the Press Photo Unit of the Department of State, wisely encouraged young photographers to pay attention to words. "News cameramen, professionals as well as amateurs, are prone to forget at times that they are not just photographers," cautioned Solomon in his guide to photojournalism. "They are photographer-reporters and as such should put as much emphasis upon getting the story in words as they do upon getting the pictorial part of it on film."[14]

Ultimately, the power of the news photograph and its ability to communicate derives from the public's continued belief in the mechanical accuracy of the camera. As Edward L. Wilson, editor of the *Philadelphia*

*Photographer,* wrote in 1876, "From its earliest days [the photograph] "has been looked upon as strictly truthful by all classes of people, with perhaps an occasional exception, as in the case of dissatisfied sitters when criticizing their own pictures."[15] The person wielding the equipment may be considered low and uncouth, what veteran photographer and editor Jack Price called "Public Pain in the Neck No. 1," but few question the veracity of the pictures that person produces.[16] Thus, while the explosive growth in popularity of illustrated newspapers and magazines late in the nineteenth century provoked numerous jeremiads on the resulting decline of morality and literary standards, the public's unwavering faith in photographs made the case for photojournalism.

As photojournalism was established as a legitimate, if disreputable profession, specialties developed. Those employed by daily newspapers were at once the most numerous and least appreciated members of the profession. Magazine photographers were a cut above, especially those connected with national publications such as *National Geographic, McClure's,* and *Vanity Fair*. Many magazine photographers even received credit for their published pictures. Those working in the new documentary tradition came to occupy a middle ground between the worlds of art and journalism. Documentary photographers were removed from the numbing grind of daily journalism, yet they still usually relied on the press to deliver their messages.

Some photographers found they could move easily between the various specialties, supplying photographs to newspapers and magazines by turns, and even delving on occasion into the heady world of documentary or the more remunerative one of advertising. Coverage of local news events sometimes augmented the work of those who were primarily studio and commercial photographers. Leading newspapers and magazines of the day ran pictures, almost always printed in black and white, and so did stereocard companies like Underwood and Underwood, the Keystone Company of Pennsylvania, and the Appletons of New Hampshire. Some photographers, recognizing the popular appeal of news photographs, made and distributed picture postcards of important events. These criss-crossed the country, providing thousands of Americans with eyewitness views combined with pithy written messages. Lantern slide shows were another popular diversion, providing photographers access to audiences hungry for visual stimulation and entertainment.

Today, in the new age of the illimitable information highway, the news photograph still has the power to mesmerize. As author and editor Vicki Goldberg writes, the public's "belief in images remains very powerful." But for how long? Contemporary news photographers sometimes wonder if their profession can survive as CD-ROMs and video disks slowly take the place of the printed page. "If it is true, as reports indicate," notes Goldberg, "that the young are not very interested in the news, doubts about its veracity will not encourage their interest."[17]

Clearly, methods of making and delivering photographs are changing. Soon the practitioner with a manual, nonmotorized camera and black-and-white film may seem as hopelessly obsolete as a wet-plate photographer in the heyday of Kodaks and Graflexes. Perhaps the morning newspaper will someday take its place alongside lantern slides and stereographs—a dusty, yellowed relic of the past. A greater threat to the power and appeal of photojournalism may lie in the temptation to use sophisticated digital techniques to seamlessly modify original images. This is not an entirely novel conundrum; altering images purporting to describe real events is an old story. But computers make manipulation easy, and the changes are undetectable. The result, as writer and critic Max Frankel suggests, is a diminution of the "evidentiary value" of news photographs. "The computer's new powers of pictorial expression will enhance the art of photography," he writes, "but erode its guarantee of realism."[18] Professor Paul Lester concurs, and warns that the digital orchestration of photographs, whether to enhance their visual impact or alter content, may ultimately degrade the power of the press. "If the manipulation . . . is accepted for any image, the public will naturally doubt all photographs and text within the publication."[19]

It is possible that in a visual world where there is no line between fact and fiction in pictures, skepticism and boredom will be the most common responses to illustrations, and the old saw that "photographs never lie" will seem quaint but irrelevant. That, at least, is the fear of Fred Richtin, who writes persuasively about digital photography. "Cultural history, political events, personal memories, all will be newly suspect while the photograph's long reign as society's high-tech but humble scribe becomes increasingly vulnerable."[20]

But we are not there yet, and I maintain my faith in the power of photographs to inform and move a mass audience. New computer-based methods of processing, sending, and receiving images, however unsettling, may not ultimately sound the death knell of photojournalism, merely send it off in a new direction. In the meantime, we should examine the work that came before this new electronic age. Photographs published in newspapers and magazines from 1880 to 1936 reverberated through American cultures, providing the public with essential daily and weekly doses of information and entertainment, of argument and intrigue. The work of photojournalists in this pivotal period is certainly worthy of study. Much of it merits veneration.

UNIDENTIFIED NEWS PHOTOGRAPHER WITH A FOLDING GRAFLEX CAMERA COVERING THE FLOODS NEAR AUSTIN, PA., OCTOBER 25, 1911. (LIBRARY OF CONGRESS)

# PHOTOJOURNALISM AT THE TURN OF THE CENTURY

Photography is now a "fad," and the "fadders" are not alone those who earn their livings by making faces, etcetera. Again, instead of the representatives of the press feeling loath to speak a word of praise for photography, or even to credit it with any of its good works and achievements, the youthful reporter of to-day, with pompadour hair and insipid moustache (to say nothing of his cheek) cannot secure a position unless he can swing a photographic vocabulary and press a button.

—*Wilson's Photographic Magazine,* April 1893.[1]

A chorus of criticism about the use of pictures by newspapers and magazines erupted in New York in the 1890s, half a century after Louis-Jacques-Mandé Daguerre introduced his magical process to the public. Woodcuts and halftones, it was said, diminished the intellectual quality of publications, thereby accelerating humanity's ruinous slide into illiteracy. Decent people shudder, wrote Dr. Royal Amidon, author and professor at Columbia Medical College in New York, when confronted by the "low literary standard and the blunting of moral refinement" that characterized the nation's newspapers in the last decade of the century. In the not too distant future, when illiteracy is universal, "the editor can substitute more pictures for the small amount of reading matter now presented." Amidon was convinced that as illustrations became ever more salacious and inane, modern newspapers would achieve a kind of mindless perfection.[2]

The editors of the *Nation,* a weekly unillustrated compendium of news and commentary added that the rise of pictorial journalism led to a gross pandering to the low tastes of the hopelessly immature. "No one who has observed New York journalism for the last few years could fail to perceive that pictures had to come sooner or later," they wrote in 1893. "The childish view of the world is, so to speak, 'on top.'"[3] William Gamble, editor of *Penrose's Annual,* the British journal of the graphic arts, though understandably in favor of the increased use of pictorial matter in the press, may have inadvertently supported those who disparaged illustrated journalism. "What can more readily convey a fact to the mind than a picture?" asked Gamble in 1898. "It is equally intelligible to the ignorant and the cultured, and requires no effort of mind to master the facts which it conveys."[4]

The intellectual elite fumed and protested, but the course of American journalism was clearly toward a mass audience that enjoyed healthy doses of entertainment and spectacle with the news of the day. The addition of photographs lent an air of authenticity and timeliness to written reports, In effect, they were used as proof and evidence, visual corroborations of what would otherwise be mere sensationalism. Nor was this trend a new story or the inevitable result of the machinations of the moguls of the Fourth Estate. As the preeminent historian of American journalism, Frank Luther Mott, points out, the "roots of sensationalism run down to the eighteenth century and below that into the unorganized newsmongering which preceded the newspapers."[5] Not even the idea of news as a commodity for the masses was new. In 1833 Benjamin Day, publisher of the *New York Sun,* lowered the price of his paper to a single penny, thereby making the news available to a vast new audience that soon was the bedrock of the industry.

By the 1890s the camera and pen were partners in daily and weekly journalism. Whether based on photographic originals or drawn by an artist, pictures by the thousands were printed in the nation's newspapers and magazines. Those offended by the increased use of visual material were vocal in denouncing the barons of the press and their minions, but the protests went nowhere. "The question of 'cuts' in the columns of the daily newspapers," noted the editors of *Harper's Weekly* in 1893, "if not exactly a burning one, excites more animated comment than many of more importance." The question was moot: pictures were now used "by every considerable morning newspaper in New York."[6] In an article written for the photographic section of the American Institute in 1886, Stephen H. Horgan, one of the inventors of the halftone process, noted that the "newspapers of the whole country are endeavoring to use illustrations." The overwhelming demand for pictures in the press was revolutionary and bound to succeed, for a "picture is the quickest and most agreeable method of conveying an idea or impression."[7]

That was precisely what aggravated the most. Pictures were everywhere, and many were published more for their lurid qualities than to inform or educate. It was the infamous era of yellow journalism, a period from 1896 to 1910 often described as wholly influenced by the flamboyant bad taste of a few greedy press barons.[8] Critics reviled both the form and content of the yellow press, contending that publishers Joseph Pulitzer, William Randolph Hearst, and others were cynical and unethical manipulators of the abhorrent appetites of the unwashed masses. To a large extent, the criticism stuck, and today yellow journalism is synonymous with the big lie and vapid sensationalism.

Author and publisher Charlotte Perkins Gilman, whose messy divorce was splashed across the pages of Hearst's *San Francisco Examiner,* attacked the yellow press with venom throughout her long and distinguished career, especially on the pages of the magazine she wrote, edited, and published, the *Forerunner*. The new journalism "plays on the lowest, commonest of its traits," she wrote in 1916, "tickling it with salacious detail, harping on those themes which unlettered peasants find attractive, and for which most people retain an unadmitted weakness."[9] The industry's principal journal, *Editor and Publisher,* also commented on the sleaze factor in yellow journalism. "The yellow journalist is just as willing to print a lie as a truth. He does not care if he injures reputations or ruins lives so long as he furnishes his public a sensational story—and that will set tongues wagging in offices, shops, or parlors."[10]

SPECIAL SUPPLEMENT
PHOTOGRAPHIC INTERVIEW
Sunday World.
A NOVELTY IN AMERICAN JOURNALISM
PAGES 1 TO 20
SUNDAY, MAY 4, 1890.

TALMAGE THE UNIQUE.

A Photographic Interview with the Best-Known Clergyman of the American Pulpit To-Day.

Camera and Pencil Combine to Record His Notable Utterances.

LIVE TOPICS OF THE DAY DISCUSSED.

He Believes in Faith-Cure and Gives His Own Extraordinary Observations.

PAYING HIS RESPECTS TO A PERSONAL DEVIL.

WOOD ENGRAVINGS MADE FROM UNCREDITED PHOTOGRAPHS OF A "PHOTOGRAPHIC INTERVIEW" WITH THE REVEREND T. DE WITT TALMADGE, A LEGENDARY ORATOR AND PASTOR OF THE BROOKLYN TABERNACLE. THIS IS THE FIRST OF FOUR PAGES OF ENGRAVINGS PUBLISHED IN THE *NEW YORK WORLD*, SUNDAY, MAY 4, 1890. (LIBRARY OF CONGRESS)

Notwithstanding such stinging rebukes, editors with a penchant for sensation and an eye on circulation began using a dizzying array of methods to amuse and startle their readers. Price made a difference; penny and two-cent papers predominated. The number of evening and Sunday papers also increased as publishers found new ways to occupy the public's leisure time. Illustrations in the form of woodcuts and engravings were used freely; many were based on photographic originals. In 1884, shortly after acquiring the *New York World* from financier and railroad speculator Jay Gould, Pulitzer responded to one critic of the new illustrated journalism in an editorial. While admitting that the pictures frequently run on the pages of his newspaper did not conform to the standards of fine art, he wrote that "still we are very proud of our pictures. We observe that the populace appreciates them, and that there is always an extra demand for *THE WORLD* when it is illuminated, so to speak. A great many people in the world require to be educated through the eye, as it were."[11]

Armed with rising circulation figures that demonstrated the public's appetite for pictorial news, Pulitzer and the *World* led the way to a new kind of journalism. Pictures of actual news events and newsmakers were soon joined by illustrations run solely to pique the curiosity of readers or sometimes to satisfy even more base instincts. Critics were not amused. When Pulitzer published woodcuts made from uncredited photographs of young women in Brooklyn, New York, in the late spring of 1884, for instance, the editors of the *Journalist,* a conservative trade journal, noted that such inherently salacious stories foster "the idea . . . that a newspaper man has no conscience, and that when he enters the house it is a good time to lock up the spoons."

The most troublesome aspect of the *World's* light-hearted piece on "Brooklyn Belles" was its lack of news value. The *Journalist*'s editors noted that illustrated newspapers were justified in the presentation of "the portraits of criminals, of politicians . . . , or any one who is either thrust forward or pushes himself before the public in a prominent manner." But there was no reason at all "for a newspaper to invade the sanctity of the home circle and hold up to public gaze and mayhap ridicule the portraits of young ladies who in nowise court publicity, and in whom the public has no interest except as they are pretty women."[12]

William Randolph Hearst also reveled in the visual. Shortly after taking over the operation of the moribund *San Francisco Examiner* from his father in 1887, he made pictures central to the paper's news operation. To be sure, the *Examiner* ran illustrations before the arrival of the younger Hearst, but they seemed more afterthought than anything else. In a letter to his father written not long before he took over as publisher, William explained the value and necessity of running pictures. "Illustrations embellish a page," he said. They "attract the eye and stimulate the imagination of the masses and materially aid the comprehension of an unaccustomed reader and thus are of particular importance to that class of people which the *Examiner* claims to address."[13] As publisher, Hearst purchased his own camera equipment, installed a darkroom in his weekend home in

Boston Sunday Journal.

TWENTY PAGES. MAY 6, 1894.

THEATRICAL LIONS OF THE WEEK

IN BOSTON

LILLIAN RUSSELL (Hollis).

THE BIG GORILLA.

MME. SEGOND-WEBER (Tremont).

HAGENBECK'S TRAINED ANIMALS (Columbia).

MOUNET-SULLY (Tremont).

JOSEPH HAWORTH (Grand).

THE *BOSTON SUNDAY JOURNAL* LED THE WAY IN THE USE OF HALFTONES OF PHOTOGRAPHS. THIS PAGE COMBINING ARTWORK AND PHOTOGRAPHS RAN ON MAY 6, 1894, AND PRESAGED THE RISE OF THE SUNDAY ROTOGRAVURE SECTION. (COLLECTION OF THE BOSTON ATHENAEUM, BOSTON)

Sausalito, and began snapping away with abandon. Thereafter, it was not uncommon to see pictures taken by the boss printed in various Hearst publications.[14]

As historian Michael Schudson notes, illustrated newspapers "responded to the changing experiences, perceptions, and aspirations of urban dwellers," and in the process significantly changed the look and feel of American daily journalism. The modern "use-paper" was born, a daily newspaper that combines news of the day with "tips for urban survival" and pure entertainment.[15] Turn-of-the-century newspapers derived what editor Arthur Kimball called their "universality of appeal" from sheer miscellaneousness. Hearst, Pulitzer, and the others were adept at providing "almost everybody with something that interests or entertains."[16] Photographs, whether sensational or staid, run singly as halftones or in splashy displays alongside drawings, were an essential part of the mix.

FAMOUS PEOPLE'S CHILDREN

SNAP SHOTS AT OUR GIRLS.

*Instantaneous Photographs of the Young Ladies of New York Faithfully Reproduced.*

WOODCUTS FROM PHOTOGRAPHS BY AN UNIDENTIFIED STAFF PHOTOGRAPHER FOR THE *NEW YORK WORLD*, PUBLISHED ON SUNDAY, MAY 25, 1890. THE PUBLICATION OF THESE AND OTHER CANDID STREET PHOTOGRAPHS RAISED SERIOUS QUESTIONS ABOUT THE INVASIVENESS OF MODERN ILLUSTRATED JOURNALISM. (LIBRARY OF CONGRESS)

PHOTOGRAPH IN THE FORM OF A CABINET CARD BY NORTH LOSEY OF OKLAHOMA CITY, OKLAHOMA, IDENTIFIED ON THE BACK AS AN "INSTANTANEOUS PHOTOGRAPH OF THE CYCLONE THAT PASSED THROUGH OKLAHOMA ON MAY 18, 1898 DESTROYING 18 HOUSES AND OTHER PROPERTY." (LIBRARY OF CONGRESS)

A key factor in the proliferation of pictures in the press was the invention and popularity of inexpensive hand cameras loaded with roll film. The public's appetite for the visual was stimulated by a vast number of images made by amateurs who liked all kinds of photographs, those made at home as much as the ones made by professionals and run in the Sunday paper. This market was catered to by George Eastman, an inventor and entrepreneur from Rochester, New York, with a keen sense of the profit potential in photography and a single-minded determination to dominate the field. "The manifest destiny of the Eastman Kodak Company," he wrote to his partner, Henry A. Strong, in 1892, "is to be the largest manufacturer of photographic materials in the world, or else go to pot." Success was not long in coming, though it was due at least in part to Eastman's practice of controlling—by fair means or foul—all patents that could be useful in developing the business.[17]

Eastman's previous experience as a manufacturer of dry plates and other photographic supplies convinced him that there could be much more to the business of photography than meeting the needs of a relatively small number of professionals. In the 1880s more amateurs began making pictures, lured in part by the availability of inexpensive cameras and factory-made films. Photography was suddenly much less arcane. In 1883 the *New York Times* reported that for the first time pictures were being taken "by private persons simply for the pleasure of it." The unnamed reporter noted that "hardly a bit of romantic landscape, river or mountain side" had escaped the notice of amateurs, and predicted that if "the craze continues with as much interest shown as in the past two years it will not be long before the whole world will be photographed."[18]

Eastman was neither the first nor the only person to take advantage of the amateur market. Small, hand-held cameras, called "detective" cameras because their size made it possible to photograph by stealth, were on the market several years before the first Kodak was introduced. Equally significant was the introduction of what came to be known as "instantaneous plates," glass-plate films that required considerably less light to produce a normal exposure. The new film made stop-action and candid photography accessible to both amateurs and professionals. Together with hand-held detective cameras it transformed the practice of photography. "Shooting photographs is getting to be common," reported the *New York Times* in 1883. "One literally and truly 'gets the drop' on persons with the instantaneous apparatus."[19]

George Rockwood, whose career began when daguerreotypes reigned supreme, was enthusiastic about the changes. "People nowadays feel that their rooms are really part of themselves," he said in 1885. "So now, instead of coming to the photographer, the photographer goes to them. He takes with him a supply of instantaneous plates, poses his subject in his or her own particular armchair, and with good taste and judgment in the arrangement of the light and pose he is likely to secure a result far removed from the conventionalities of the 'gallery picture.'"[20]

Cornelia J. Needles, a highly regarded amateur from Philadelphia who specialized in at-home photographs of children, wrote enthusiastically about how the new cameras and films improved portrait photography. "Compare with the graceful and much more animated positions of today the stiff and unnatural poses of our own baby portraits," she wrote. In the old days, before fast plates, children sat with "arms plastered at the sides, . . . perched in a perilous position on the arm of a chair or sofa with the 'wait for the bird' expression."[21]

All kinds of activities could now be photographed. The mysteries of animal locomotion, which so interested Eadweard Muybridge in California, continued to fascinate.[22] So, too, did the possibility of capturing on film the vagaries of nature, a sudden storm, perhaps, a spring flood, or even the dark and menacing stem of a tornado. Everyday life also opened itself to photographic exploration. Especially in America's burgeoning cities, the hard facts of urban living were documented by the curious as well as by agents of reform.

Of course, there were risks associated with photographing in the open air; stalking the unwary or ill-disposed could be dangerous. But that only added to the allure. The possibility of losing life, limb, or just equipment in the pursuit of elusive instantaneous views made it all seem daring and heroic. Outside the studio, life was unpredictable, and photographers could get hurt, but the inherent value of a single fleeting image balanced the books.

In 1885 the editors of *Anthony's Photographic Bulletin* cautioned readers that "it behooves every man, woman and child to walk circumspectly while on the streets, for it is impossible to tell when they may be confronted with a photograph showing them in some ridiculous or embarrassing position." The situation was exacerbated by newspaper publishers who embellished their pages with the likenesses of persons caught unaware by amateurs and professionals armed with detective cameras.[23] In 1884 an editorial in the *New York Times* likened the spread of amateur photography to that of a pernicious disease. "The appearance of cholera in Europe has to some extent diverted public attention from the spread of the camera in this country," intoned the editors sarcastically. "Sporadic cases of camera . . . have occurred in various parts of the United States at intervals during the last six or eight years, but it is only within three years that the disease has assumed an epidemic form, and only within the last year that it has become a national scourge."[24]

What was plague for the *Times* was opportunity for George Eastman. In the mid-1880s he began experimenting with hand-held, point-and-shoot cameras, and by 1888 he had a prototype machine, the Kodak #1, ready for patenting. Unlike its many competitors, Eastman's handy little camera was loaded at the factory with enough roll film to produce one hundred pictures. Eastman's Kodak entered the marketplace early the following year, and was an instant success. Sales were encouraged by an extensive national advertising campaign based on the slogan "You press the button, we do the rest," that demystified the process and promised an endless supply of good, if not perfect results. In effect, Eastman took the science out of photography and gave the medium to the people. Messy chemicals, fragile glass plates, and the mysteries of the darkroom were things of the past: when all one hundred pictures were taken, the entire camera was shipped back to the factory, the film developed and printed, the camera reloaded with fresh film, and returned.

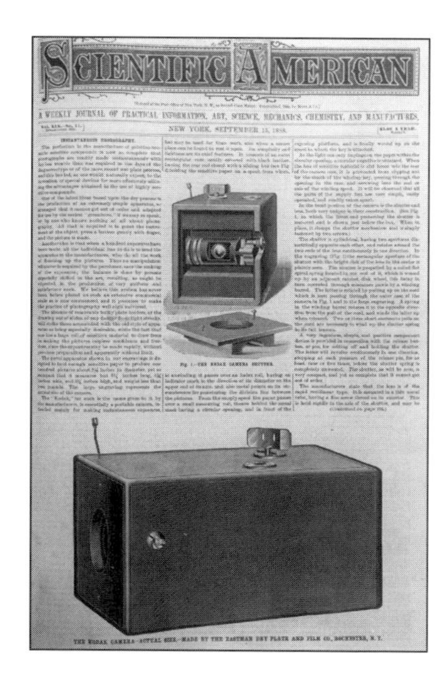
SCIENTIFIC AMERICAN
A WEEKLY JOURNAL OF PRACTICAL INFORMATION, ART, SCIENCE, MECHANICS, CHEMISTRY, AND MANUFACTURES.
NEW YORK, SEPTEMBER 15, 1888.

THE FRONT-PAGE STORY IN *SCIENTIFIC AMERICAN*, SEPTEMBER 15, 1888, ANNOUNCING THE INTRODUCTION OF GEORGE EASTMAN'S FIRST KODAK. (OTTO RICHTER LIBRARY, UNIVERSITY OF MIAMI)

From his earliest experiments with dry plates in the 1870s, Eastman believed that the camera and lens were ultimately less significant than film. What was truly revolutionary about the Kodak #1 was not its small size or its ease of operation or its lens; there were many other small, simple cameras on the market. Rather, it was all that roll film. "That which is most important is the substance—the film, the plate—that receives the image," Eastman wrote. "That is the starting point of photography."[25]

THE COVER OF A 1916 CATALOGUE DESCRIBING KODAK CAMERAS AND SUPPLIES. THE UNCREDITED PHOTOGRAPH, SHOWING A WOMAN WITH A FOLDING BROWNIE CAMERA PHOTOGRAPHING TWO CHILDREN AT THE BEACH, REFLECTS THE COMPANY'S DETERMINATION TO EXPAND THE PHOTOGRAPHIC MARKET BY ENCOURAGING WOMEN TO PURCHASE AND USE PHOTOGRAPHIC EQUIPMENT. (PRIVATE COLLECTION)

*If it's a Kodak—it's an Eastman.*

Did you ever miss a particularly attractive picture because the subject slipped away while you were getting a plateholder into position?

Kodak Convenience

does away with the possibility of this. No cumbersome plateholders, no heavy, fragile glass plates, no bothersome dark-slides.

*Just turn a Key—*

All Kodaks use our light-proof film cartridges (which weigh but ounces where plates weigh pounds) and can be loaded in daylight. Seven styles use either plates or films.

Kodaks, $5.00 to $35.00.

EASTMAN KODAK CO.

*Catalogues free at the dealers or by mail.* Rochester, N. Y.

AN EARLY EASTMAN KODAK ADVERTISEMENT STRESSING THE EASE AND PRACTICALITY OF GELATIN-BASED ROLL FILM, THE HEART OF GEORGE EASTMAN'S BURGEONING INDUSTRIAL EMPIRE. (PRIVATE COLLECTION)

By 1896 Eastman's factories in Rochester and Harrow, England, had built and sold more than one hundred thousand cameras and measured the production of roll film, glass plates, and photographic paper in hundreds of miles.[26] The Kodak #1 was joined by numbers 2, 3, and 4, and a host of others, from folding Kodaks with Bausch & Lomb shutters, to the Kodet, a Kodak clone loaded with glass plates.[27] Eastman derided as hopelessly out of touch the scoffers who characterized amateur photography as a momentary craze. "If the bulk of the pictures taken by amateurs were taken as a mere pastime, there would be something in the argument," he wrote to one of his investors in England, "but such is not the case." The business of making film, paper, and cameras would decrease only when "the desire for a pictorial record of daily life disappears, and not until then."[28] Unlike the skeptics who contended that amateur photography was but a temporary fad, Eastman knew that the public's fondness for instant photographic record would not soon diminish. What Eastman called "the biz" was perfectly secure.

Given Americans' enthusiasm for photography, the increased use of pictures in the press was hardly surprising. For one thing, publishers and editors who elected to print photographs had little to lose, for the law was mostly silent on the publication of candid photographs. In 1890 Samuel D. Warren and Louis Brandeis noted as much in an article published in the *Harvard Law Review*. Although in the early days of photography the state of the art "was such that one's picture could seldom be taken without his consciously 'sitting' for the purpose," modern cameras changed all that. Formal permission, which Warren and Brandeis characterized as a verbal contract, was no longer required "since the latest advances in photographic art have rendered it possible to take pictures surreptitiously." In the end, the two legal scholars suggested with the merest hint of remorse that "no fixed formula can be used to prohibit obnoxious publications."[29]

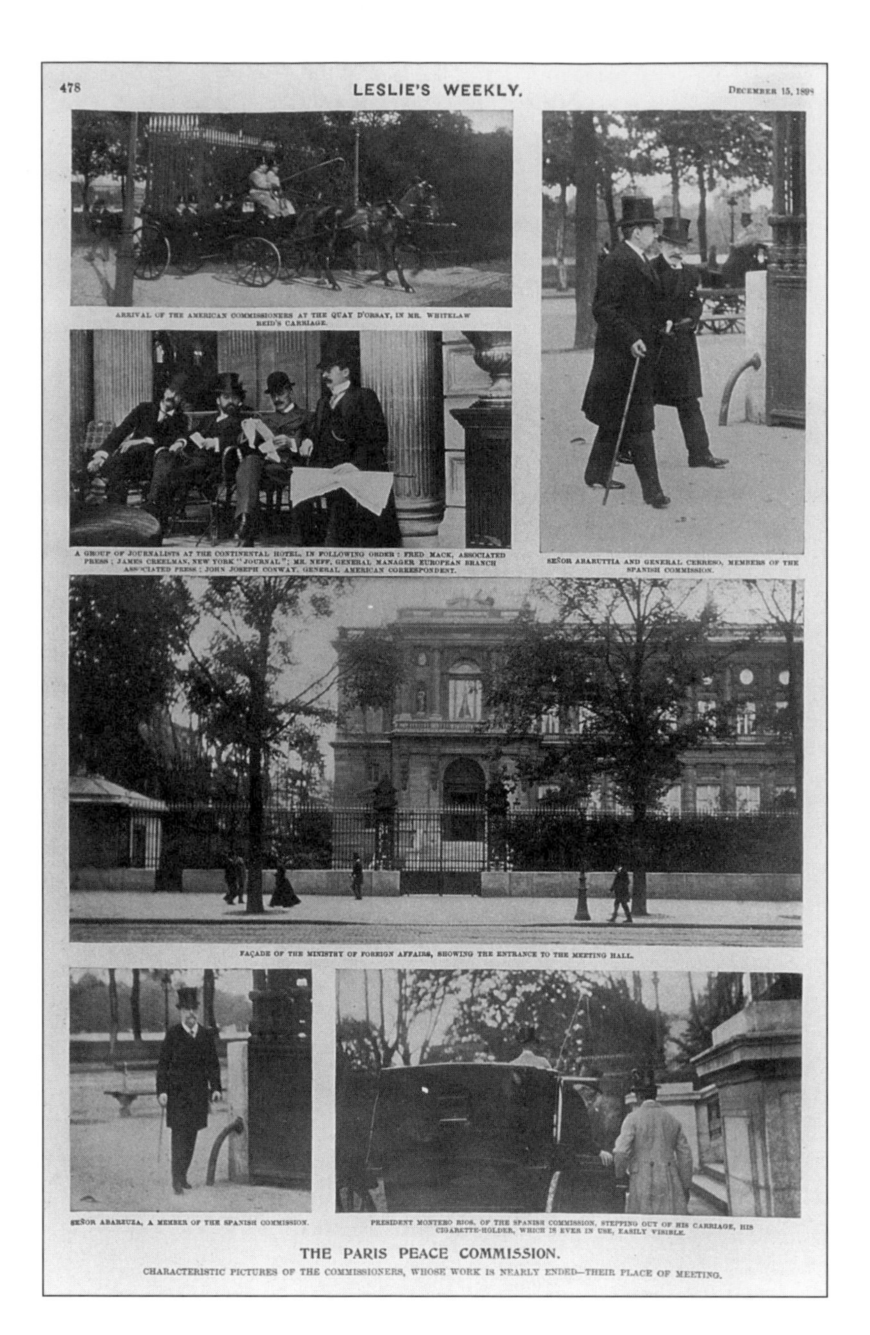

478 LESLIE'S WEEKLY. DECEMBER 15, 1898

ARRIVAL OF THE AMERICAN COMMISSIONERS AT THE QUAY D'ORSAY, IN MR. WHITELAW REID'S CARRIAGE.

A GROUP OF JOURNALISTS AT THE CONTINENTAL HOTEL, IN FOLLOWING ORDER: FRED MACK, ASSOCIATED PRESS; JAMES CREELMAN, NEW YORK "JOURNAL"; MR. NEFF, GENERAL MANAGER EUROPEAN BRANCH ASSOCIATED PRESS; JOHN JOSEPH CONWAY, GENERAL AMERICAN CORRESPONDENT.

SEÑOR ABARUTTIA AND GENERAL CERRESO, MEMBERS OF THE SPANISH COMMISSION.

FAÇADE OF THE MINISTRY OF FOREIGN AFFAIRS, SHOWING THE ENTRANCE TO THE MEETING HALL.

SEÑOR ABARZUZA, A MEMBER OF THE SPANISH COMMISSION.

PRESIDENT MONTERO RIOS, OF THE SPANISH COMMISSION, STEPPING OUT OF HIS CARRIAGE, HIS CIGARETTE-HOLDER, WHICH IS EVER IN USE, EASILY VISIBLE.

THE PARIS PEACE COMMISSION.

CHARACTERISTIC PICTURES OF THE COMMISSIONERS, WHOSE WORK IS NEARLY ENDED—THEIR PLACE OF MEETING.

CANDID PHOTOGRAPHS BY UNIDENTIFIED PHOTOGRAPHER(S) OF AMERICAN AND SPANISH OFFICIALS INVOLVED IN NEGOTIATIONS ENDING THE SPANISH-AMERICAN WAR, PARIS, 1898. PUBLISHED AS HALFTONES IN *LESLIE'S WEEKLY,* DECEMBER 15, 1898. (OTTO RICHTER LIBRARY, UNIVERSITY OF MIAMI)

The fact that many persons could now produce their own photographs merely quickened the craving for pictures. The amateurs who fanned out across the country, shooting pictures of just about anything that would remain still momentarily, helped to create a culture of the visual that regarded the image as more important than the methods used to get it. "The camera 'fiend' is certainly ubiquitous, for you see him or her everywhere and under all circumstances," wrote Emma Seckle Marshall in 1896. A charter member of the California Editorial Association, Marshall deplored the loss of privacy occasioned by omnipresent photographers. "If we, our homes, and our very goods and chattels, are not sacred to the camera fiend now what will the future reveal?"[30] Any of the growing number of professional news photographers at the turn of the century might have supplied the answer: in the inevitable conflict between Victorian notions of propriety on the one hand and the pictorial needs of daily newspapers and weekly and monthly magazines on the other, privacy and decorum came in second. Getting the picture, *any* picture, was and usually still is considered the primary goal of the photojournalist, even if in the process feelings are hurt and manners temporarily forgotten.

In the case of an intrepid amateur named Robinson in Detroit, Michigan, instantaneous photography led to sudden immersion but no lasting damage. Determined to procure dramatic, water-level shots of the steamer *Alaska,* the photographer rowed into the Detroit River one spring day in 1885. Equipped with two plates and a single holder, Robinson made one picture of the ship coming directly toward him, then prepared to make another as it went by, but the steamer's mighty wake violently rocked his small boat, and Robinson "took that unlucky step forward and myself and the plates—camera and all—took headers into the river."[31]

Occasionally, even studio work proved hazardous. Such an incident occurred in 1883, and caught the somewhat bemused attention of a reporter for the *New York Times*. When a career criminal by the name of Thomas Davis was arrested, he was taken to a local portrait studio so that his picture could be added to the police department's notorious rogue's gallery. According to the reporter, "Mr. Davis, curiously enough, did not wish to have his photograph taken . . . , so he seized his chair, and, using it as a club, irretrievably smashed the camera." Since neither Davis nor the police was willing to pay for the broken equipment, the photographer, one L. Coe, was said to be "in a discontented and gloomy frame of mind."

STEREOGRAPH COPYRIGHTED BY B. L. SINGLEY OF THE KEYSTONE VIEW COMPANY OF MEADVILLE, PA., SHOWING A MAN WITH A KODAK PHOTOGRAPHING THE RUINS OF THE CATHOLIC CHURCH IN KIRKSVILLE, MO., DESTROYED BY A TORNADO ON APRIL 27, 1899. (LIBRARY OF CONGRESS)

In this case, the *Times* sympathized with the criminal. The insinuation of cameras into every aspect of life, with or without the consent of the photographed, was an abomination. "If this sort of thing happened in Russia we should call it intolerable tyranny. A man may be a habitual criminal and yet have some rights, and among these is clearly the right to be protected from outrages like that to which Davis was subjected."[32] The increasingly common practice of catching people unawares, of preserving on film candid or even embarrassing moments of everyday life, concerned even the editors of the *Illustrated American,* a weekly news magazine that relied heavily on the pictorial. "There are many nice points that might be raised as to the relative rights of the photographer and of society at large," the editors wrote in their inaugural issue in 1890. "Probably none of us would like it to be in the power of every fiend with a camera to decorate his rooms with unwilling likenesses of our sisters or our wives."[33]

The army of amateurs wielding Kodaks and other small cameras changed the way pictures were made and viewed. Informality and relaxed poses began to replace the frozen, grim-faced portraits typical of daguerreotype and wet-plate days. Spontaneity increasingly came to be seen as a prerequisite of authenticity. "I was determined to show people a new kind of photography," wrote San Francisco's best-known studio photographer, Arnold Genthe. "I would try to take my sitters unawares, at a moment when they would not realize that the camera was ready."[34] A new photographic aesthetic evolved, emphasizing the unguarded moment and natural settings. Photographs taken by friends and family members seemed more realistic, and the public responded. "It was the snapshot camera that showed us what ought to be done," recalled Gotthelf Pach, youngest of the three brothers who ran one of New York's most famous commercial and portrait studios. "People began to discard artificial photographs for snapshots. We found that our best likenesses were those taken when we were off guard."[35]

In an address to the 1885 convention of the Photographers' Association of America, the group's president, George Gentile, reported enthusiastically that "the detective camera is now called into play when any important event occurs." Later, he predicted that "it will not be long before every newspaper of any importance will have a photographer attached to its staff."[36] Gentile's successor, Arthur H. Elliott, also spoke warmly of the potential of hand-held cameras. Detective cameras, he said at the annual meeting in 1886, enable photographers to take "pictures without making any special demonstration and without previously focusing upon the object to be caught."[37] The ability of photographers to make pictures of unwitting and even unwilling subjects and to record the most troublesome events provoked criticism, but it could not slow the use of photographs by the periodical press.

Not surprisingly, portable, point-and-shoot cameras soon made their way into the newsroom by way of amateurs and reporters who illustrated their own stories. The increasing demand for publishable pictures ensured their use. "In these days of modern journalism," wrote one

UNCREDITED KODAK-LIKE PHOTOGRAPHS SHOWING THE SEARCH FOR BODIES FROM THE CAPSIZED EXCURSION STEAMER *SEA WING*, PRINTED IN HALFTONE BY THE *ILLUSTRATED AMERICAN*, AUGUST 9, 1890. (LIBRARY OF CONGRESS)

142 THE ILLUSTRATED AMERICAN. AUGUST 9, 1890.

WRECK OF THE "SEA WING."

FEW summer seasons pass without the country being shocked by the story of some terrible disaster on one of the picturesque lakes of the Northwest. And with few exceptions these disasters can be directly attributed to human recklessness and an utter disregard of the experiences of the past. On the night of Sunday, July 13, Lake Pepin, an enlargement of the Missouri lying between Wisconsin and Minnesota, was the scene of one of these awful tragedies, more terrible than any that had preceded it on the northwestern lakes. The *Sea Wing*, an excursion steamer with two hundred and fifteen passengers, mostly women and children, on board, was wrecked, and over one hundred of the excursionists lost their lives.

The *Sea Wing*, with the barge *Jim Grant* in tow, started on the morning of that fatal Sunday from Red Wing to take the excursionists to the camp of the First Regiment Minnesota National Guard, which was pitched a little below Lake City. It was a magnificent day, and the placid waters of the lake gave scarcely any evidence of the fury of the storm which had created such havoc the night before. After a pleasant day had been spent at the camp, Captain Wotheren, of the *Sea Wing*, prepared to return. He was asked to postpone his departure, as there was a storm approaching, and some of the excursionists knew well that Lake Pepin was noted for its ugly seas when swept by a wind of any violence. Besides this, the steamers that ply on the upper Mississippi—and the *Sea Wing* was no exception—are not built to weather a gale. Owing to the shallowness of the waters near shore the draught of the steamers is light; they are smooth-keeled, and their bulk and weight are almost entirely above water-line. Their engines are not powerful, and they present a huge surface above the water to resist the blast of a storm. But Captain Wotheren was stubborn. He did not believe the storm would be serious, and at eight o'clock in the evening started off up Lake Pepin toward Red Wing. The wind was already blowing a gale, against which the *Sea Wing* could make hardly any headway. Just above Lake City a point runs out from the Minnesota shore. To get around this point the steamer had to turn slightly toward the Wisconsin shore. While doing this the

ARRIVAL OF SEARCH-PARTY.

hurricane seized her, and in a second she was beyond the control of her engines and crew. The barge in tow, which had a quarter of the excursionists on board, was struck by the gale at the same time, and most of her passengers were thrown into the seething waste of waters. An attempt was made to beach the *Sea Wing*, but it failed. The steamer righted herself for a moment, but an instant later she keeled over and lay helpless, the great waves breaking over her. She drifted a short way back to the point and then sank, with most of those on board. The barge had meanwhile broken loose from the *Sea Wing* and floated down opposite Lake City, where about twenty people who were still on board were rescued.

Then followed an awful scene. From the waters of the usually peaceful lake, now lashed into fury by the wind, arose the shrieks of men, women, and children who were struggling in the angry waves. Every now and then a flash of lightning lit up the grand but terrible sight; revealed the waves lashed into mountains by the fury of the wind and the strugglers in the water. "Here and there," relates a survivor, "could be seen the white dress of some poor woman or child. One poor creature I saw go down clinging to her child, whom she had been trying to save. The mother—for mother she evidently was—had fastened a life-preserver about her waist, and with its aid was trying to keep herself and child afloat until help could reach them. Suddenly I saw the woman release the hold she had upon

WRECKED STEAMER "SEA WING."

observer in 1902, "there is an absolutely endless demand for photographs as illustration." Magazine and newspaper editors were often "very hard put . . . to discover suitable pictures wherewith to fill their pages," and most were unconcerned who made their pictures. The single most common criticism, in fact, was that amateurs tended to lack sufficient "businesslike enterprise," and thus sometimes failed to market their most publishable pictures.[38]

Some editors, no doubt aware of the public's fondness for snapshots, used round Kodak-like pictures in their layouts. Although usually there is no way of knowing if the printed images were originally made with Kodaks, most of them seem genuine, which is precisely the point. In an 1890 article describing the capsizing during a violent summer storm of the *Sea Wing*, an excursion steamboat that plied the waters of Lake Pepin on the

Minnesota-Wisconsin border, the editors of the *Illustrated American* used six round pictures to tell the grim story. The illustrations, which describe the wreckage of the steamer and the search for bodies, are uncredited, and some have been retouched, but they have an aura of authenticity about them, like pictures made by an amateur with a Kodak.[39]

Professionals who admired the informality of snap-shot photography did not immediately trade in their heavy view cameras for one of the new hand-held models. Perhaps in part to distinguish their pictures from those produced by mere amateurs, commercial and journalistic photographers continued to use bulky 8×10 cameras for at least a decade after Eastman introduced his little Kodak. All that changed in 1898, however, when William F. Folmer introduced the Graflex camera, an instrument that did for professionals what the Kodak had done for amateurs. The Graflex used either 4×6- or 5×7-inch film. A mirror behind the lens reflected the image onto a plate of ground glass at the top of the camera, and a tall leather hood kept out extraneous light. The shutter was a focal-plane type, located just in front of the film, which made speeds as fast as one thousandth of a second possible. "Here was a camera a man could hold in his

PHOTOGRAPH BY JAMES HARE OF PHOTOJOURNALISTS WITH THEIR GRAFLEX CAMERAS COVERING THE AFTERMATH OF A DISASTROUS DYNAMITE EXPLOSION IN COMMUNIPAW, N.J., IN 1911. (PHOTOGRAPHY COLLECTION, HARRY RANSOM HUMANITIES RESEARCH CENTER, UNIVERSITY OF TEXAS, AUSTIN)

hands, focusing by looking into a hood, and seeing his picture up to the instant of opening the shutter," remembered veteran press photographer Jack Wright. "Revolutionary is a mild word to describe such a camera."[40]

At the end of the nineteenth century, even those who complained about the pushy omniscience of cameras admitted that in some areas at least, press photography could be useful. Few objected, for example, to the photographic coverage of the rise and fall of political figures. Politicians had long since discovered the camera's ability to publicize, and by 1880 the public was used to seeing and perhaps even owning portraits of their favorite candidates. Illustrated newspapers and magazines ran photographs of politicians as a kind of public service, knowing full well that the public wanted to ponder the faces of their leaders. In July 1880, for instance, the editors of *Harper's Weekly* thanked the well-known portrait photographers Gotthelf Pach and Napoleon Sarony for the "excellent photographs from which the portraits of the Republican candidates for President and Vice President were engraved." The previous week's issue contained engravings of James Garfield and Chester Arthur but no credit; the July 3 blurb was thus both acknowledgment and apology.[41]

Just a few months after his inauguration on March 4, 1881, Garfield was shot and critically wounded by Charles Guiteau, who was distraught by his failure to procure work in the new administration. All summer long the slow decline of the president was front-page news. When Garfield finally died in Elberon, New Jersey, on September 19, 1881, interest in his portrait peaked. "Nothing has ever found so extraordinary a market as the Garfield pictures," a leading dealer of photographs told a reporter from the *New York Times* in 1882. "The day after the President died the rush for them . . . trebled." Asked by one New York City wholesaler for a million "cheap photographs of Gen. Garfield," the dealer declined somewhat reluctantly, but still "kept 300 negatives running, got out 10,000 a day for three months, and couldn't begin to fill the orders."[42]

Of course, not all office-holders were photogenic, nor did they all relish the attentions of the press. After Grover Cleveland's defeat by Benjamin Harrison in 1888, for instance, there were complaints about pictures of the new president and his family. One dealer in Washington, D.C., told a reporter for the *Philadelphia Telegraph* that "Harrison has hardly any sale; Mrs. Harrison practically none; and I have not had any of the Cabinet on sale for two months. It has been a dead loss." In this case the dealer assured the reporter that poor sales had nothing at all to do with politics: "it was merely a matter of youth and beauty."[43]

Judge Alton Brooks Parker, who defeated William Randolph Hearst for the presidential nomination of the Democratic Party in 1904, was decidedly unenthusiastic about the news photographers who dogged his every move during the campaign. Finally, he announced a new policy: beginning in July, no candid photography would be permitted. "I reserve the right," Parker said, "to put my hands in my pockets and assume comfortable attitudes without being everlastingly afraid that I shall be snapped by some fellow with a camera."[44] The judge's strategy stemmed, no doubt,

UNCREDITED PHOTOGRAPHS MADE FOR UNDERWOOD AND UNDERWOOD AND DISTRIBUTED BY THE ELLIOT SERVICE COMPANY. THE ACCOMPANYING CAPTION EXPLAINS THAT THE IMAGES ARE "NEWS PICTURES FOR USE IN WINDOW DISPLAY" AND IDENTIFIES THE SUBJECT AS AARON S. WATKINS, NOMINEE OF THE NATIONAL PROHIBITION PARTY IN THE 1920 PRESIDENTIAL CAMPAIGN. "DR. WATKINS IS A COLLEGE PROFESSOR, AND AS PROFESSORS' SALARIES THESE DAYS ARE LESS THAN MOST MECHANICS' WAGES, HE OFTEN LENDS A HAND WITH THE CHORES." (LIBRARY OF CONGRESS)

from a realization that unplanned photographs could do much more harm than good. He was right. "If I could photograph a presidential candidate with a cigarette in his mouth I'd guarantee him defeat, no matter how strong might be his party," crowed one veteran press photographer during the 1904 campaign. "If I could photograph him with his hair parted in the middle, or with his trousers rolled up, or with a full-dress evening suit on, he'd be defeated again." This was Judge Parker's worst nightmare, a virtual guarantee that one's message could be fatally compromised by a few candid pictures in the press. Americans "won't stand nonsense," concluded the unnamed photographer. "They want for their representatives plain men, not whippersnappers. There isn't a farmer in America that would vote for a cigarette smoker if the fellow was only running for municipal night watchman."[45]

Parker's reticence was applauded in some circles, but against Theodore Roosevelt, who clearly appreciated the publicity value of photographs, it made no political sense at all. No American politician was more savvy about the press and photography than Teddy Roosevelt, who eagerly acceded to those wishing to record his likeness. None of the Roosevelts was camera shy, according to Gotthelf Pach, though his first encounter with Teddy was distinctly nonphotographic. As a child, Roosevelt was a "regular caution," and one day he hurled a sizable rock through the skylight of the Pach brothers' fancy Broadway studio. They refrained from ratting on young Teddy, since the family were such good customers.[46]

Especially during his national campaigns, first as William McKinley's running mate in 1900, then as president in 1904, and finally as the standard-bearer of the Progressive Party in 1912, Roosevelt made sure that

UNCREDITED PHOTOGRAPH MADE FOR UNDERWOOD AND UNDERWOOD OF PRESIDENT ROOSEVELT SPEAKING IN BRATTLEBORO, VT., C. 1902. (CALIFORNIA MUSEUM OF PHOTOGRAPHY AT THE UNIVERSITY OF CALIFORNIA, RIVERSIDE)

news photographers had plenty of access. Views of Roosevelt speaking to crowds of rapt citizens from the rear platform of his campaign train were particularly popular. At each stop, photographers accompanying the candidate rushed back to record the scene, then elbowed their way back to the train. If they tarried, they were likely to be left behind. Once, Jimmy Hare, the tireless photographer for *Collier's* magazine, was about to be abandoned when he "jumped and managed to get a precarious 'toe-and-finger hold' on the last car." The train rumbled several miles down the track before Hare was able to get the attention of his somewhat amused colleagues inside.[47]

Roosevelt's friendly relations with the picture press apparently extended to his running mate in 1904, Indiana senator Charles Warren Fairbanks. One of those who accompanied Fairbanks on his various cross-country campaign swings was Robert L. Dunn, whose experience included stints with both McKinley and Roosevelt as well as several months covering the Russo-Japanese War. Dunn worked like a one-man wire service. His specialty was the candid view, and according to the editors of the *Photographer* magazine, Dunn produced hundreds of prints each day in the train's darkroom, sometimes mailing sets of "twenty to twenty-five pictures each . . . to a score of big daily papers in different parts of the country."[48]

STEREOGRAPH BY AN UNIDENTIFIED PHOTOGRAPHER AND PUBLISHED BY UNDERWOOD AND UNDERWOOD. "AWAY FROM THE CASES OF STATE—PRESIDENT ROOSEVELT READY TO ENTER YELLOWSTONE NATIONAL PARK, WYOMING. (CALIFORNIA MUSEUM OF PHOTOGRAPHY AT THE UNIVERSITY OF CALIFORNIA, RIVERSIDE)

Ironically, the pictures supplied by Dunn and other press photographers were often run as engravings or woodcuts well after the introduction of the halftone process in 1880. During the 1880s and 1890s, halftone process work was slowed chiefly by the vigorous objections of those employed as sketch and graphic artists. Even at the *New York Daily Graphic,* which introduced halftones in 1880, the process made little headway. In daily journalism halftones were thought to be impractical, though as historian Sally Stein rightly points out, upscale monthlies like *Harper's* and the *Century* ran halftones in addition to traditional sketches and other hand-drawn illustrations.[49]

Newspaper artists argued that readers cherished and responded to art, not to the quick and cheap pictures produced by cameras. As R. Smith Schuneman notes, graphic artists insisted that pictorial journalism was fine as long as published pictures maintained a certain level of aesthetic purity. In the end there was but "one key requirement: that the work be accomplished by hand."[50] As a result, for a decade and a half after Stephen Horgan published the first halftone, pictures of news events, whether originally drawn by an artist or made with a camera, were most often printed as woodcuts or engravings.

Photographers and some publishers argued that the process engraving, the halftone, is far better suited to journalistic illustration because it is machine-made and therefore more accurate than any hand-drawn picture. Horgan, the halftone's most vocal early supporter, told the members of the photographic section of the American Institute in 1886 that newspapers in the business of informing the people about the events of the day could no longer afford to publish illustrations based more upon fertile imagination than fact. "The newspaper aims to give a faithful picture of current history. How much more truthful would that record be if it were made by the unprejudiced and impartial camera?"[51]

Timeliness was another consideration, especially at daily newspapers. The creation of a detailed engraving or woodcut could take many hours, or even days, and in a profession governed by the iron logic of the deadline, speed is essential. "A cut which formerly required several days to produce can now be turned out in a few hours," argued Harry Jenkins on behalf of the Inland Printer Company in 1896.[52] Combined with its greater fidelity to the original image and comparatively low-cost, the halftone was bound to succeed. Publishers could not long resist the cheapness, speed, and accuracy of halftones, and by the turn of the century the process was firmly established in the newspaper business.

To emphasize the importance of photographs in daily journalism, the May 1900 issue of *Wilson's Photographic Magazine* carried an unsigned

FRANK LESLIE'S ILLUSTRATED NEWSPAPER

No. 1,387.—Vol. LIV. NEW YORK—FOR THE WEEK ENDING APRIL 22, 1882. [Price 10 Cents.

MISSOURI.—JESSE JAMES, THE NOTORIOUS DESPERADO, KILLED AT ST. JOSEPH, APRIL 3d.

AN ENGRAVING MADE BY AN UNIDENTIFIED ARTIST FROM A PHOTOGRAPH BY ALEXANDER LOZO OF THE "NOTORIOUS DESPERADO," JESSE WOODSON JAMES. PUBLISHED IN *FRANK LESLIE'S ILLUSTRATED NEWSPAPER*, APRIL 22, 1882. (NATIONAL PORTRAIT GALLERY, SMITHSONIAN INSTITUTION) article extolling their use at the *New York Tribune*. Beginning on January 21, 1897, when the paper published a halftone portrait of Thomas C. Platt, the new Republican senator from New York, there was an effort among the city's major newspapers to publish more photographs and run them as halftones. The author claimed that the *Tribune*'s photographic illustrations "have been the marvel of other newspaper proprietors, both in this country and Europe." Using the latest high-speed presses, the *Tribune* could now furnish the public with words and pictures of events just a few hours after the last click of the shutter.[53]

As editors and publishers soon found out, technological improvements made photography more accessible to the press and the public, and the slow acceptance of halftone engraving completed the equation. After 1900 illustrated journalism increasingly meant photojournalism. "The demand for illustrations for periodical publications is . . . so imperative," wrote amateur Walter Sprange in 1897, "that almost every possible device is exercised by the publishers . . . to secure original prints." Amateurs as well as professionals now could find numerous outlets for their work, and the volume of pictures being reproduced meant that the reading public began to recognize and appreciate the "individual characteristics of known workers."[54] Photographers may not have been welcomed into the newsroom with open arms—most of them were still viewed with a mixture of derision and suspicion—but the pictures they made were vital.

"Stories are good," wrote Charles Watson Meade in 1904, "but illustrable stories are better." This meant that the lowly photographer's needs frequently outweighed those of reporters. After all, continued Meade, "the reporter can get his facts after the act from eye witnesses and others. The photographer must catch the act itself with the camera."[55] Hearsay and second-hand reports are useless to photographers. Even the most word-bound editors began to realize that in order to procure and run effective photographs, moribund newsroom practices had to change.

Instead of relying on amateurs and the occasional professional to furnish suitable pictures on a freelance basis, newspapers and magazines began hiring full-time staff photographers. Jack Price, for many years the chief of photography at the *New York Morning World* and later an editor and columnist for *Editor and Publisher,* described the extraordinary physical demands placed on these first professional news photographers. Despite the popularity of Kodaks and other small automatic cameras, they needed to carry a daunting array of equipment and supplies to ensure success in the most adverse conditions. "The news photographer of the tin type era was a sturdy lad who carried around a dog house facetiously called a camera," recalled Price. But the camera and a collection of glass plates was only the beginning. In order to get suitable results inside and at night, photographers also toted a tripod and "some heavy hardware known as a flash/gun . . . [with] enough high-explosive magnesium powder to blow his whiskers off." Encumbered by equipment and pressured by rigid deadlines and the absolute need to always return with a picture, *any* picture, the press photographer was "a much handicapped and misunderstood

UNCREDITED PHOTOGRAPH OF PRESS PHOTOGRAPHERS GATHERED AROUND PAULINA LONGWORTH, DAUGHTER OF NICK AND ALICE LONGWORTH AND GRANDDAUGHTER OF TEDDY ROOSEVELT, AND HER NURSEMAID. (LIBRARY OF CONGRESS)

grown-up in an infant department of journalism that was just beginning to look at life through the lens of a camera."[56]

Professionals developed an informal working rationale, a methodology based as much on the pictorial needs of their employers as on their own skill and stamina. "It is obvious that the news photographer must have a fine nose for news, must not flinch where others flee, and always look alive, [and] give no quarter even to people who do not wish to be photographed," wrote Gilson Willets, a reporter and camera aficionado, in 1900.[57] The fact that some subjects are unwilling or even openly hostile is immaterial. So, too, is the possibility that viewers might be shocked, repulsed, or saddened by the printed image. Whereas studio and commercial photographers rightly cater to the wishes of their clients; press photographers need only please their editors. Those who complained about pictures were most often assured that cameras are purely objective and that photographs never lie.

"When you pull the trigger on a news picture you are recording the unadorned truth," wrote Sammy Schulman, longtime staff photographer for the picture division of Hearst's International News Service. "That black box we wield is a terribly revealing weapon. Ours is a trade as uncompromising as our lenses, but people can't give a lens hell—so we photographers get it whenever our truthful pictures are painful to the subject."[58] Schulman's defense is as old as photography itself, but in light of common newsroom practices in the early years of the twentieth century, it needs some revision.

Photographs printed in newspapers and magazines were often altered in order to make them more palatable to the public or to enhance their effect. Graphic artists added filigrees and bold type, pictures were cropped, gerrymandered, and stuffed into dense pictorial layouts. However accurate the original image, what actually appeared on the printed page sometimes bore only the most tenuous connection to fact. Retouching was common practice, especially among the yellow papers, and there was seldom any printed acknowledgment of the changes.

Harry Coleman, who worked as a photographer and graphic artist for various Hearst newspapers, noted that early in the twentieth century "a great moral light dawned" suddenly on the editors who ran the *Chicago American* and *New York Journal*. Artists at each paper were ordered to remove or paint over material deemed risqué or otherwise problematic. Apparently, the editors felt that family newspapers must not subject their readers to even a hint of nudity, no matter how innocent the exposure. "Nipples on the hairy breasts of fighters were ordered painted out on sports-page pictures and athletes of any variety had to be scrutinized carefully for over-exposure," according to Coleman, who did as he was instructed.[59]

Official prudery in some departments did not appreciably lessen the fondness of editors for photographs of shapely young women. Images of models and actresses were a staple of popular daily journalism at the turn of the century, notwithstanding the professed moral purity of the management. "As for photographs—what offenses were committed in their name!" wrote Will Irvin in a broadside against the Hearst and Pulitzer papers. The radicals who seem most eager to replace words with pictures, he said, "are conservative about giving up their pictures; and pictures the yellows must have, especially for 'pretty girl stories.'"[60]

Actually, illustrated newspapers needed all kinds of pictures, not just ones meant to titillate or amuse. As Cleveland press photographer James Kincaid wrote in 1936, "news is anything new or of general interest." He conceded that such a broad definition "covers a multitude of assignments"—everything from society balls to air races. "In between these extremes we run the gauntlet of accidents, murders, trials, celebrities, fires, features and general news stories."[61] Gradually, photographers divided the news into two principal categories: spot news referred to random and unplanned events, and features were everything else. Much later, after the establishment of the National Press Photographers Association in 1946, these divisions were refined and broken down into several discrete subcategories including sports news and features, portraits, fashion, and pictorial.

"Always be on the lookout for oddities," advised a writer for the British magazine *Amateur Photographer* in 1904. "The public loves

UNCREDITED PHOTOGRAPH OF THE HEAVYWEIGHT BOXING CHAMPIONSHIP BETWEEN JOHN ARTHUR (JACK) JOHNSON *(LEFT)* AND JESS WILLARD. (NATIONAL PORTRAIT GALLERY, SMITHSONIAN INSTITUTION)

HALF OF A STEREOGRAPH BY WILLIAM A. RAU OF PHILADELPHIA SHOWING WRECKED ENGINES AT THE MISSOURI-PACIFIC RAILROAD ROUNDHOUSE IN KANSAS CITY, MO., AFTER THE JUNE FLOOD OF 1903. (LIBRARY OF CONGRESS)

anything bizarre and unusual, and if it sees something of the kind in a photograph . . . it must be true." The public's apparent appetite for the sensational, and the willingness of publishers to satisfy it, offered ambitious photographers plenty of opportunities. "A big sporting meeting, a review of troops, a royal visit, a railway accident are all grist to the photographer's mill."[62]

Modern hand-held cameras, fast films, and flash powder made it possible to document all aspects of daily life, the placid as well as the dramatic. Such resources, according to writer Ellerslie Wallacc, "render the pictorial transcriptions of such scenes as railway accidents, marine collisions and wrecks, collapsed bridges and buildings, the dire effects of floods, cyclones, and fires an easy matter, comparatively."[63] Finding outlets for such pictures was simple, for the increasing use of photographs by the press assured enterprising photographers of quick sales of relevant material. And after the turn of the century, several companies that specialized in the dissemination of news pictures were established, thereby affording photographers nationwide access to newspapers and magazines.

Like today's wire services and photo agencies, syndicates provided the press with timely photographs of events and persons in the news, and in the process created a national market for freelance photographers. The first, and one of the most influential of these new firms was the brainchild of a midwestern journalist with an eye for pictures. George Bain was born in 1865, and after receiving a law degree he began working as a reporter in 1883 on the staff of the *St. Louis Globe-Democrat*. A year later he transferred to its rival, the *Post-Dispatch*; much to his surprise he was assigned to the paper's bureau in Washington, D.C. Bain began including photographs with the stories he sent back to the paper. He had picked up a smattering of photographic knowledge while a student at St. Louis University; the enthusiastic response of his editors to his pictures, especially candid views of politicians made with hand-held cameras, convinced him of the importance and market potential of news photography. He left the *Post-Dispatch* to become Washington manager of the United Press Association, and there learned how to serve the varying pictorial needs of newspapers across the country. Bain began to purchase and collect photographs made of news events and notable persons from around the world. According to Emma Little, his biographer, Bain amassed more than one million pictures by 1905. Each image was meticulously catalogued and cross-indexed, though rarely credited. Bain got his pictures from a variety of sources, purchasing some from established freelance photojournalists like Frances Benjamin Johnston, and others from a team of young photographers that he hand-picked and trained. Thus began the Bain News Service, a key player

UNCREDITED PHOTOGRAPH MADE FOR AND DISTRIBUTED BY THE BAIN NEWS PHOTOGRAPHIC SERVICE SHOWING THE MASSACHUSETTS STATE MILITIA GUARDING THE APPROACH TO TEXTILE MILLS IN LAWRENCE DURING A STRIKE BY MILL WORKERS IN JANUARY 1912. (GEORGE GRANTHAM BAIN COLLECTION, LIBRARY OF CONGRESS)

UNIDENTIFIED PHOTOGRAPHER FOR HARRIS AND EWING MAKING A PORTRAIT OF CLIFFORD A. BERRYMAN, EDITORIAL CARTOONIST FOR THE *WASHINGTON STAR*. (HARRIS AND EWING COLLECTION, LIBRARY OF CONGRESS)

in the news industry for nearly four decades.[64] Before the introduction of reliable wire service transmission of photographs, syndicates provided newspapers and magazines with photographs of news events and personalities from around the world. They were not the only source of news pictures—stereo card producers such as Underwood and Underwood also distributed pictures—but they occupied a vital niche in the news business.

Bain's success inevitably attracted competitors. One of the best was George W. Harris, who began his career as a photographer on the staff of the *San Francisco Examiner*. In February 1905, Harris and Martha Ewing, an artist and fellow Californian, established their own picture agency in Washington. Years later, Harris recalled that his decision to move east and explore the possibilities of syndication was spurred by his editor at the *Examiner*, Andrew Lawrence. Upon returning to the office from an unproductive trip to photograph the volcano Mauna Loa in Hawaii, Harris ran into Lawrence, who was in a rage over his failure to locate even a single usable photograph of one of California's United States senators. Lawrence's advice was prophetic: "Any young fellow," he said, "could build up a splendid business in Washington if he could keep this idea in mind: just let the newspapers know that if he didn't have the photograph they wanted, he'd get it."[65]

Business was slow at first and the two partners worked alone, Harris as photographer and Ewing as colorist, receptionist, and business manager. In later years, Harris often recalled an assignment at the White House when the fortunes of the young company took a decided turn for the better. Harris was asked to photograph a meeting of Teddy Roosevelt's cabinet in session, an image which he believed was the first of its kind. When he arrived, however, he hesitated because the room was small and poorly lit. He related his misgivings to the president. "When anybody asks you if you can do anything in photography, tell them, 'Certainly, I can,' then find a way to do it," suggested the president, who knew a thing or two about photography and a great deal about self-confidence. Harris wisely took his advice and made the picture. Thereafter, the doings of the government provided Harris with endless photographic opportunities. At one point, for instance, Clifford Berryman, an award-winning editorial cartoonist for the *Washington Star,* hired Harris to make a portrait of every member of Congress. Eventually, the firm employed more than a hundred persons, and operated five studios in addition to its international news photography service.[66]

Rivaling the Bain and the Harris and Ewing syndicates was an eminently successful agency run by Paul Thompson, who began his career in journalism in 1901 as a reporter for the *New York Sun.* He turned to photography after making a series of candid portraits of Mark Twain during a day-long visit to the writer's home in Redding, Connecticut. Thompson sold the pictures of Twain for over a thousand dollars, more than enough to bankroll his entry into the photo-syndication field. His firm specialized in coverage of sporting, society, and news events, and images carrying the credit "photo by Paul Thompson" were run in newspapers and magazines across the country during the first decades of the twentieth century.

The credit line was deceptive, however, for Thompson was always more businessman than photographer. He hired those who made the pictures, and marketed their work, but only rarely clicked the shutter. According to the *New York Times,* "Many people naturally assumed that Mr. Thompson was, or had been an expert cameraman himself, but such was not the case." On one memorable occasion Thompson was hired to provide coverage of an important international yacht race. He was present as observer, but the real work of the firm was handled by an employee. At the end of the race, Thompson's photographer announced sadly that his film was ruined—"light struck"—and Thompson went home depressed. The next morning he was pleasantly surprised to see the New York papers chock-full of race pictures credited to Paul Thompson. Apparently, an office boy shot the event on his own and saved the day. Still, the only name under the pictures was that of the boss.[67]

Illustrated newspapers and magazines provided sure outlets for news pictures, especially given the energetic marketing of the syndicates, but there were others as well. Stereographs and postcards were popular con-

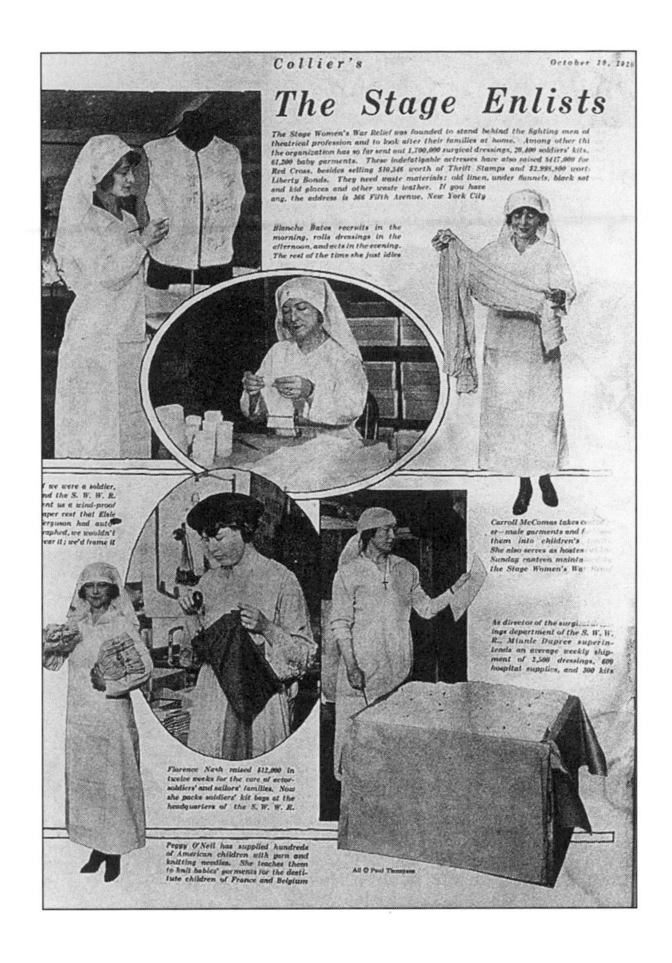

Collier's October 19, 1918

# The Stage Enlists

*The Stage Women's War Relief was founded to stand behind the fighting men of theatrical profession and to look after their families at home. Among other thi the organization has so far sent out 1,700,000 surgical dressings, 20,400 soldiers' kits, 61,200 baby garments. These indefatigable actresses have also raised $417,000 for Red Cross, besides selling $10,546 worth of Thrift Stamps and $2,998,800 wort Liberty Bonds. They need waste materials: old linen, under flannels, black sat and kid gloves and other waste leather. If you have any, the address is 366 Fifth Avenue, New York City*

*Blanche Bates recruits in the morning, rolls dressings in the afternoon, and acts in the evening. The rest of the time she just idles*

*f we were a soldier, nd the S. W. W. R. ent us a wind-proof aper vest that Elsie erguson had auto raphed, we wouldn't ear it; we'd frame it*

*Carroll McComas takes c er—male garments and f them into children's She also serves as hostes Sunday canteen mainta the Stage Women's Wa*

*As director of the surgi ings department of the S. W. W. R., Minnie Dupree superintends an average weekly shipment of 2,500 dressings, 600 hospital supplies, and 300 kits*

*Florence Nash raised $12,000 in twelve weeks for the care of actor-soldiers' and sailors' families. Now she packs soldiers' kit bags at the headquarters of the S. W. W. R.*

*Peggy O'Neil has supplied hundreds of American children with yarn and knitting needles. She teaches them to knit babies' garments for the destitute children of France and Belgium*

All © Paul Thompson

PHOTOGRAPHS CREDITED TO PAUL THOMPSON BUT PROBABLY MADE BY A MEMBER OF HIS STAFF DESCRIBING THE ACTIVITIES OF ACTRESSES WORKING FOR THE STAGE WOMEN'S WAR RELIEF GROUP IN NEW YORK CITY. PUBLISHED IN *COLLIER'S*, OCTOBER 19, 1918. (MIAMI-DADE PUBLIC LIBRARY)

sumer items at the turn of the century, and both were made and distributed in large numbers by news-minded photographers. During the last years of the nineteenth century, the trade in stereographs was enhanced by coverage of the Spanish-American and Boer Wars as well as by new methods of manufacturing and marketing the cards. As always, travel views predominated, but cards that described major news events also did well. Cards in boxed sets were endorsed by leading educators and used as teaching aids at all levels. Major firms such as Underwood & Underwood, the Keystone View Company, Griffith & Griffith, and the H. C. White Company, used machines to print, mount, and package cards that were produced by staff as well as freelance photographers.[68]

Local stereo coverage of floods along French Creek in the northwestern corner of Pennsylvania, just south of Erie, in early June 1892, launched the fabulously successful career of B. Lloyd Singley. An enthusiastic amateur, Singley made enough money on his flood pictures to found the Keystone View Company, which eventually became the largest producer of stereos in the country.[69] Perhaps because of his success with the French Creek series, Singley's company continued to sell stereos of news events from around the world. One of its most prolific staff photographers, Philip Brigandi, traveled extensively and sometimes risked his life, to make stereos for the company. In 1940 *Everyday Photography* magazine

STAFF PHOTOGRAPHER PHILIP BRIGANDI OF THE KEYSTONE VIEW COMPANY USING HIS COMPANY CAR AS A PHOTO PLATFORM. (CALIFORNIA MUSEUM OF PHOTOGRAPHY AT THE UNIVERSITY OF CALIFORNIA, RIVERSIDE)

published a tribute to Brigandi's long and storied career. Frank Cunningham, the author, described Brigandi as an inveterate chronicler of the news, at once brazen and tenacious.

Brigandi covered the news for Keystone for nearly half a century, producing stereos of labor riots in France, of young American soldiers on the way to the front, and of the scarred battlefields of Russia and the Balkans just after the First World War ended. He photographed the treaty signing at Versailles and later made the first stereograph of a cabinet meeting in progress during Calvin Coolidge's tenure in the White House. His regular excursions into news photography augmented the more placid and much safer business of making landscape and architectural views. The news was never a full-time occupation for either Brigandi or Singley, but both saw the potential for profit in making and marketing pictures of dramatic events.

Late in the nineteenth century, photographs were disseminated in an entirely new form, one which is very much in evidence today. Although usually overlooked as a significant element in the history of photojournalism, the proliferation of postcard views of news events just after the turn of the century suggests that the lowly postcard ought not be dismissed as mere curiosity or collectible. As historian Frank Staff rightly notes, "Whenever a train crashed, a tram car turned over, a ship became stranded on the rocks, or an aeroplane fell into the branches of a tree, the local photographer was there on the spot, and in a very quick time a picture postcard recorded the occasion."[70]

Postcards originated in 1869, when Dr. Emmanuel Hermann, professor of political economics at the Military Academy of Wiener-Neustadt, wrote to the *Neue Freie Presse* in Vienna suggesting that inexpensive cards with an address on one side and message on the other would facilitate communication and improve commerce. Apparently the government concurred, for the first card was issued by the Austro-Hungarian Empire on October 1, 1869. Crude illustrated cards began to appear in Europe in the early 1870s, and by 1890, picture postcards were popular consumer items.[71]

In the United States, picture postcards first appeared in large numbers in 1893, when several manufacturers issued cards commemorating the World's Columbian Exposition in Chicago. Formal congressional approval of privately printed cards came five years later, in May 1898. It should be noted that picture postcards, which are privately or commercially printed and affixed with a separate stamp, are not identical to postal cards. The latter are produced by the government and usually carry no decoration except for a printed stamp. The development by George Eastman and others of printing paper precut to postcard size (approximately five by three inches) helped expand the industry, as did the institution of free delivery of mail to outlying rural areas. And in 1906 Congress passed a law that permitted users to divide the back of the card: the right half for the address, and the left for a message. Now that pictures no longer had to share space with words, the business of making and selling photographic postcards, especially of news events and other matters of local or regional interest, flourished. In 1908 the Post-Office Department reported handling

UNCREDITED STEREOGRAPH OF CLARA BARTON, FOUNDER OF THE RED CROSS. THE IMAGE WAS COPYRIGHTED BY UNDERWOOD AND UNDERWOOD BUT PUBLISHED BY THE KEYSTONE VIEW COMPANY. (NATIONAL PORTRAIT GALLERY, SMITHSONIAN INSTITUTION)

PHOTOGRAPHIC POSTCARD OF A FATAL ACCIDENT ON THE CENTRAL VERMONT RAILROAD NEAR BARRE, VT., IN 1912. THE CARD IS ADDRESSED TO MRS. CHARLES WILLEKE, NO. 2 EAST STREET, ROCKVILLE, CONN. THE MESSAGE READS "THIS IS THE POST CARD SHOWING THE RECK WHARE MY SON WAS KILLED YOU SEE THE BRIDGE GAVE AWAY AND THEW ENGINE ROLLED OVER THE BANK ARE YOU WELL I WOOD LIKE TO SEE YOU AGAIN DONT FORGET TO RITE ALL IS WELL FROM SIMMONS MONTPELIER VT. RITE SOON FROM MR JJ SIMMONS." (PRIVATE COLLECTION)

nearly 668 million cards; five years later the number was 968 million.[72]

Although Americans living in cities had access to a variety of illustrated periodicals, many small newspapers continued to report the news primarily with words until the 1920s. Few small-time publishers could afford modern photo-engraving equipment and high-speed stereotype printing presses, so most made do without. Moreover, as journalism historian Kevin Barnhurst points out, nineteenth-century editors were wedded to firmly literary ideas; many refused to believe pictures were either serious or useful.[73] What was economically and philosophically daunting for newspapers in small towns and cities, however, was made to order for enterprising photographers. Postcards were inexpensive to make, and in the absence of any competing medium of visual communication, profit was practically guaranteed. During the first two decades of the twentieth century, local photographers who recorded hometown news were most likely to sell the images in the form of postcards. Local stores displayed and marketed their cards, often using the revolving steel display rack invented in 1908 by E. I. Dail, a traveling salesman from East Lansing, Michigan.[74]

Most postcards were produced by photographers who augmented the routine work of the studio with coverage of local news events. However, a few found that the postcard business was so good that they could specialize in it. Such was the experience of Wilfred Dudley Smithers of Alpine, Texas. Early in the twentieth century Smithers churned out postcards describing life along the border with Mexico. "I set myself up as a postcard manufacturer and became a booming regional success," he wrote. During flare-ups of fighting on the border, he was barely able to keep up with the demand. "Using pictures I had made in Texas, Mexico, New Mexico, and Arizona, I produced two thousand cards in [one] eighteen hour period," he recalled.[75]

Smithers' success in the Big Bend region was not unique. American companies that operated in Mexico attracted the attention of photographers, particularly during periodic conflicts between labor and management. And American military installations along the border offered numerous outlets for postcard makers like Walter H. Horne, a neophyte photographer who began making cards in earnest when fighting accelerated between Mexican soldiers and rebels led by Francisco Madero in 1911. For the next ten years, until the tuberculosis from which he suffered finally took his life, Horne produced thousands of views along the border. They were the foundation of his fortune.[76]

Horne sold his cards locally and through wholesale houses in Los Angeles, Atlantic City, and New York. As long as fighting percolated along the border, he was happy, but he fretted during the lulls. "The pictures of the Mexican Revolution don't amount to anything now," he wrote to his mother in September 1911. "Am in hopes that there will be more trouble across the river, but it is quiet there now."[77] When American troops landed at Vera Cruz in 1914, interest in Mexican-American relations soared, and Horne and other photographers had an easy time selling their pictures. He even expanded his postcard operation to include out-of-town newspapers.

Local events that caught the attention of major metropolitan newspapers provided a bonanza for postcard photographers. When the bulky, top-heavy steamer *Eastland* capsized in the Chicago River on July 24, 1915, drowning hundreds of excursionists from the Western Electric Company's Chicago plant, photographers flocked to the docks to record the disaster. The egregious loss of life combined with stories concerning the ship's questionable fitness and the ineptitude of the crew attracted

A PHOTOGRAPHIC POSTCARD MADE AND DISTRIBUTED BY JUN FUJITA SHOWING A DIVER AT WORK RECOVERING BODIES FROM THE CAPSIZED STEAMER *EASTLAND*, CHICAGO, 1915. (CHICAGO HISTORICAL SOCIETY)

national attention, and postcards of the ship, the survivors, and the dead sold well. The public was fascinated and appalled by the tragedy, and postcards provided an inexpensive opportunity to commemorate and comment.

Securing compelling photographs that day in Chicago was not easy. Frantic rescue workers, medical personnel, and the police were loath to either hold still or make way for photographers in search of a few good pictures. Press photographers such as Fred Eckhardt of the *Chicago Daily News,* Jun Fujita of the *Evening Sun* (perhaps the first Asian American photographer at a mainstream newspaper), and many others worked into the night, providing their papers with on-the-spot views.[78] Some of these were later distributed as postcards. Amateurs tried as well. One of the several who captured the scene on film was Leonard O. Inland, who described his experience in a letter to the *Camera* magazine later that summer.

Inland finally got his picture in the early morning of July 25, a full day after the *Eastland* rolled over and settled into the muck at the bottom of the river. "I had to run to get away from the policemen who were guard-

PHOTOGRAPH BY JUN FUJITA OF THE *CHICAGO DAILY NEWS* SHOWING A RESCUE WORKER WITH THE LIFELESS BODY OF A CHILD FROM THE *EASTLAND* DISASTER, JULY 23, 1915. (CHICAGO HISTORICAL SOCIETY)

ing the boat and the bodies," he wrote. "No one except the divers and doctors were allowed on the wharf. I sneaked in, but was chased out." Inland was using an Auto Graflex, the standard press camera of the day, and 4×5 film fast enough to make an exposure at a sixtieth of a second. The single image he made while backpedaling away from the police served him well. "I have sold over 20 dozens postcards at five cents each, and could have sold more but cannot make them fast enough, having no printing machine nor dark-room."[79]

Inland's experience with the police was not unusual. As photographers sought greater access to scenes of public and private turmoil, they often ran afoul of those determined to prevent such exposure. "Train wrecks offer greater obstacles than auto crashes," wrote James Kinkaid in 1936. For one thing, the railroad crash site is likely to be strung out over several hundred square feet, and thus difficult to capture in a single telling shot. More important, as Kinkaid and many others found out, vigilant and unsympathetic railroad detectives specialize in the rough eviction of photographers since pictures of "train wrecks are not good advertising for the railroad."[80]

Efforts to keep photographers and other members of the press at bay sometimes backfired, making them all the more determined to tell the story in pictures and words. Revealing the forbidden and uncovering what some would keep forever hidden were major preoccupations of journalists at the turn of the century.[81] News photographers increasingly saw themselves as embattled and misunderstood tribunes of the people. When news happened they rushed to tell the story; and if their pictures sickened or enraged or saddened, that was proof of their effectiveness and necessity.

With the encouragement of editors ever on the lookout for scandal, sensation, and amusement, photographers were given license to pursue and pester. Intense competition between newspapers at the turn of the century—most cities had several morning and evening papers—filtered down to the photographers, and the doctrine of the scoop was born. Even those most interested in the art of photography could see and appreciate that speed was essential. "I was eager to see how fast I could take, develop and print a picture," remembered Alfred Stieglitz of an experiment in the early 1880s. From start to finish, the process took him thirty-four minutes. When asked what he was trying to prove, Stieglitz replied that "newspapers would reproduce photographs with increasing frequency, [and] . . . speed would be of ever greater importance."[82] He was right. Providing the editor with a printable picture before the competition had one became a central tenet of turn-of-the-century press photography, and for most situations, a single picture that could tell the entire story was sufficient. Beating one's rivals mattered more than anything else. "Money, time, the rest of the paper, sometimes even men's lives do not seem to count against that insane desire to get something of importance in the sheet which all the rest want and can't get," commented one photographer dryly, convinced that racing after scoops really was insane.[83]

The press of time and the absolute imperative to return to the newsroom with usable pictures led inevitably to conflicts between photojournalists and the public, except, of course, when the subject was no longer among the living. One intrepid photographer for the Hearst empire made postmortem photography something of a specialty. He arranged to keep a certain amount of equipment—a starched shirt-front with bow tie attached, and a coarse-toothed comb—in a special drawer at the city morgue, and when the paper needed a quick portrait, he went to work. "I had invented a device which made this outfit instantly adjustable, and . . . [it] could be snapped around the Adam's apple of any cadaver that happened to be newsworthy." He noted that other papers "were content to print their pictures from sketches of these cold-storage stiffs." But that just would not do for Hearst. "My system was to roll the departed on his slab out upon the morgue floor, where I could prop him up slantwise, clamp on my false haberdashery, comb out the disheveled locks, then straddle the body with my camera focused downward." Occasionally, the deputy coroner would allow him to "prop open the eyes so that my portraits would have a more homey look," he said. When such manipulation was prohibited or impossible, the paper's art staff simply retouched the photograph, painting the eyes open and even adjusting the clothing. So much for verisimilitude.[84]

Sometimes all the guile and perseverance in the world could not assure access. In early June 1911, Norman Alley of the *Chicago Tribune* was caught trying to make a photograph in the courtroom of U.S. District Court Judge Kenesaw Mountain Landis during a grand jury investigation of price fixing in the lumber industry. The young photographer was publicly rebuked before being escorted out. Alley, who later went to work making newsreels for Hearst's News Photo Syndicate, was not on assignment at the time; this was his own idea, not his editor's. Landis, who would one day be commissioner of major league baseball, set him straight. "Young man, such conduct in this court constitutes contempt of the gravest nature. This is a dignified hall of American justice, not a playground for curious Kodakers. Had you asked your employers, I'm sure they could have saved you from all this."[85]

Alley's courtroom adventure was not without precedent. The sordid details of spectacular crimes were manna for the yellow press, and whenever possible, pictures accompanied the written reports. Steamy stories involving men and women tangled in violent and illicit love affairs were especially prized. When Harry Coleman worked as a staff photographer at the *New York Journal*, the case of Florence Burns, a young and pretty woman tried in 1902 for the murder of her lover, Walter S. Brooks, a salesman, attracted national attention. For Coleman the extensive photographic coverage of the trial marked the true beginning of candid courtroom photography. "The spicy trial, itself, ran to type," wrote Coleman. The accused murderess, "dazzling, peach-jowled, high-pompadoured, strawberry blond . . . , sat demurely in court while conflicting tales of passion and virtue were argued before a goggle-eyed audience." The trial, which ended in Ms. Burns's acquittal, was "one of the first turn-of-the-

PHOTOGRAPH CAPTIONED AS THE "DREAMLAND FIRE" AT THE CONEY ISLAND AMUSEMENT PARK IN NEW YORK CITY, MADE BY AN UNIDENTIFIED PHOTOGRAPHER FOR UNDERWOOD AND UNDERWOOD, OCTOBER 5, 1911. (LIBRARY OF CONGRESS)

century paramour murder cases to be adequately pictured for the press," and it obviously led to many others.[86]

Although the picture press relished stories that involved crime, sex, or better yet, both, their coverage of the news was not limited to the lurid and profane. Many of the yellow journals were liberal in their politics, and stories that pilloried the great industrial and commercial interests of Gilded Age America were published with considerable enthusiasm. During this period many blue-collar Americans were increasingly at odds with the managers and owners for whom they worked, and publishers such as Hearst, Scripps, and Pulitzer sympathized with the workers.

Of particular importance for editors of illustrated newspapers and magazines were pictures of natural and man-made catastrophes. Critics contended that such coverage resulted from a cynical belief that "misery sells," but often there was considerably more to the story than a ghoulish delight in the misfortune of others. Some of the most riveting disaster stories had subtexts that spoke directly to the political and social concerns of Americans at the turn of the century.

On May 31, 1889, floodwater swept through Johnstown, Pennsylvania, a major steel-producing center not far from Pittsburgh. More than 2,200

HALF OF A STEREO VIEW BY WILLIAM A. RAU FOR UNDERWOOD AND UNDERWOOD SHOWING THE FREIGHT YARDS AND WAREHOUSES IN KANSAS CITY, MO., DURING THE JUNE FLOOD OF 1903. (LIBRARY OF CONGRESS.)

STEREOGRAPH BY AN UNIDENTIFIED PHOTOGRAPHER FOR THE KEYSTONE VIEW COMPANY OF STRANDED AND WRECKED VESSELS ON THE GALVESTON, TEXAS, WATERFRONT AFTER THE HURRICANE OF 1900. (PRIVATE COLLECTION)

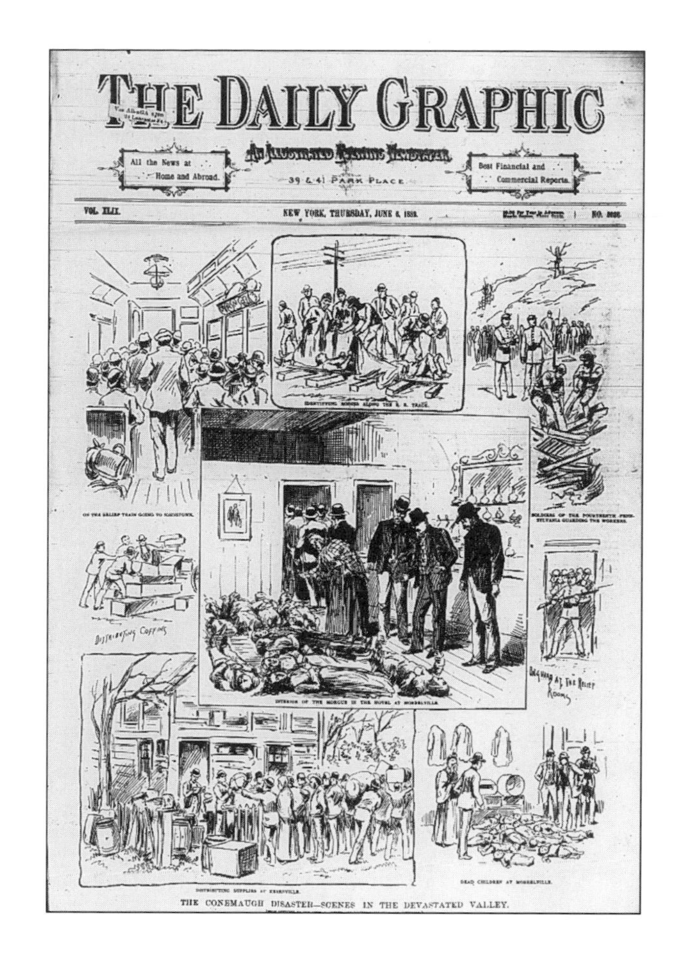

THE DAILY GRAPHIC

All the News at Home and Abroad.

39 & 41 Park Place

Best Financial and Commercial Reports.

NEW YORK, THURSDAY, JUNE 6, 1889.

INTERIOR OF THE MORGUE IN THE HOTEL AT MORRELLVILLE.

SOLDIERS OF THE FOURTEENTH PENNSYLVANIA GUARDING THE WORKERS.

Distributing Coffins

THE CONEMAUGH DISASTER—SCENES IN THE DEVASTATED VALLEY.

WOOD ENGRAVINGS PUBLISHED BY THE *NEW YORK DAILY GRAPHIC* ON JUNE 6, 1889, SOME OF WHICH WERE MADE FROM PHOTOGRAPHS BY DAVIS OF PITTSBURGH, SHOWING THE AFTERMATH OF THE FLOOD IN JOHNSTOWN, PA. (LIBRARY OF CONGRESS)

people drowned, many of them the wives and children of immigrant steel workers. The story gripped the national press, and not merely because of the terrible toll in human lives. The flood occurred when the earthen dam that created a private trout-fishing preserve burst, sending an enormous wall of water, muck, and debris into the narrow streets of Johnstown, fourteen miles downstream. The lake was owned and used exclusively by the South Fork Fishing and Hunting Club, an elite group of Pittsburgh industrialists, bankers, and lawyers including Andrew Carnegie and Henry Clay Frick. Although forewarned of the dam's weakness, the club's directors did nothing, and heavy spring rains that year sealed Johnstown's fate. The popular press saw proof of meanness and criminal neglect among the potentates who presided over America's burgeoning industrial empires. "The dam served no useful end, beyond the pleasure of a few rich men," wrote the editors of the *New York Daily Graphic*. "The owners of the dam neglected it and paid no attention to the complaints that it was structurally weak. Then the awful catastrophe came."[87]

Evidence of Dickensian selfishness and official corruption combined with the stirring accounts of eyewitnesses and survivors made the Johnstown tragedy famous almost overnight. The flood and its aftermath was news for months, and photographs of the wreckage sold well, though several newspapers in Pennsylvania complained bitterly about all the sightseers, gawkers, and other nonessential personnel. Still, they came, many armed with cameras to document the tragedy for posterity. In fact, so many pictures were made and published that critics began discussing which pictorial qualities were most effective. One noted that images "are anything but interesting when the camera was directed to the heaps of miscellaneous *debris* in and near the rivers." Pictures of unidentifiable flotsam could neither move nor inform. "But it is different," he added, "when we see the pictures of houses pierced by tall trees and streets filled with wreckage as high as the third-story windows."[88]

Pictures of one broken house with the trunk of a large tree protruding from an upstairs window, surrounded by the shattered remains of other buildings, were published nationwide and issued as well in stereo format. The house became the preeminent visual symbol of the flood. Another view showed the body of a man lying face down in the rubble, but as historian David McCullough points out, this one is undoubtedly a fake. By the time it was made, bodies so exposed would have been found and buried. And the man's neat white shirt is a glaring anomaly.[89]

Efforts to investigate and publicize the cause of the flood in Johnstown, to examine the precise role and responsibility of the well-heeled members of the South Fork Fishing Club, led to lasting bitterness and suspicion, which was aggravated in the heyday of yellow journalism. Photographers were the most visible members of the press, with an infinite capacity to ruffle feathers and antagonize. Early in the century, so common were attacks upon lowly press photographers that some of them began to fight back in the courts. In July 1911, Wade Mountford Jr., staff photographer for the American Press Association, filed suit against Whitney Warren of Newport, Rhode Island, and New York City. Mountford was working on Bailey's Beach in Newport, making pictures of society ladies, among them Warren's wife and her friend, Elsie French Vanderbilt. When Mountford refused to go away, Warren attacked. Mountford sued him for a thousand dollars. In a nearly identical case earlier that same year, a Boston-based newspaper photographer named Richard Sears was awarded one hundred dollars in Newport's Superior Court.[90]

Although in some quarters sympathy was expressed for the beleaguered press photographer, who was, after all, merely trying to make a living, others blamed the invasive tactics of modern journalism. "The argument set up by a certain portion of the press, that if a person is willing to be seen in public, whether in conventional attire or bathing-costume, he or she cannot reasonably object to being so pictured in the newspapers, is not altogether illogical," admitted the editors of *Photo-Era Magazine* in the fall of 1911. But, they added, "the subject should have the privilege to decide this point for himself."[91] Complaints and even physical intimidation did little to dissuade or inhibit press photographers. The pursuit of pictures in a hostile environment made the job seem that much more heroic and noble, and the number of professionals steadily increased. Women began entering the field as well, though in newsrooms dominated by men, women were at best grudgingly tolerated. An editorial in one

HALF OF A STEREOGRAPH BY GEORGE BARKER SHOWING "A SLIGHTLY DAMAGED HOUSE." THIS WAS ONE OF THE MOST WIDELY REPRODUCED IMAGES OF THE WRECKAGE LEFT BY THE JOHNSTOWN FLOOD. (LIBRARY OF CONGRESS)

popular photographic magazine suggested that women might be a useful addition to the profession in part because of their "natural instinct for neatness, system and order." These were essential qualities for the running of a photographic studio; the editors were silent about the possibilities in photojournalism.[92]

Many male editors felt that daily journalism was simply too coarse for the naturally refined and gentle tastes of women. "I would rather see my daughters starve than that they should have ever heard or seen what women on my staff have been compelled to hear and see," wrote one editor to Edward Bok at the *Ladies' Home Journal* in 1901. He did not say whether his daughters concurred. Another said that not one in twenty women was able to navigate the troubled waters of modern journalism successfully, and in any event, the pay was so bad that such work was hardly worthwhile.[93] Still, women persevered. In major American cities, competition between newspapers created job openings, and women were among those who benefited. The number of women employed by major American newspapers averaged about five, wrote Anne O'Hagan in 1898, though on "some conservative sheets there are but two or three, reserved for such dainty uses as the reporting of women's club meetings and writing weekly fashion and complexion advices." It was different at the yellow papers. O'Hagan noted that on progressive newspapers as many as eight or ten women could be seen "scurrying breathlessly through the town to see bankers or murderers, to report teas or trials, to interview the latest strike leader or to ask the newest divorcée questions which she will decline to answer unless she needs advertising for some post-matrimonial venture."[94]

The proliferation of equipment designed for amateurs undoubtedly encouraged women to think seriously about careers in photography. Moreover, the women's rights movement propelled a number of them to seek admittance to what was essentially a fraternity.[95] "Ladies also use the camera nowadays," reported the *New York Times* in 1883, "and they take great delight in them, too." The efforts of women, added the reporter, was no longer limited to populating the family album. Galleries around the country displayed photographs made by women, and their best pictures found "ready purchasers."[96]

Eventually, even the most intransigent publishers and editors discovered that women were capable of competing with men in the newsroom. What counted, after all, was the picture, not the gender of the person who made it. In certain situations women reporters and photographers found they could actually gain greater access and achieve better results than their male colleagues. "I seem to have been regarded with less suspicion," wrote Mildred Ring upon her return from a photographic excursion among Native Americans in Wisconsin. Despite their well-known and justifiable antipathy to whites, especially those with cameras, Ring secured effective portraits of tribal members, and concluded that in this case "being a woman has proven an advantage."[97]

Frances Benjamin Johnston achieved considerable fame as a journalistic photographer late in the nineteenth century, and she encouraged other women to enter the field. She had no illusions about what it took to be productive and prosperous. "Photography as a profession should appeal particularly to women, and in it there are great opportunities for a good-paying business." She was convinced that in order to flourish as a journalist, a woman must possess "good common sense, unlimited patience to carry her through endless failures, equally unlimited tact, good taste, a quick eye, a talent for detail, and a genius for hard work."[98]

Johnston's emphasis on diligence and tenacity was mirrored by Jessie Tarbox Beals, the first American woman to work as a full-time staff photographer at a daily newspaper. Her hiring in November 1901 by the *Buffalo Inquirer,* and her success at the paper, paved the way for women who craved the excitement and drama of daily journalism. In an article in the *Focus,* a journal for amateur photographers published in St. Louis, Beals wrote that newspaper work offers intellectual stimulation as well as profit. "If one is the possessor of health and strength, a good news instinct . . . , a fair photographic outfit, and the ability to hustle, which is the most necessary qualification, one can be a news photographer." But for women, it was not easy. "Mere feminine, delicate, Dresden China type of women, get nowhere in business or professional life," Beals wrote in her diary. "They marry millionaires, if they are lucky." For the rest, competition demanded qualities that polite Victorian society usually deemed wholly masculine.[99]

For Beals and many other professional women, the rigors of the marketplace were sometimes less daunting than achieving some balance between family and work. In a May 1912 interview with Margaret Hubbard Ayer, a reporter for the *New York Evening Journal,* Beals spoke wistfully of what she missed at home. "I spend an hour with my daughter every morning and then leave her with the nurse. In the evening—for I work nearly every night in my office—she is sound asleep, so I have no time for lullabies, or cuddling her." Guilt and frustration were difficult for Beals to bear, but there seemed no real alternative. "I have to work," she said, "and I am away a great deal, but it is not the right thing for the child."[100]

What was difficult and frustrating for the first women photojournalists was much more difficult for the members of various racial and ethnic minorities. For African, Hispanic, Native, and Asian Americans, employment in journalism was limited to small-circulation periodicals directed at particular ethnic audiences. There were numerous black photographers at the turn of the century, for instance, but their work was confined to the segregated districts in which the vast majority of them lived. Although mainstream newspapers and magazines occasionally published illustrated stories dealing with minority cultures, the photographs were almost always made by persons of white European stock and usually expressed the prevailing racist attitudes of the dominant culture.

Chinese communities in California attracted national attention in the 1890s. Immigration policy on the Chinese and other ethnic groups was a

PHOTOGRAPH BY JESSIE TARBOX BEALS OF JEWISH CHILDREN LISTENING TO THE NORTH AMERICAN INDIAN LEGEND OF THE NORTHERN LIGHTS AT THE SEA-SIDE BRANCH OF THE QUEENS BOROUGH PUBLIC LIBRARY, C. 1905. (WARREN AND MARGOT COVILLE PHOTOGRAPHIC COLLECTION, BLOOMFIELD HILLS, MICH.)

AFRICAN AMERICAN PHOTOGRAPHER JAMES VAN DER ZEE'S IMAGE OF YOUNG MEN IN HARLEM DISTRIBUTING THE *CHICAGO DEFENDER,* THE LARGEST-CIRCULATION, BLACK-OWNED AND OPERATED NEWSPAPER IN AMERICA, 1928. (METROPOLITAN MUSEUM OF ART, GIFT OF THE JAMES VAN DER ZEE INSTITUTE, 1970 [1970.539.54])

hot political topic, and much of the debate centered on the use of opium among Asians. Several photographers using fast film and magnesium flash managed to invade the dens and come away with images of this practice, images that seemingly offered proof of lawlessness and a pernicious resistance to American values. Combined with written reports that skewered the Chinese, the articles added fuel to the arguments of those seeking to curtail or even end immigration. "A Chinaman is not violently eager to pose as an object lesson at any time especially when no benefit accrues to him," reported Henry W. Canfield in 1892. "He might be induced to sit for his photograph in the robes of a mandarin, but to expect him to give his likeness to posterity . . . clad in tattered garments and with an opium pipe in his hands is a picture from which his mind would recoil in horror."[101] The photographer in this case was Frank Davey, an assistant in Isaiah W. Taber's renowned studio. His photographs are effective, capturing the oppression of cramped quarters and the shock of those bathed in the sudden blinding light of magnesium flash. But one wonders how any one of the successful Chinese photographers in San Francisco might have handled the assignment.

Just before dawn on April 18, 1906, little more than a decade after the flurry of stories on opium use among the Chinese, San Francisco nearly perished altogether in a ruinous earthquake and subsequent fire. The city was home to a thriving photographic community, and those whose equipment was not utterly destroyed wandered into the ruins with their cameras. Photographic coverage of the disaster was so extensive that many may have assumed that the photographic community was miraculously unscathed. A brief article in the June issue of the *Photo-Beacon* told the real story. "Men who the day before . . . were considered to be well off are now endeavoring to raise enough money to pay their expenses east," wrote the editors, "and are looking for almost any kind of position to keep the wolf from the door." Photographers across the country were urged to do whatever they could to help their fellows on the coast.[102]

Some managed to resume work within hours of the disaster, and those employed by newspapers and magazines immediately set about recording the aftermath of the quake. Commercial photographers such as A. C. Pillsbury and Oscar Maurer, press photographers George Haley of the *Chronicle*, Edward A. Rogers of the *Morning Call*, and George Parmenter and Harry Coleman of Hearst's *Examiner*, as well as fine-art and portrait photographers, recorded every aspect of the devastation, providing contemporary viewers with a complete visual history of the event.[103] Photographs of the ruins, of the great fire, and of the charred remains of such notable structures as city hall were published in magazines and newspapers, including a special combined issue of the San Francisco papers entitled, appropriately, the *Call-Chronicle-Examiner*. Postcards and stereo views also sold well.

Among the best-known views of San Francisco in the hours and days immediately following the earthquake were those made by the city's leading portrait and fine-art photographer, Arnold Genthe. However, if not for

21% More Piano Ads. Last Tuesday.

18% MORE Real Estate Offers Made last week through The American Than were made the same week last year.

Sunday American Circulation Over 800,000.

New York American

EDITION FOR THE TWENTIETH CENTURY NEWSPAPER GREATER NEW YORK

Government Weather Report. Tuesday, fair; diminishing north winds; Wednesday, fair and warmer.

Sunday American Circulation Over 800,000.

No. 8376. —NEW YORK, TUESDAY, APRIL 24, 1906.—20 PAGES. PRICE ONE CENT

# FIRST PHOTOGRAPHS FROM SAN FRANCISCO!

## FIERY DESTRUCTION OF SAN FRANCISCO AS SEEN FROM OAKLAND.

THIS remarkable picture was taken by Photographer Howe from the end of Long Wharf, in Oakland, and shows the two big pillars of flame and smoke that marked the location of the great fire that ate up the Latin Quarter and along the Barbary coast, the entire business district from the water front far up Market street.

The pillar of fiery smoke on the left shows the location of the fire that destroyed the Examiner Building, Newspaper Row, and the other great office buildings in the heart of the business section. Thousands of anxious watchers in Oakland who had friends or relatives in San Francisco crowded the Oakland wharves and begged every newcomer for news of the burning city. The earthquake was forgotten in the terror of the flames.

COPYRIGHT, 1906, BY W. R. HEARST, AMERICAN-JOURNAL-EXAMINER.

*Any person reproducing this picture without permission will be prosecuted to the full extent of the law.*

Photographs by John D. Howe, of Oakland, California. "On account of lack of water with which to develop in Oakland and San Francisco," writes Mr. Howe, "I am sending these plates on the first train. I hope you will be able to get good results from these, as I am positive that these are the first out of Oakland."

## CALIFORNIA'S GOVERNOR THANKS W. R. HEARST.

*Oakland, Cal., April 23.*

*Hon. W. R. Hearst, New York:*

*Permit me to express to you the deep sense of gratitude I feel for the good work you have done and are still so ably doing. I tender you my heartiest thanks personally and on behalf of the people of San Francisco and the State at large.*

*GEO. C. PARDEE, Governor of California.*

THE FRONT PAGE OF HEARST'S *NEW YORK AMERICAN*, APRIL 24, 1906, WITH A PHOTOGRAPH OF THE SAN FRANCISCO WATERFRONT IN FLAMES BY JOHN D. HOWE OF OAKLAND, CALIF. (LIBRARY OF CONGRESS)

PHOTOGRAPH BY GEORGE W. HALEY OF THE *SAN FRANCISCO CHRONICLE* SHOWING A REPORTER SENDING THE LAST TELEGRAPH MESSAGE FROM A MAKESHIFT STATION IN FRONT OF THE HALL OF JUSTICE AS THE FIRE APPROACHES. STAKES SHOW WHERE BODIES WERE HASTILY BURIED. (STILL PICTURES BRANCH, NATIONAL ARCHIVES)

A PANORAMIC VIEW OF THE SAN FRANCISCO WATERFRONT AFTER THE DEVASTATING EARTHQUAKE AND FIRE, MADE BY GEORGE R. LAWRENCE FROM A BALLOON HOVERING SOME TWO THOUSAND FEET ABOVE SAN FRANCISCO BAY. LAWRENCE SOLD THIS VIEW TO NEWSPAPERS AND MAGAZINES AROUND THE WORLD. (LIBRARY OF CONGRESS)

the largesse of camera store owner George Kahn, Genthe might have been much less productive. "I found that my hand cameras had been so damaged by the falling plaster as to be rendered useless," he recalled. Kahn provided replacements, free of charge. "'Take anything you want,'" he told the famous photographer, "'This place is going to burn up anyway.'" Genthe selected a 3A Kodak Special and filled his pockets with film. During the next several weeks he made many views of the devastation, including several memorable images of San Franciscans watching their city burn.[104]

After years of making pictures for the *New York Journal*, Harry Coleman transferred to the *Examiner* early in 1905. After shooting what little film he had on hand on the day of the quake, Coleman spent hours aiding fire and rescue personnel. The next day, resupplied with equipment and film from intact stores in Oakland, Coleman went back to photographing his beloved adopted city, accompanied much of the time by Jack London,

AN UNCREDITED STEREOGRAPH PUBLISHED BY THE H. C. WHITE COMPANY OF NORTH BENNINGTON, VT., OF THE VIEW DOWN MARKET STREET IN SAN FRANCISCO, AFTER THE EARTHQUAKE AND FIRE. (PRIVATE COLLECTION)

whose reminiscence of the disaster was published in *Collier's*. "I photographed funerals winding through long bread lines," Coleman wrote later, "and cinder-smeared congregations singing hallelujahs and seeking solace as they knelt before ashcan pulpits where ministers held street services in the shadows of crumbled altars."[105]

The breadth of coverage of the San Francisco disaster offered proof of the value of news photography. Books, pamphlets, magazines, and newspapers used countless photographs from both artists and commercial photographers to document the destruction and rebuilding of the city.[106] The public's unabated fascination with the pictures indicated the growing importance of the mediated image in American culture. Three years later, James Boniface Schriever asserted the central place of photography. "Without the camera, the lens, and the sensitized plate and paper," he wrote, "the business of the world, the amusements of a large part of the population, the instruction of the school children, the expeditious selling of material, and the spreading of news, would be vastly hindered, if not at a standstill."[107] As president of the American School of Art and Photography in Scranton, Pennsylvania, Schriever's remarks are somewhat self-serving. But for those who braved the fires in San Francisco, and Americans elsewhere eager to see and understand the tragedy, photographs provided dramatic and detailed evidence of the city's dreadful condition.

A MASS-PRODUCED POSTER ADVERTISING MOVIES, PHOTOGRAPHS, AND LANTERN SLIDES MADE DURING AND JUST AFTER THE 1898 WAR WITH SPAIN (PRIVATE COLLECTION)

CHAPTER TWO

# COVERING WAR

The man behind the camera has come to the front in recent years to bid for the laurels of the war-correspondent, the explorer and the hunter. The demand for pictures caught in odd corners of the world, or on the firing-line, has bred a new race of heroic adventurers ready to take any chances in any clime. The Spanish War first showed what could be achieved by daring and resourceful photographers who were ready to touch elbows with soldiers and sailors in action. The public at home welcomed this new manner of illustration, and the newspapers and magazines made it profitable for the men who could "deliver the goods," to make war-photography a profession.

—*Outing Magazine,* September 1905[1]

On April 26, 1898, Richard Harding Davis wrote to his family from the battleship *New York,* the flagship of the United States naval squadron stationed off Havana, Cuba. For Davis, a young ambitious reporter on assignment from no fewer than three major news organizations—the *New York Herald,* the *London News,* and *Scribner's Magazine*—war with Spain promised adventure, romance, and almost certain celebrity. He was pleased with the accommodations on Admiral William T. Sampson's ship, since they surpassed even the plush quarters on board the *Smith,* the racing yacht owned and operated by the *New York Herald,* where Davis had spent the preceding weeks. The *New York* was like "a luxurious yacht,"

PICT
TION
IN THE ART OF
LIFE AND MOTI
SESSIO
GREATEST INVE
nimated
FE-LIKE MOTI
THE WONDERFUL MOVIN
WILL REP
s and Incidents from
way Trains Going at
nes, Comic Scenes,

but "with none of the ennui."[2] There was not much to report in the way of real action—a few deafening salvos from the ship's guns with practically nothing in return from the Spanish garrisons ashore, no torpedoes or mines, and thus no casualties—but he was not the least bit bored. "There is a band on board that plays twice a day," he explained. "The other night, when we were heading off a steamer and firing six-pounders across her bows, the band was playing the 'Star' song from *The Meistersinger*." The anticipation of righteous war overlaid with gentle tropical breezes and Richard Wagner's stirring music struck Davis as something quintessentially fin de siècle, and he swore that he was having "a magnificent time."[3]

What John Hay, the American ambassador to Great Britain, called "our splendid little war" gave Davis and his fellow correspondents their largest audience to date, and one that was increasingly enamored of titillating gossip, dramatic flourishes, the sensational, and the pictorial. Davis asked rhetorically who would benefit from the coming conflict: "To whom would it bring honor, to whom honor with death, to whom would the chance come, and who would seize it when it came?"[4] For many publishers in America, the Cuban revolution had already paid rich dividends, for the vast circulations controlled by Hearst, Pulitzer, and Scripps were built at least in part on news from Spain's unhappy colonies in the Caribbean and Pacific. If war on behalf of the insurgents was morally justified, it was also a prodigious economic windfall. Hearst and Pulitzer in particular made every effort to keep it that way.

Early in 1897 Hearst sent Richard Harding Davis and the celebrated artist Frederic Remington to Cuba, announcing their arrival in a banner headline on page one. The accompanying story noted that the two stellar journalists "have reached the insurgent army in the island. . . . Mr. Remington is making sketches of the life and activity of the patriot army as he finds it, and Mr. Davis, acting as war correspondent, will have a new field of effort for his trenchant and brilliant pen." The story contained a great deal of bombast and hyperbole, and it promised that in Cuba Remington would find "a new background for his vivid sketch work." He did not. After two weeks of frustration and boredom, Remington was ready to come home. According to fellow *Journal* correspondent James Creelman, the artist sent the following plaintive cable to Hearst in New York: "Everything is quiet. There is no trouble here. There will be no war. I wish to return." Hearst is said to have responded immediately. "Please remain. You furnish the pictures. I'll furnish the war."[5]

The story may be apocryphal (neither Hearst nor Remington would ever confirm it), but the pictures supplied by illustrated magazines and newspapers caught the attention of the public, and photographers nationwide took note. "It's an ill wind that don't blow somebody good," wrote T. H. Cummings in *Photo Era* magazine in June 1898, "and from a photographer's point of view, the war will prove a real blessing." He noted that while studio photographers busied themselves with portraits of departing soldiers and views of placid stateside encampments, many amateurs in the ranks equipped themselves with cameras and film in order to provide their

See Our Superb Christmas Number Next Week, with Colored Cover.—Price, 10 Cents.

LESLIE'S WEEKLY

ILLUSTRATED

UNIFORMS AND TYPES OF THE ARMY AND NAVY.—PLATE X. ROUGH RIDERS.

LESLIE'S WEEKLY.

ROOM IN WHICH FORTY SPANISH SOLDIERS WERE KILLED BY THE EXPLOSION OF AN AMERICAN SHELL AFTER IT HAD PENETRATED SEVEN FEET OF MASONRY.

A THOUSAND SPANISH SOLDIERS AT SUPPER.

SQUAD OF SPANISH PRISONERS UNDER GUARD OF AMERICAN SOLDIERS.

SPANISH FORT AT CAVITE AFTER IT HAD BEEN SHELLED BY ADMIRAL DEWEY.

THE ISABELLA BRIDGE IN OLD MANILA.

MANILA AFTER ITS SURRENDER.

DESTRUCTION WROUGHT BY ADMIRAL DEWEY'S FLEET—HOW THE SPANIARDS WERE CARED FOR.

ABOVE LEFT: UNCREDITED COVER PHOTOGRAPH OF ROUGH RIDERS, PRESUMABLY IN CUBA. ABOVE RIGHT: A PAGE OF UNCREDITED PHOTOGRAPHS MADE IN MANILA, PHILIPPINES, AFTER ADMIRAL DEWEY DEFEATED SPANISH FORCES DURING THE SPANISH-AMERICAN WAR. PUBLISHED IN *LESLIE'S WEEKLY*, DECEMBER 8, 1898. (OTTO RICHTER LIBRARY, UNIVERSITY OF MIAMI)

own instant documentation. In addition, he said, "publishers have sent their representatives to the war to secure photographs of scenes, and incidents of public interest, which they reproduce and sell as *war pictures*." The day of what Cummings called the "pen picture, unaccompanied by words," was over.[6]

The possibility of profiting from and perhaps even becoming famous through war correspondence made it easy to lose sight of the difficulties and dangers of such work. Pictorial coverage of the Civil War was a distant memory. Then, pictures were supplied by sketch artists and a small, determined group of photographers, but for the most part their images showed the terrible aftermath of war, not actual fighting. In Cuba, Puerto Rico, and the Philippines, however, photographers could record war as it happened, up close and very personal. Covering modern war, as both reporters and photographers discovered, could have disastrous consequences.

The well-publicized case of Ridgway Glover, photographic correspondent for *Frank Leslie's Illustrated Newspaper* and the *Philadelphia Photographer* magazine, who was killed by Sioux and Cheyenne warriors near Fort Phil Kearny in Wyoming Territory in 1868, might have served as both lesson and warning to those clamoring for war work. So, too, the more

HARPER'S WEEKLY

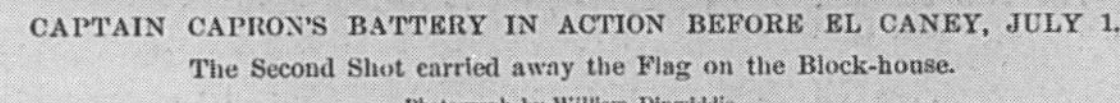

CAPTAIN CAPRON'S BATTERY IN ACTION BEFORE EL CANEY, JULY 1.
The Second Shot carried away the Flag on the Block-house.
Photograph by William Dinwiddie.

9TH INFANTRY FIRING IN THE RAIN, FROM INTRENCHMENTS, AT FORT SAN JUAN, JULY 9.
Photograph by James Burton.

BEFORE SANTIAGO—PHOTOGRAPHS TAKEN UNDER FIRE.

here and enjoy ourselves without people talking our reason for coming!"
ou don't mean to say," cried Mrs. Perkenpine, now r feet, "that you two elderly ones is the honey-ers?"
es," said Mr. Archibald, looking with amusement astonished faces about him, "we truly are."
Vell," said the she-guide, seating herself, "if I'd an old maid as long as that, I think I'd stuck it out. erhaps you was a widow, mum?"

find people who are willing to assert their individuality, and when they are found I always want to talk to them. I suppose, Mr. Matlack, that your life is one long assertion of individuality."
"What, ma'am?" asked the guide.
"I mean," said she, "that when you are out alone in the wild forest, holding in your hand the weapon which decides the question of life or death for any living creature over whom you may choose to exercise your jurisdiction, absolutely independent of every social trammel,

PHOTOGRAPHING UNDER F

[SPECIAL CORRESPONDENCE OF "HARPER'S WEEKL

SAN JUAN, *July*

JULY 1 will forever be a memorable day in A history. On that day the United States army, un eral Shafter, stormed and took, after several hou ing, the two Spanish strongholds El Caney a Juan. I was with the Seventh United States I

PHOTOGRAPHS BY WILLIAM DINWIDDIE *(LEFT)* AND JAMES BURTON SHOWING AMERICAN TROOPS IN ACTION DURING THE SIEGE OF SANTIAGO, CUBA. PUBLISHED IN *HARPER'S WEEKLY,* AUGUST 6, 1898. (OTTO RICHTER LIBRARY, UNIVERSITY OF MIAMI)

recent case of an amateur photographer named Morris, manager of Donald Mackenzie's ill-fated North West Africa Company at Tarfaya in far southwestern Morocco. Morris brazenly attempted to photograph a group of soldiers of the sultan of Morocco, Moulay Hassan I, in 1888. The *New York Times* reported that he was in the process of aiming, or perhaps focusing his camera, when he was killed. The Moroccans, according to the *Times*, were not entirely to blame, for "when they found him leveling against them an instrument looking suspiciously like a machine gun, some of the party stole up and brained him, perhaps while his head was under the cloth." The moral was obvious: photographers ought not to "take aim with a lens at a group of natives without first carefully assuring them that it is not loaded."[7]

Despite the obvious risks, journalists covering the war with Spain seemed somewhat surprised at their own vulnerability in combat situations. "I suppose everyone has a different sensation when for the first time he finds himself with bullets whistling around him on all sides, yet seeing nothing, only hearing them as they rush by, crashing through the leaves and twigs on their deadly errand," recalled photographer James Burton, on assignment in Cuba from *Harper's Weekly*. Nothing in his previous experiences as a photojournalist prepared him for what he found during one deadly skirmish outside Santiago. Somehow "the danger of the situation did not strike me until I heard several heavy thuds near me, and, on looking around me, saw some of our men on the ground, dead or wounded." He wondered if he would be next.[8]

Jimmy Hare from *Collier's* was similarly affected by his initial experience of combat, at least according to novelist and neophyte war correspondent Stephen Crane, who was working for Pulitzer's *New York World*. During their first real battle, the two accompanied troops advancing toward Santiago when suddenly "the crash of Spanish fire became uproarious, and the air simply whistled." Hare seemed at once frightened and undaunted. "He looked at me with eyes opened extremely wide. 'Say,' he said, 'this is pretty hot, ain't it?'" Crane, who was just as new to combat as his colleague, assured the photographer that this was the real thing, not some paltry affair. Apparently, Hare felt that if the fighting was serious, "then he was willing to pay in his fright as a rational price for the privilege of being present." He accepted Crane's assurances "with simple grace, and deported himself with kindly dignity as one moving amid great things."[9]

Crane's descriptions of fighting in Cuba had the power to mesmerize in no small part because he made it clear that his were the recollections of an eyewitness. The same was true of the photographs made by Hare and others who managed to get to the front. The work of American soldiers and sailors during the war was endlessly glorified by the press; it is not surprising that a good bit of the glory stuck to the correspondents themselves. After all, in many of their dispatches, they were heroes as well. For months after the war ended, soldiers, sailors, and journalists published stirring accounts of their experiences. American involvement in the war lasted just a few months, but a year later, according to William Dean Howells, "troops of heroes of all shapes and sizes are writing themselves up or being written up with tireless activity in the magazines."[10]

The deluge of coverage to which Howells referred is understandable given the number of reporters, photographers, and artists who managed to secure press credentials. Yet the largesse of the War Department toward the fourth estate was not universally appreciated, even by representatives of major news organizations. In an article for *Overland Monthly*, James F. Archibald, who was wounded early in the war, complained that "our Government issued innumerable passes to correspondents, and in consequence there were all sorts and conditions of writers gathered in Tampa." He noted contemptuously that even an obscure agricultural publication sent a reporter to Cuba, and writers from religious weeklies were common. The problem was that most eager would-be war correspondents were bereft of military experience. "Hardly a score in the entire lot knew a spare wheel from a cavalry brigade, and yet they were, in many cases, the best writers from their respective journals."[11]

After the war some well-connected journalists suggested that only reporters from important publications or press syndicates and those with established reputations should be given credentials. Such a policy would ease the troublesome glut of journalists seeking passage and access, as well as ensure that war would be covered by experts friendly to the service. "The War Department might furnish a list of names of those men acceptable to it," Richard Harding Davis proposed, and the leading journals could propose a second list. The two lists would constitute the entire press corps. These reporters, he said, "are men well known to the army and navy and to the reading public. They have been together in many campaigns; they are trained to observe; brilliant, descriptive writers and historians; and of their own reputation for responsibility they are properly jealous." All others need not apply.[12]

American military forces in Cuba numbered approximately 17,000 men, and after hundreds of journalists flocked to Key West and Tampa, Florida, in the first days of the conflict, 165 were issued credentials to cover the fighting. That was just the beginning. Many more would ask for and receive credentials in coming weeks, though not many would be allowed access to frontline areas. For Davis the "generosity in the bestowal of passes was absurd," because it meant that the news gathered by the few journalists who managed to get to the front had to compete constantly with the "hysterical, half-baked news sent north" by correspondents who watched the war from comfortable accommodations far behind the lines.[13] After the sharp fight at Las Guasimas, for instance, the first reports sent

PHOTOGRAPH BY *HARPER'S* WILLIAM DINWIDDIE OF SOLDIERS RELAXING DURING A TRUCE IN THE AMERICAN TRENCHES NEAR SANTIAGO, CUBA. (LIBRARY OF CONGRESS)

back to the United States declared that General Joseph Wheeler's men had been routed. But those stories came, according to Davis, "from correspondents three miles away at Siboney, who received their information from the wounded when they were carried to the rear, and from an officer who stampeded before the fight had fairly begun."[14] Davis contended that none of the artists who depicted the battle got it right either, for they also based their sketches on second-hand reports. Like other correspondents, Davis carried a simple camera, and frequently illustrated his own stories.[15] He made sure his readers knew he had been there and that the things he wrote about were true because he had seen them with his own eyes and captured them on film.

The size of the press corps and its insatiability created enormous logistical problems. In the end it took perseverance, and sometimes military connections, to get to the front. To make matters much worse, at least from the point of view of the high command, inexperienced reporters and photographers sometimes got in the way. Frederic Remington described what could happen when noncombatants found themselves in a firefight. "Russian, English, and Japanese correspondents [and] artists, . . . were flushed, and went straddling up the hill before the first barrel of the Dons. Directly came the warning scream of No. 2, and we dropped and hugged the ground like star-fish. Bang! right over us it exploded. I was dividing a small hollow with a distinguished colonel of the staff."[16]

For Remington providing accurate pictures of the war for the mighty Hearst empire took a toll on both body and spirit. In November 1898 he reflected on the role of journalists in war for *Harper's Monthly*. "It is well to bear in mind the difference in the point of view of an artist or a correspondent, and a soldier." The latter has a particular job to do, and presumably the training and equipment necessary to do it. On the other hand, the journalist "stalks through the middle distance, seeing the fight and its immediate results, the wounded; lying down by a dead body . . . ; he will share no glory; he has only the responsibility of seeing clearly what he must tell; and he must keep his reserve." In the end Remington thought that the "soldier sleeps better nights."[17]

Remington's reminiscence describes photojournalists and artists as cool and steadfast eyewitnesses working tirelessly and without fanfare on behalf of the public. It is a powerful image, and one that still has power. A year after the war with Spain ended, one observer commented that the "popular conception of the photographer in war-time is one of a man in the midst of the fray calmly focusing scenes of carnage for newspaper illustration." The place of the peripatetic combat photographer, he continued, was assured. "The war photographer of the future will be a well paid, live, all-round man. His work will be demanded by the people, and newspapers will not ask the price of a man, but his quality."[18]

There is some truth in this description, but despite technological innovations in cameras and films as well as the phenomenal success of illustrated journalism, photojournalists during the Spanish-American War faced a host of nearly insurmountable problems. Not the least of these was the difficulty of making effective photographs during battle. Small cameras and fast film made action pictures possible in theory, but success in the field was not automatic. James Burton discovered as much during one sharp skirmish outside Santiago, and he admitted and explained his failure in a brief article. "Although I was thus on the first firing line, and many men were wounded and killed all about me, as you will see by my photographs . . . I found it impossible to make any actual 'battle scenes,' for many reasons—the distance at which the fighting is conducted, the area which is covered, but chiefly the long grass and thickly wooded country."[19] Burton made sure his audience knew he was there, at the front, dodging bullets with the best of them. But being there did not—could not—guarantee pictures.

Naval activities were equally problematic. Albert Greaves, who served as a lieutenant with the fleet during the war, explained that both amateurs and professionals were confounded by great clouds of smoke during even routine naval engagements, as well as by thick deposits of "saltpetre and powder gases" that often coated their lenses. After the climactic battle of July 3, when the Spanish fleet commanded by Admiral Pascual Cervera y Topete finally emerged from Santiago harbor only to be dispatched by the American fleet under Admiral Sampson, one set of "valuable and historic pictures" was ruined "by the careless submergence of the camera and roll in one of the ship's boats."[20]

Neither personal hazards nor the myriad difficulties of photographing the war discouraged the army of amateur and professional photographers determined to catch a bit of action on film. Soldiers and sailors were inspired to record the war by newspapers and magazines anxious to run pictures—any pictures—of the fighting, and by camera advertisements that promised ease of operation and good results. "Among the 90,000 soldiers now at Tampa, Chickamauga, and other places," reported T. H. Cummings in June, "there are, at the lowest calculation, several hundred who are thoroughly prepared to take snap shots."[21] Lieutenant Greaves concurred. "Photographic material was in demand in those days, and the little stationery shop near the hotel [in Key West] did a thriving business in Kodaks of all kinds among the junior officers of the fleet, some of whom secured many valuable pictures of the memorable events that took place in the succeeding months."[22]

Although most newspapers and magazines ran photographs of the war taken by professionals, a few made an effort to obtain publishable pictures from the men in the ranks. Arthur Brisbane, stalwart editor of the *New York Journal,* recalled one proposal to send a "first-class camera" to every ship in the American fleet. The man who got the equipment would be promised up to five hundred dollars for the negative of "a good battle-scene" provided, of course, "it should reach the home office before any other newspaper got it."[23] The editors at *Leslie's Illustrated* put this idea into practice. They announced in May that "prizes aggregating $100" would be awarded "for the best pictures taken by amateurs, of scenes, on land or sea, connected to the present war Excitement."[24] Such generosity probably had more to do with circulation than any altruistic regard for the pictorial output of the armed forces. In any event, the ads in *Leslie's* encouraged some to make photographs with real news value, to do more than compile simple mementos for the family photo album.

In one case, a midshipman aboard the battleship *Iowa* was so caught up with the photographic possibilities of the naval battle at Santiago that he put himself at considerable risk in order to secure a view of the action. The ship's commander, Captain Robley D. Evans, described how the young sailor set up his tripod on top of the turret of one of the ship's guns during action against the Spanish armored cruiser *Colon*. He was "busily engaged in 'getting the focus,' . . . unmindful of the hurricane of shot and shell around him." The young man may have finally succeeded in procuring a snapshot of the distressed Spanish ship, according to his outraged captain, but he also would "remember for many years to come the few words I addressed to him."[25]

Although soldiers and sailors photographed aspects of the war, most of their pictures were routine snapshots made of men relaxing in camp. The real business of compiling a pictorial record of military activities for newspaper and magazine readers back home was left to professionals. Of these, Jimmy Hare from *Collier's Weekly* emerged with a reputation as the preeminent American war photographer. He seemed to be everywhere in Cuba, and his exploits were breathlessly related by correspondents from his own and rival publications. Long after the war, at a testimonial dinner in Hare's honor, Robert J. Collier told how his favorite photographer changed the course of the magazine business. He remembered that shortly after the battleship *Maine* exploded and sank into the mud of Havana Harbor on February 15, 1898, Jimmy burst into his office, demanding to be sent to Cuba. "Sending Hare to Havana that morning involved me in more troubles and wars and libel suits than any one act in my life," the publisher said. "It turned me from the quiet paths of a literary career into association with war correspondents, politicians, muckrakers, and advertising men. If it had not been for Jimmy Hare, I do not think *Collier's* would have been troubled by any advertising." In effect, he said, the "*Maine* BLEW UP, and Jimmy BLEW IN."[26]

Hare's father was a well-respected British camera-maker, and in his youth Jimmy was endlessly drilled in the mechanical and optical intricacies of the trade. Relations between father and son became strained, however, and in 1899 Jimmy immigrated to the United States. After working briefly as a technical advisor for the company originally established by the Anthony brothers, he turned his attention to making pictures instead of equipment. From the beginning Hare used small, portable cameras, and he did well as a freelance photojournalist, selling pictures of sporting and news events to a variety of publications.

In 1895 Hare began working at Lorrillard Spencer's *Illustrated American*, a slick weekly magazine that prided itself on a sophisticated use of photographs. In the first issue the editors promised to employ the best artists and engravers in the country, but the magazine's "special aim will

STEREOGRAPH BY AN UNIDENTIFIED PHOTOGRAPHER FOR THE KEYSTONE VIEW COMPANY OF MEADVILLE, PA. "SEARCHING FOR THE DEAD ON WRECKED BATTLESHIP MAINE. HAVANA HARBOR, CUBA." FEW AMERICAN PHOTOGRAPHERS NEGLECTED TO MEMORIALIZE THE RAGGED STEEL SUPERSTRUCTURE THAT JUTTED OUT OF THE WATER (PRIVATE COLLECTION)

be to develop the possibilities, as yet almost unexplored, of the camera and the various processes that reproduce the work of the camera." Illustrations in the magazine provide the most accurate and timely chronicle of contemporaneous history, for there exists "no greater artist than the sun; he binds upon paper the evanescent grace of the life around us, the men and women among whom we move, the familiar scenes that we love, the landscapes that we admire."[27]

For three years, Hare's photographs ran in most issues, but in 1898, his job went up in flames. When he arrived at the office one cold January morning, he found the building ablaze; it was soon gutted from cellar to roof. Almost all his equipment was inside: cameras, lenses, and film gone forever. His reaction was swift. According to one of his biographers, within minutes the initial despair wore off, and Hare borrowed a camera, "photographed the fire from the most effective angles, and sold to several newspapers the pictures of the holocaust that had ruined him."[28]

A few weeks later he was in Cuba. Like many of his fellow photographers, he made images of the eerie, evocative wreckage of the *Maine*—twisted steel looming out of the still water—as well as conditions in the infamous *reconcentrados,* where rebel prisoners of war and other enemies of Spain were kept. He also teamed up with Sylvester ("Harry") Scovel, the well-known reporter for Pulitzer's *World,* on a clandestine mission to study and photograph Spanish fortifications near Havana.

In late April, Hare joined Henry James Whigham and Francis H. Nichols, reporters with the *Chicago Tribune,* on a secret mission that was part journalistic enterprise and part pure espionage. The stated purpose of the foray was to take word to rebel leader General Máximo Gómez y Baez in Santa Clara province of the official entry of the United States into the war. The stories written by Hare and the others confirmed their status as top war correspondents, and Hare's gritty images of the ragged but undaunted insurgents provided seemingly irrefutable evidence of the need for American involvement.

During his brief sojourn with the rebels, Hare demonstrated both persistence and guile in obtaining a rare photograph of General Gómez. The rebel commander was loath to have his portrait taken, by Hare or anyone else. Whigham argued that such a picture would further the cause of international relations, and Nichols insisted that the world would doubt the entire story "if they didn't bring a picture of the Cuban patriot back with them," but Gómez refused.[29] He had posed for pictures in the past, he said, and every time the results were wretched and terrifying; no amount of gentle persuasion on the part of the Americans would change his mind. Since a formal portrait was out of the question, Hare decided to work by stealth. While the commander was engaged in conversation with the American reporters, Hare quietly made a single image with one of his small, unobtrusive cameras. Later he made another from behind the general as he relaxed in a hammock. Gómez never knew, and *Collier's* got its scoop.[30]

HALFTONE OF A PHOTOGRAPH SHOWING JOHN C. HEMMENT, ACCOMPANIED BY HIS ASSISTANT, DOCUMENTING THE WRECKAGE OF THE *MAINE*. PUBLISHED IN THE *AMERICAN ANNUAL OF PHOTOGRAPHY FOR 1900*. (PRIVATE COLLECTION)

Not every press photographer in Cuba was as enamored as Hare with the possibilities offered by candid photography. There was a certain reluctance to use simple box cameras to record significant events. Detective cameras might do for avid amateurs, but professionals used large, bulky equipment that confounded the Sunday snapshooter. One of the best-known and most highly respected photographers in Cuba, John C. Hemment, who worked for the *New York Journal* as well as *Leslie's Weekly*, publicly eschewed small cameras. Hemment always traveled in style, equipped with the finest view cameras and usually accompanied by one or more assistants. The unguarded moment was out of the question for Hemment since each photograph necessitated an elaborate series of grand gestures and commands barked to both subjects and assistants. As a result, fast-moving events such as the deadly seesaw of opposing armies were usually beyond his control.

During the long, tedious march to Santiago, Hare happened upon Hemment unexpectedly. The man from the *Journal* offered his rival a bit of lunch, a gesture that was not atypical; for all Hemment's grandiloquence, he was well liked by many photographers. Hemment was accompanied by a Japanese assistant who carried both equipment and provisions. "There's fried chicken," Hemment offered, "and I even have napkins." The aide held a large umbrella over Hemment's head, shielding him from the harsh tropical sun. After lunch Hemment lit a choice Cuban cigar and announced he was through for the day. Shortly thereafter he and his servant departed for more comfortable accommodations in the rear.[31] Hemment emerged unscathed from his stint as war photographer in Cuba; his servant, however, did not. While holding Hemment's horse as the photographer attempted to make a picture of the Spanish fort at El Caney, he was wounded in the face by a bullet that "just furrowed out the flesh."

Hemment was unfazed; he did not record the feelings of his helper.[32]

Backed by the considerable power of Hearst, Hemment was a high-profile presence at the turn of the century. Traveling through the war zone with his heavy cameras and tripods, accompanied by assistants, Hemment naturally attracted attention. Part of his success was undoubtedly due to charisma; he established cordial if not outright friendly relationships with editors, publishers, and fellow photojournalists. However, an incident in Europe in 1899 involving Hemment, Admiral George Dewey, the hero of Manila Bay, and Frances Benjamin Johnston reveals a more sinister approach to the business of photojournalism.

At the time, Johnston often augmented the income from her studio by supplying photographs to the George Bain News Service and other syndicates. Before she left for a vacation in Europe, Bain suggested she photograph Dewey during his triumphal tour of ports on the continent; there were few photographs of Dewey available, and fewer still of him on board his battleship, the *Olympia*. "I have canvassed the situation and I honestly believe that if you cover this subject in your best style and quickly you can make enough out of it to pay for your entire European tour," wrote Bain in July 1899. She also agreed to supply photographs of the admiral to Charles Culver Johnson of the United News service. The problem was getting permission to board Dewey's ship. That, apparently, was not much of an obstacle for Johnston, who was both well-connected and resourceful. She tracked down Theodore Roosevelt, then assistant secretary of the navy, at the family estate in Oyster Bay, New York, and after a brief interview came away with the necessary entrée. On the back of one of her business cards Roosevelt scrawled, "My dear Admiral Dewey, Miss Johnston is a lady, and whom I personally know. I can vouch for [her], she does good work, and any promise she makes she will keep."[33]

Johnston met the *Olympia* in Naples, Italy, early in August, presented her card with the greeting from Roosevelt, and received permission to tour and photograph the ship. The following day she took a great many pictures, perhaps as many as 150, including portraits of the admiral, interior and exterior views of the ship, and studies of the sailors. At about the same time, John Hemment also made photographs of Dewey and his ship, and in the process met Johnston. Both sets of films were developed in Naples, but at that point the saga of Johnston's images becomes somewhat murky.

Johnston apparently agreed to let Hemment deliver her pictures to Bain in New York since he was returning to the United States immediately, whereas she was just beginning her long-awaited vacation. Bain had warned her about Hemment before she left. Her fellow photojournalist was talented, according to Bain, but there were rumors of certain tricky practices, and she was told to be on her guard. Bain's caution was well-founded. When Hemment returned to the United States, he began marketing his own images of Dewey energetically, but there was no sign of Johnston's film. For nearly a month he had the market pretty much to himself; her negatives were still in London. Bain was furious. "And WHY did you entrust your negatives to the only person who was working against you?" he asked.

UNCREDITED PHOTOGRAPH OF FRANCES BENJAMIN JOHNSTON SHOWING ADMIRAL GEORGE DEWEY A SELECTION OF HER IMAGES ABOARD THE U.S.S. *OLYMPIA* IN NAPLES, ITALY, 1899. (LIBRARY OF CONGRESS)

Johnston never explained her faith in Hemment, nor did she offer any explanation as to the precise nature of their agreement. In the end her photographs—though tardy—arrived and sold well, and perhaps even George Bain was placated. He certainly should have been. Bain sold one of Johnston's photographs of Dewey to *Leslie's* for $100, at the time a record sum for a news picture.[34]

The case of Johnston's overdue negatives—whether from Hemment's deviousness or some innocent lapse—underlines the competitiveness of photojournalism at the turn of the century. It may also speak to a certain dissatisfaction in some circles with the mere presence of women in journalism. By then the ranks of reporters and photographers included a number of talented and prominent women. This was due in no small measure to the public prodding of Johnston and others. "As a rule the beginner will find her best opportunity and her chances of success greatly multiplied if she is able to originate and exploit some special field of work," Johnston advised in 1897.[35] Specialization could provide a neat stepping stone to success in journalism; Johnston's own career was proof of that.[36]

As women became more active in magazine and newspaper journalism, some sought access to stories that were formerly the private domain of men. Such was case with Johnston's photographs of Dewey and the *Olympia* in 1899, and with Anna Benjamin's reports from Cuba and the Philippines for *Leslie's Illustrated Weekly*.[37] The success of these and other women rankled a few of their male colleagues. Reporter James Creelman, who was seriously wounded during the fighting at El Caney, wrote after the war that women brought great sorrow to the corps of intrepid males who used to have war all to themselves. He bitterly denounced the idea that women reporters be allowed to cover war, and concluded that any success they enjoyed must be due to nefarious scheming, not excellence in reporting. "The swish of the journalistic petticoat on the edge of the military camp meant the hidden leaking of news," he wrote after the war. "For a woman, when she cannot drag forth the secrets of an army by strength, will make a sly hole in some man's discretion, and the news will run out of itself."[38] Creelman's acid complaint had little effect, however, and after 1898 the idea that women could accompany armies in the field, reporting on and photographing their activities, was no longer either novel or cursorily dismissed. After all, what counted for many editors was not the gender of the photographer but the quality of the images. This was certainly the case with a series of photographs of Spanish prisoners of war made by Sarah Kneller Miller at the naval base in Annapolis, Maryland. She sold one image of three Spanish officers to *Leslie's Illustrated Weekly* and was offered in return what she called a "roving commission" by the editors. For the next twenty years, Miller provided *Leslie's* with photographs from around the world.[39]

During the Cuban and Philippine campaigns, the best efforts of correspondents—regardless of gender—were stymied most often by unforeseeable natural circumstances and by the efforts of various military authorities to control and monitor the flow of information about the war. The bulky equipment that some photographers insisted on using also presented daunting logistical problems. After leaving Cuba, Hemment advised photographers to leave their giant machines at home and cover war with hand cameras. Though fitted out in style and accompanied by an assistant, he must have envied the ease with which many of his colleagues moved through the war zone. Yet sometimes even the most portable equipment could not guarantee success, as Jimmy Hare discovered shortly after the victory of Roosevelt's volunteers at San Juan and Kettle Hills. During the assault of the Rough Riders, Hare shot six rolls of 5×7 film, each consisting of twelve exposures. It was good work. But on the trip back, his horse suddenly bolted, and two rolls were lost forever. On another occasion, Hare was the only photographer present at an impromptu meeting between Generals Gómez, Nelson A. Miles, and Joseph Wheeler near Santiago, and he shot one roll of twelve 5×7 exposures. But once again Hare had a nasty riding accident. This time the photographer managed to salvage the film and sent the entire film pack to New York, where *Collier's* technicians were able to develop and print an image. The August 20 issue included a double-page drawing by Gilbert Gaul made from Hare's negative as well as a brief explanation. "The photograph from which this drawing was made . . . was taken on a celluloid 'film' of a roll of twelve. On his way to the rear, Mr. Hare fell from his horse while crossing a stream, and the roll of films became soaked, and it remained wet more than two weeks, reaching New York in a solid mass, apparently. After days of effort the outer portion of the roll was removed and the remainder 'developed' and printed."[40]

In the end neither the technical limitations of photography nor the occasional brush with nature deterred those determined to produce images of war for the periodical press. "We had certain . . . handicaps then which made it necessary to develop pictures while at the battle front, and early cameras and the first types of film were hard to work with—almost as hard as the modern military censor," Hare recalled in 1940.[41] Nevertheless, photographs of men in action were produced and published widely, giving Americans at home a reasonably realistic view of the brief war, and one that provided a vivid contrast to the romantic hyperbole of political leaders and military publicists.

During the Civil War, photographers were unable to do much more than depict objects and men at rest. In 1898, however, they could show things as they happened. For the first time, Americans at home were eyewitnesses of war. It was a revelation. Photographs of men on the march, of soldiers hunkered down during skirmishes with the enemy, of officers peering at maps and discussing strategy, and of artillery pieces being fired were published with considerable fanfare by the popular press. An avid public was suddenly privy to actual combat, at least vicariously.

This supposedly accurate and on-the-spot view of war was not, however, entirely free from the work of censors—both civilian and military. During the early days of the revolution in Cuba, American reporters and photographers chafed under rigid guidelines for the press established by Spanish authorities, especially those enacted by General Valeriano Weyler y Nicolau, the last military governor appointed by Spain. As the situation in Cuba worsened, criticism from the American press and the government increased and access to Spanish prisoner-of-war camps and rebel-held areas decreased. American reporters who were caught defying the rules were likely to be treated harshly. When Thomas Dawley, a photographer for *Harper's Weekly*, was arrested for crossing the Mariel's infamous *trocha*—a vast, fortified barrier that cut across the island—in order to interview and photograph rebel leader Antonio Maceo, he was transported back to Havana in chains, lashed to another prisoner in an unventilated boxcar with a sheet-metal roof. Once back in the capital, Dawley was paraded through the streets, then unceremoniously thrown into prison at Morro Castle. Five days later, in a gesture designed to mollify the new American consul, Fitzhugh Lee, the photographer was released.[42]

Dawley's brush with the Spanish authorities only escalated the amount of written and pictorial material sent north to newspapers and magazines. Cuba was news, and daily infusions of words and pictures were vital. Editors and publishers back home, locked into vicious circulation wars, insisted on a constant flow of dramatic words and pictures from the

HARPER'S WEEKLY
A JOURNAL OF CIVILIZATION
NEW YORK, SATURDAY, SEPTEMBER 24, 1898.
TEN CENTS A COPY. FOUR DOLLARS A YEAR.
COLONEL THEODORE ROOSEVELT, U.S.V.

UNCREDITED COVER PHOTOGRAPH OF TEDDY ROOSEVELT, COMMANDER OF THE ROUGH RIDERS, IN CUBA, 1898. (OTTO RICHTER LIBRARY, UNIVERSITY OF MIAMI)

Caribbean. Stephen Crane recalled that reporters were urged by their editors "to remember that the American people were a collection of super-nervous idiots who would immediately have convulsions if we did not throw them some news—any news." Crane disagreed with this snide characterization, but did as he was told. He and his colleagues in Cuba made sure the folks stateside had a steady diet of war news. "We told them this and we told them that, and I warrant you our screaming sounded like the noise of a lot of sea-birds settling for the night among the black crags."[43] Evading censors thus became part game and part way of life, especially among those working for Hearst and Pulitzer, a way for patriotic, freedom-loving reporters to help the cause of democracy in Cuba while boosting readership at home.[44] Before the arrival of American troops in Cuba on June 22, correspondents went to extraordinary lengths to ensure that their stories got past the Spanish censors. Elaborate codes were devised, recalled author and reporter Ray Stannard Baker, "whereby messages may seem to say one thing when they mean quite another." Newspapers that could afford it bought or hired speedy dispatch boats to ply the Florida Straits, picking up stories and photographs from correspondents in Cuba, sometimes in the dark of night, and racing with them to Key West.[45] The

PHOTOGRAPH BY GEORGE ROCKWOOD OF NEW YORK, COPYING THE PORTRAIT PUBLISHED EARLIER BY *HARPER'S WEEKLY,* AND USED TO ADVERTISE ROOSEVELT'S MEMOIRS OF THE WAR WITH SPAIN. (OTTO RICHTER LIBRARY, UNIVERSITY OF MIAMI)

press corps in Cuba was active and intensely partisan; most reporters felt that evading censorship helped in a noble cause.

This attitude was easily transferred to the American military when it established its own set of rules and regulations regarding press coverage. General William Shafter, the bovine and choleric commander of the American ground forces in Cuba, was not thrilled by the prospect of unrestrained access, and he insisted on a certain measure of military control. "It is my opinion that newspaper men should not be allowed to accompany an army," he wrote after the war, "but they all came with credentials from the Secretary of War, and I gave them passage." He really had no choice. American participation in the Cuban revolution was fueled by the daily deluge of words and pictures that was delivered to and printed by American newspapers and magazines despite the best efforts of Spanish authorities. There was no way a few beleaguered American censors could restrain a press corps enamored both of its own power and of cloak-and-dagger methods of gathering the news. Shafter admitted as much: "I recognized that, with a people like ours, it may be better to risk the injury their news even under censorship may do than cause the dissatisfaction their exclusion would give rise to at home."[46]

As war extras and special editions flooded the streets back home, American correspondents flocked into every encampment and battle site, eager to relay detailed accounts of military activities and even proposed military activities. "Any feeble opposition put up by the browbeaten authorities on the score of secrecy was imperiously brushed aside," wrote historian Walter Millis in 1931. "After all, if it was not the newspapers' war, whose was it?"[47] And not everyone in the military viewed the press with disdain and suspicion, since timely publicity could often provide the perfect impetus for advancement. "Most of the newly appointed general officers of the American army owe their advance to the reports of the correspondents," wrote James Archibald smugly shortly after the war. Although these officers were neither untalented nor undeserving, Archibald insisted that "it takes the special writer to bring their deeds and value before the public. If it depended upon the official dispatches and reports to make them famous they would go to their last rest without any special reward."[48]

No military personage was more knowledgeable and appreciative of the power of the press than Teddy Roosevelt, commander of the Rough Riders. He established cordial relations with correspondents and photographers, allowing a few of them both access and special privileges. In return, his exploits and those of his men on San Juan Hill became the glittering centerpiece of coverage of the land war in Cuba. Pictures of Roosevelt in action flooded the press, making him an icon, instantly recognized and unforgettable. In September *Harper's Weekly* ran a photograph of Teddy Roosevelt on the cover. In the uncredited picture, the future president stares sternly into the camera, his eyes shielded by a rumpled cowboy hat rakishly pinned up on the left side; his gloved left hand is perched imperiously on his hip, and a kerchief around his neck blows slightly in the breeze. Apparently Roosevelt or those in his entourage realized the value of the picture, for when *Scribner's Magazine* advertised the publication of Teddy's memoirs, the text of the ad was accompanied by an uncanny copy of the *Harper's* photograph. But the new picture was made in a studio far from Cuba, and it was copyrighted by the well-known New York studio photographer George Rockwood.

The popular press reveled in its power after the war. A new generation of seasoned war correspondents congratulated themselves and each other for first providing irrefutable evidence of Spanish perfidy, then furnishing the public with lively and detailed descriptions of the overwhelming American victory. "The siege of Santiago developed other heroes than those who wore the blue," the editors of *Munsey's Magazine* reminded their readers in September 1898. The wounds suffered by reporters James Creelman and Edward Marshall exemplified "courageous devotion to duty," demonstrating the courage and determination of civilian reporters who accompanied the military. According to the story, both men, though grievously wounded (Marshall was paralyzed), insisted on dictating their stories before they were taken from the field to receive treatment.[49]

Not everyone agreed that the wartime press deserved praise, or, for that matter, that the war itself was either noble or necessary. Harvard scholar William James castigated the popular press as well as the government. "In 1898 our people had read the word WAR in letters three inches high in every newspaper for three months," he wrote in 1910. "The pliant politician McKinley was swept away by their eagerness, and our splendid war with Spain became a sordid necessity."[50] Even during the war, friction between the press and the military belied the contention that coverage was simple, direct, and universally approved. At the ceremonies marking the surrender of Santiago to American forces, antipathy between the high command and those who covered the high command surfaced publicly. General

Shafter and *New York World* reporter Harry Scovel were arguing about some matter, when suddenly the general slapped the reporter. Oblivious to the ranks of armed men standing nearby in silent formation, Scovel struck back. The men were pulled apart and the matter seemed closed, though an undercurrent of bitterness remained on both sides.[51] The incident was practically lost in the public's euphoria over the swift and decisive victory. Shafter's sudden rebuke received scant coverage in newspapers and magazines, although many reporters witnessed it and the entire press corps soon learned of it. Perhaps the press was reluctant to append a sour note to what was widely viewed as an unmitigated military achievement.

The power of the press and the degree to which it could choose what to cover was in large part due to its active involvement in the Cuban Revolution long before the United States military showed up. Indeed, as a number of reporters and publishers boasted later, the war might not have happened at all were it not for them. As a result, military authorities were hamstrung in the establishment of strict controls. Moreover, notwithstanding stories that criticized specific actions of army or naval personnel, American correspondents were generally positive about the role and goals of the military. Ultimately, the press and the military established a kind of uneasy partnership in 1898. There was censorship, to be sure, but for most journalists it seemed manageable. "We had some censors in those days . . . ," remembered Jimmy Hare, "but they had not attained to their present colossal proportions so a fellow could sometimes 'put it over' them."[52]

The access given to the press in the Spanish-American conflict would not soon be repeated. It would, in fact, become something of an anomaly. During the Russo-Japanese War early in the century, for instance, both sides effectively contained the press, and the Japanese were especially adept at controlling coverage. In addition to the steadfast refusal of both sides to allow unrestricted access, conditions were often appalling. *Collier's* magazine, which published several pictorial histories in book form after the war, enumerated the problems confronting photographers. "Since the days of the telegraph and the modern war correspondent, there has never been a war in which the work of the chroniclers was beset with such difficulties," wrote the editors. Images "were taken only after long marches over frozen and wind-swept country, the films developed in zero weather with the help of Korean servants or Japanese commissary officers, and they reached *Collier's* office only after being carried scores and perhaps hundreds of miles by coolie runners through a country where a mail service was unknown."[53]

Early in the war such obstacles proved daunting to even the most enterprising photographers. Most of them spent months in Tokyo, waiting in vain for permission to travel to the front. Later, when the Japanese instituted a system requiring all journalists to be accompanied by official military escorts, and to pay liberally for this service, the cost of covering the war increased dramatically. Only those with significant financial backing could now afford to remain in the war zone.

One who did stay was Jimmy Hare. The *Collier's* veteran war photog-

JOURNALISTS WISHING TO COVER JAPANESE MILITARY ACTIVITIES DURING THE RUSSO-JAPANESE WAR WERE ACCOMPANIED BY MILITARY PERSONNEL WHO CAREFULLY SCRUTINIZED AND CENSORED THEIR WORDS AND PICTURES. THIS UNCREDITED STEREOGRAPH, COPYRIGHTED IN 1905 BY T. W. INGERSOLL OF ST. PAUL, MINN., SHOWS *(LEFT TO RIGHT):* MAJOR YAMAGUCHI, CHIEF INTERPRETER AND PRESS CENSOR FOR THE JAPANESE MILITARY; RICHARD BARRY, A PHOTOGRAPHER FOR THE INGERSOLL VIEW COMPANY; AND MAJOR ODA, ASSISTANT TO GENERAL NOGI. (LIBRARY OF CONGRESS)

rapher, now nearly fifty, continued to astonish his colleagues with an ability to make successful pictures in the most adverse of circumstances. The magazine's chief reporter, Frederick Palmer, described Hare's activities early in the war. "When we stood on the heights of Wiju, the soldiers appeared only as the veriest specks to a camera lens. Jimmy wanted to see the charge as much as the rest of us. But the detail had to be shown and the photographer must be near the detail, so Jimmy slipped away when the censor wasn't looking." Later, near the Yalu River, Hare made exclusive pictures of groups of wounded Japanese soldiers. "He was the first of the correspondents' corps to cross the river," according to Palmer. "He trudged through miles of sand up to his knees. His pony was worn out; his weary servant promptly resigned. But Jimmy himself was up the next morning at daybreak, ill and pale, developing the first photographs of the army at the front."[54]

Although output from the Orient was paltry when compared to the abundant work produced by photographers in Cuba and the Philippines, those who persevered in covering the war did manage to come away with a few startling views that earned them both money and a measure of fame. One of the best known was James Ricalton, staff photographer for Elmer and Bert Underwood, publishers of stereo cards and news pictures since 1882. By 1901 the firm was producing 25,000 photographs a day, many of them views of news events. In fact, the business of supplying periodicals with pictures was so good that in 1921 the Underwoods sold their stereo operation to Keystone and concentrated all their efforts on collecting and disseminating news pictures.[55] Ricalton, described in the *Outing Magazine* as "a little, modest, bespectacled man," had made a number of grotesque

JIMMY HARE'S TENT AND ASSISTANTS SOMEWHERE IN KOREA DURING THE RUSSO-JAPANESE WAR. (HARRY RANSOM RESEARCH CENTER, UNIVERSITY OF TEXAS, AUSTIN)

A WOUNDED RUSSIAN SOLDIER IN KOREA, PHOTOGRAPHED BY HARE FOR *COLLIER'S MAGAZINE*. (HARRY RANSOM RESEARCH CENTER, UNIVERSITY OF TEXAS, AUSTIN)

and chilling views of carnage in Canton, China, during the Boxer Rebellion at the turn of the century. In Korea he managed to procure an image of an eleven-inch mortar at the instant of its firing, though he nearly lost his life doing so. During a fierce bombardment, one Japanese gunner on whom he trained his camera was decapitated by a Russian shell, and others nearby were riddled with shrapnel. Ricalton somehow emerged without a scratch, still determined to capture the action. A short time later, he made a stereo showing a projectile from a Japanese mortar frozen in flight. According to historian Christopher Lucas, the newspaper rights alone for this view earned the company "the lavish sum of $5000. Hundreds of copies were made in a matter of weeks," and the Underwoods announced plans to publish a complete boxed set of stereo views of the Russo-Japanese conflict.[56]

The rigid controls placed on Hare, Ricalton, Robert Dunn, James Archibald, and other reporters and photographers so aggravated some journalists that they departed. In May 1904, Juan C. Abel, editor of the *Photographer* magazine, reported that cameramen "sent out to follow the Russo-Japanese war seem to be having a hard time of it." One photographer "has already returned to this country in disgust," he wrote, "and others are likely to follow him unless the Japanese officials change their tactics."[57] But the hope that the threat or fact of leaving would lead to some diminution of the military's press policies came to nought. The concerns of a group of demanding and disgruntled reporters from western news organizations carried little weight in Korea, and in any event, neither the Japanese nor the Russians relished extensive news coverage of their operations.

What was condemned by the journalists was viewed by others with great interest. The Japanese success in restricting and manipulating the flow of information regarding military movements impressed most western military attachés. The practice of insisting that journalists be accompanied by military personnel as they went about their business was looked on with special favor by military men. Such a policy virtually guaranteed positive coverage, while placating those who persisted in demanding access to the front. Captain Peyton C. March of the United States Army wrote to his superiors that "it is not improbable that the day of the war-correspondent

HALF OF AN UNDERWOOD AND UNDERWOOD STEREOGRAPH MADE DURING THE BOXER REBELLION IN CHINA, PROBABLY BY JAMES RICALTON. THE PRINTED CAPTION READS, "THE GRIM EXECUTIONER TAKING THE LABELED HEAD TO EXHIBIT AS A WARNING, CANTON, CHINA." (LIBRARY OF CONGRESS)

A PHOTOGRAPHIC POSTCARD MADE FOR AND DISTRIBUTED BY THE INTERNATIONAL NEWS SERVICE, A SYNDICATE, SHOWING AMERICAN TROOPS RELAXING AFTER THE SHARP FIGHTING IN VERACRUZ, MEXICO, IN APRIL 1914. (PRIVATE COLLECTION)

who sends daily or weekly dispatches to his paper is over." He urged that similar procedures be adopted by American forces.[58] Also in attendance was Douglas MacArthur, then a first lieutenant assigned to the staff of his father, General Arthur MacArthur, an official observer. Just before the United States joined the Allies in World War I, the younger MacArthur would propose wartime guidelines for the press that were eerily reminiscent of Japanese policies during their war with Russia.[59]

Official governmental and military antipathy toward the press during wartime was global by the first decade of the twentieth century. The consensus among rulers around the world was that a free flow of information and criticism invariably compromised military success. Reporters and photographers were tightly corralled, their words and pictures pored over, shaped, and reshaped by ever-vigilant and suspicious censors. For some correspondents, the new restrictions made it impossible to work at all. When Jimmy Hare traveled to Serbia during the First Balkan War in 1912, for instance, he found that military chaperons and censors were unbending in their determination to restrict coverage. By early 1913 Hare was thoroughly frustrated and dissatisfied, and he left abruptly, convinced that the few images he managed to procure were hardly "worth the time, trouble and expense."[60]

There was a respite of sorts for the press in America during the long revolution in Mexico. Beginning with Francisco Madero's overthrow of dictator Porfirio Díaz in 1911, Mexico attracted the attention of reporters, photographers, and an enthusiastic corps of newsreel cameramen. For several years enterprising Americans filed stories and made moving and still pictures with comparatively little oversight from military authorities. During Madero's struggle to oust Díaz, for instance, freelancer Walter Horne, William Gunn Shepherd of the United Press, Earl Harding of the *New York World*, Hare, and several others hired cars and drivers to take them to Madero's various camps along the border. There among the rebels

UNCREDITED PHOTOGRAPH OF WILLIAM FOX, STAFF PHOTOGRAPHER FOR THE UNDERWOOD PHOTO NEWS SERVICE AND OFFICIAL PHOTOGRAPHER WITH THE U.S. EXPEDITIONARY FORCE IN MEXICO, 1916. (LIBRARY OF CONGRESS)

UNCREDITED PHOTOGRAPH FOR THE AMERICAN PRESS ASSOCIATION OF A U.S. MILITARY ENCAMPMENT IN MEXICO DURING THE PURSUIT OF PANCHO VILLA IN 1916. (STILL PICTURES BRANCH, NATIONAL ARCHIVES)

they collected information and views, then hurried back to the telegraph office and photographic labs in El Paso.[61]

After an American fleet steamed into Veracruz in April 1914, precipitating a brief but costly firefight between U.S. Marines and cadets of the Mexican naval academy loyal to Victoriano Huerta, correspondents arrived in droves. Some were already celebrities of a sort; others soon would be.

COLLIER'S FOR JULY 22, 1916 11

THE MEXICAN MESS

BY PORTER EMERSON BROWNE

MY friend had just returned from the Mexican border.

"Well," I said as he sank into a chair and lighted a cigar, "how did you find things?"

He shook his head.

"It certainly was a surprise to me," he said.

"Conditions?" I queried.

"This is a large country," he went on with apparent irrelevance, "a most large country. And it's incomprehensible to the point of inconceivability how almighty little any one part of it seems to know about all the other parts.

"To the sovereign State of Maine," he continued, "the affairs of the equally sovereign State of Cali-

"But the National Guard," I objected. "Surely they—"

"Their spirit is fine," he interrupted; "their response to the call inspiring. But soldiering is a profession. You can't make soldiers in a minute, any more than you can make lawyers or doctors. Also you can't take men out of offices and banks and department stores and clubs and expect them to do active duty in a country like Mexico. For the first six months it'll be all the National Guard can do to keep alive. And, anyway, this is no job for a national guard in the first place. It's a task

alcohol, and killing Indians and the common forms of amusement dance halls and lynching horse thieves, and that the farther you go into Mexico the worse it gets."

I smiled: I will admit ruefully.

"What is it like?" I asked.

"As concerns the border, just about diametrically the reverse of what you thought," he replied.

"San Antonio and El Paso are cities that much resemble Springfield, Mass., or Portland, Me., or Atlanta, Ga. They run to banks and department stores and trolley cars and moving-picture theatres and automobiles and laundered shirts and five-o'clock teas. You might live in any of 'em for years and

HALFTONE PUBLISHED BY *COLLIER'S* OF WALTER HORNE'S BEST-SELLING PHOTOGRAPH OF THE EXECUTION OF JUAN AGUILAR BY FEDERAL TROOPS IN CIUDAD JUAREZ, MEXICO, ON JANUARY 15, 1916. AGUILAR AND TWO OTHERS WERE ACCUSED OF STEALING MILITARY SUPPLIES; ALL THREE WERE SHOT. HORNE MARKETED HIS EXCLUSIVE IMAGES OF THE EXECUTIONS IN THE FORM OF POSTCARDS AND SOLD COPIES TO NEWSPAPERS AND MAGAZINES ACROSS AMERICA. (MIAMI-DADE PUBLIC LIBRARY)

Writers Richard Harding Davis, Frederick Palmer, and Jack London, as well as the peripatetic Hare, all veteran war correspondents, were often seen and photographed together. Hare's biographer, Cecil Carnes, writes that the "quartet of men who had gone through so many campaigns together . . . , whose work was well known to millions of stay-at-homes, . . . were a group that every photographer was eager and proud to picture."[62]

There was a huge market for photographs of the principal actors in the revolution. Mexico's proximity encouraged those who wished to report on events, as did the relative lack of official censorship of American reporters, at least early on. But what made circumstances especially appealing to photographers and writers was the fluid situation in Mexico and the willingness of many of the participants to accommodate representatives of the American press. All that changed, however, after March 9, 1916, when Francisco (Pancho) Villa mounted a surprise attack on Columbus, New Mexico, a tiny town just three miles north of the border and home of the 13th Cavalry Regiment at Camp Furlong. President Wilson's decision to pursue Villa with American troops under the command of General John J. Pershing meant that the press would now be controlled and monitored by American military forces. Strict censorship became an unpleasant fact of life almost immediately.

Walter Horne, the Texan whose specialty was the production of news pictures in postcard format, wrote to his mother a little more than a week after Villa's raid. "We were the first ones into Columbus with cameras," he said, "and the first ones out with negatives, consequently we beat them all to the newspapers; got our stuff into Chicago, New York, Boston, Atlanta, San Francisco, over twelve hours ahead of the others." But he added ominously that the new military censor was making life difficult, particularly for photographers just arrived on the scene. Movement on both sides of the border was now restricted, though Horne was able to keep his clients supplied with relevant views from his vast store of negatives depicting the life and times of border communities.[63]

During Pershing's frustrating Mexican expedition, the army honed its policies regarding photography and the press. The Signal Corps became an increasingly important producer of images, in direct competition with non-military photographers. Army personnel often had access to events and persons that were otherwise restricted, and the Signal Corps began supplying editors and publishers around the country with seemingly exclusive illustrative material. In addition, work produced by civilian photographers was tightly controlled by military censors. All images intended for publication had to be approved by a military censor, stamped on the back with an official permission to publish.

During the Mexican campaign, and later in Europe, each image produced by military photographers was scrutinized and approved before being released for distribution to the press. Assignments were doled out with great care; subjects deemed potentially problematic were simply not covered. By restricting access on the one hand, and providing its own carefully controlled coverage on the other, the army finally was able to manage and direct the visual representation of war. In order to accommodate the pictorial needs of both the press and the military, the army even established its own school in San Antonio for training still and motion-picture photographers. Instruction was led by Sergeant William Groat, the official military photographer of Pershing's Mexican campaign.[64]

With the increasing determination of military officials to monitor and ultimately to control press coverage, conflicts between those who reported on war and those responsible for its planning and execution were inevitable. In this century no conflict was more rigidly censored than the First World War. All sides restricted the press; the activities of the Allies were no more open to public scrutiny than those of the Central Powers. The consensus among the warring parties was that press coverage is more harmful than helpful, and so, from the outset, much of the global bloodletting occurred outside the view of the public. Independent visual and written reports from the front were systematically suppressed. In part to make up for the sudden decline in coverage, governments became adept at disseminating their own views, many of which were wholly fabricated or sanitized. As historian Paul Fussell writes, official euphemism and outright prevarication characterized much of the material presented to the public during the Great War. "It was perhaps the first time in history, that official policy produced events so shocking, bizarre, and stomach-turning that the events had to be tidied up for presentation to a highly literate mass population."[65]

Photographers, amateur as well as professional, were seen as especially troublesome since modern cameras could easily produce views of "sensitive" subjects. In the hysterical, paranoid atmosphere of wartime Europe, even the most innocent photographic excursions often attracted the authorities. "Photographers in London and other European cities must be more careful than ever how they take snapshots during wartime,"

PHOTOGRAPH BY WILLIAM FOX SHOWING GENERAL PERSHING AND AN INSPECTION PARTY FORDING THE SANTA MARÍA RIVER IN MEXICO, 1916. (STILL PICTURES BRANCH, NATIONAL ARCHIVES)

OFFICIAL WAR DEPARTMENT PHOTOGRAPH BY ARMY PRIVATE WILLIE WYNN OF CORPORAL BECKETT AND HIS CYCLE GRAFLEX IN FRONT OF "THE STUDIO" AT THE ENCAMPMENT OF THE 16TH INFANTRY DIVISION, EL PASO, TEXAS, ON NOVEMBER 3, 1916. (STILL PICTURES BRANCH, NATIONAL ARCHIVES)

advised the editors of the *Photographic Journal of America* in 1915, "for a thoughtless use of cameras may easily cause them to find themselves in prison for a few days." The mere presence of camera-toting amateurs in the vicinity of some military activity or installation was enough to warrant swift official action. "There are probably many thousands of amateur photographers who, wishing to snap scenes in the neighborhood of barracks or other military or naval places, find themselves arrested as if they were spies."[66]

What was occasionally difficult and even dangerous for amateurs was not much easier for professionals. In every theater of the war, the actions of photographers were sharply curtailed. "In the first months of the war our General Staff . . . treated British war correspondents as pariah dogs," wrote Charles Edward Montague in 1929. "They might escape arrest so long as they kept out of sight; that was about the sum of their privileges."[67] Attempts to view combat at first hand, to see life in the trenches and witness the deadly ebb and flow of great battles, were forbidden. Military and social connections were crucial to obtaining even temporary permits allowing limited access to the fighting. "To get to the front is the correspondent's chief object in life," wrote William Gunn Shepherd in an article published in *Collier's Magazine*, "and to attain this object it is often necessary to pass through a sea of social activities, including teas, calls, and conferences."[68] And, once at the front, there was no guarantee that a reporter or photographer could work or write freely.

Although the most common justification for the suppression of information was that the lives of fighting men would be endangered by unrestricted press coverage, there were other considerations as well. Military officials were unwilling to assume responsibility for the transportation, care, feeding, and protection of journalists, some of whom were probably critical of the armed forces anyway. And experience proved that modern warfare could cost the lives of those who reported on it. According to one observer, during the British army's bloody operations against the Boers in South Africa in 1899, a remarkable "thirty-three per cent of the correspondents have been killed or wounded, or have died of disease incurred in the line of duty."[69] Many journalists and especially their publishers were willing, even eager, to take the risk, but the military was much less enthusiastic. They had their own men to worry about.

The ability of media early in twentieth century to gather information and disseminate it to mass audiences quickly and efficiently convinced high commands around the world that success on the battlefield depended on utter secrecy and total control of the press. Reporters simply could not be trusted to keep plans and operations secret. In a statement regarding the need for military censorship during the First World War, Douglas MacArthur, now a major and the official censor for the War Department in Washington, D.C., contended that during the war with Spain "the success of the Cuban expedition . . . was seriously menaced by the news in the American press concerning the concentration in Tampa. Every military movement was reported in the American newspapers, and the Spanish government had, within two or three hours, complete accounts of the American preparation for war."[70] As far as the War Department was concerned, the press would not again enjoy unfettered access to military operations.

MacArthur enumerated the ways that press coverage might seriously impair military operations. By thoughtlessly publishing detailed accounts of victories or defeats and the names of particular outfits and organizations, reporters "furnish information to the enemy that will enable him to detect the strength and location and intended movements of our own troops." Equally important, the penchant of some reporters and publishers to criticize the actions and plans of certain military personnel invariably under-

A FRENCH WOMAN IN FRONT OF THE REMAINS OF HER HOME IN THE SOMME REGION, 1916. AN ACCOMPANYING CAPTION BLAMES THE GERMAN MILITARY FOR THE DESTRUCTION AND WARNS THAT THIS UNDERWOOD AND UNDERWOOD PHOTOGRAPH "MUST NOT BE USED FOR ADVERTISING WITHOUT WRITTEN PERMISSION." (LIBRARY OF CONGRESS)

mines their effectiveness. "They cry for and obtain new Generals and new plans of campaigns," MacArthur complained, although their reports are naturally devoid of "expert knowledge and thought." The result could be disastrous: "a consequent lengthening of the war or even defeat."[71] This was not a novel idea. The French general staff, for one, continued to blame the press for the army's defeat during the Franco-Prussian conflict of 1870. Reports of intended troop movements and other plans imperiled French soldiers, they felt, and stories about unsanitary conditions and low morale undermined the average soldier's willingness to fight.[72]

Early in the war, both the Allies and Central Powers adopted policies severely restricting access of the press to the front. In addition to rigid censorship, correspondents were supplied with bits of wholly optimistic and salutary news and disinformation. Meanwhile, photographers were allowed to train their cameras only at approved subjects. Any deviation resulted in swift punishment: arrests were not uncommon, though uncooperative correspondents were more likely to find themselves blacklisted.[73]

William Shepherd of the United Press Association, described what could happen to a reporter who failed to heed the strict rules:

> He would be taken back to London or Paris or Berlin or Vienna and turned loose there. But his name would go down in the correspondents' black book. Soon would come the day when Monsieur Ponsot of the French Foreign Office, or Mr. Montgomery of the British Foreign Office, [or] Mr. Zimmmerman of the German Foreign Office, or Count Montlong in Vienna, would be arranging a trip to the front. Our hero would appear at the Foreign Office and request that his name be put on the list. He would be met, smilingly, perhaps, but he wouldn't take the trip. Days would pass and weeks and months without summons to the frontward expeditions, and then the truth would dawn upon him that his name was in the black books, and that never again in the Great War would he be permitted to see the front.[74]

All published work was scrutinized for material indicating the rules of censorship had been evaded. Only official accounts of events and approved photographic subjects were tolerated in domestic as well as foreign press reports. Oliver Gramling, historian of the Associated Press, recalled that in Germany early in the war a summary of news, "giving the High Command's version, was issued three times weekly by the General Staff office in Berlin, and correspondents were held personally responsible not only for the dispatches they wrote, but also for headlines and pictures which might accompany these dispatches when they were printed in America."[75]

American journalists complained bitterly about the restrictions, but to no avail. A reporter for the *New York Sun* stationed in France proclaimed sadly that the very profession of war correspondent was lost, "for no one is allowed within thirty miles of a battle." Connections, influence, and official neutrality apparently meant nothing; in fact, even "French correspondents are kept away."[76] There were also rumors that those caught with cameras on or near the front were subject to immediate execution or imprisonment without trial for the duration of the war. "The story has never been told as to what happened during the last few weeks in Belgium," wrote John D. Tippett, the London representative for Universal Film Manufacturing Company, in a letter to Universal's president, Carl Laemmle, in September 1914, "and men from America, and people from other neutral governments, have disappeared, and will never be heard of again."[77] This story and variations of it, though apocryphal, were told throughout the war, and may have helped persuade some journalists to accept, if grudgingly, the dictates of censors.

In spite of well-publicized difficulties and dangers, there was no shortage of American journalists and adventurers willing to try their luck in Europe. The war was front-page news, and illustrated newspapers and magazines desperately needed a steady supply of words and pictures. Just about anyone willing to take the risk could procure a press pass, though even the most impressive credentials could not guarantee access. At the insistence of military commanders, journalists were kept far behind the frontlines, and thus had to be content with information supplied by the army and whatever feature stories and pictures they could glean from non-

316 LESLIE'S WEEKLY *September 7, 1918*

# Our Men Who Fly *for* Italy

*Photographs by* JAMES H. HARE, Staff War Photographer

The latest type of bombing Caproni airplane, which United States aviators in Italy are flying, about to start on a raid. It carries a great number of bombs; several are suspended beneath the plane, others are inside.

American aviators in Italy inspecting a machine before starting on a trip over the Austrian lines. The officer facing the machine is Lieutenant Paton MacGilvary. Lieutenant G. P. Bogert has his hand on his hip.

Lieut. Norman Downs, Jr. Lieut. W. S. Wilson. Lieut. A. M. Beach. Lieut. W. A. Patthoff. Lieut. W. S. Fitch.

PORTRAITS OF AMERICAN AVIATORS FLYING FOR ITALY, AND VIEWS OF THE AIRPORT IN NORTHERN ITALY, MADE BY JAMES HARE FOR *LESLIE'S WEEKLY*. (LIBRARY OF CONGRESS)

SECOND LIEUTENANT PAUL WEIR CLOUD, A STILL PHOTOGRAPHER WITH THE 89TH DIVISION DURING THE WAR, DEMONSTRATES GRAFLEX TECHNIQUE NEAR KYLLBURG, GERMANY, JUST AFTER THE ARMISTICE. (NATIONAL ARCHIVES)

combat areas. The result was that stories and images were published with great fanfare, but few of them told the real story. "Of all records of war, photographs are the most interesting and the most valuable in aftertimes," wrote Francis J. Reynolds in the foreword to a postwar anthology of photographs published by *Collier's*. "From collections like this one people in the homes throughout the world can learn what the war was like—in the trenches and the camps, at sea, in the air."[78] Reynolds' statement was more bluster than anything else, for the photographs were mostly staid behind-the-lines scenes and training-camp views. The policy of all participating governments assured that the real war would take place far from the unblinking eye of the camera. The result was predictable: "News, lies, local color, human interest, fakes, all went down the great public gullet in Gargantuan gulps," wrote one disgusted reporter in 1917.[79]

For some old hands, covering war was practically routine, and they arrived on the continent with a sense of journalistic noblesse oblige only to find that they, too, would be kept in the rear. Early in the war, armed with a letter of introduction from Theodore Roosevelt to President Raymond Poincaré of France, Richard Harding Davis sailed to Europe with his wife, the former actress Bessie McCoy, aboard the plush, ill-fated liner, *Lusitania*. Davis had designed his own uniform, which he wore in Mexico and during the Balkan Wars. The natty coat was similar to that of a British officer, and it was decorated with campaign ribbons attesting to his veteran status.[80] Neither the letter nor the uniform persuaded the French to allow Davis to wander about the front.

Eventually, he and several compatriots attached themselves to British forces in eastern Europe, where the rules were somewhat less strict. One day the group, which included Jimmy Hare and reporters John McCutcheon and John Bass, came under desultory fire from a battery of Bulgarian guns, much to the delight of the Americans. William Shepherd recalled that Davis was especially ebullient. "Well," he said, "I've been a war correspondent long enough to have the right to say I like it. There's a thrill about it that's pleasant."[81] Perhaps most important, all of them could now proclaim, truthfully, that their words and pictures were obtained at the front and under fire. During World War I, not many could say that.

But one who could—and often did—was Donald C. Thompson, a native Kansan who began the war as a press photographer in Canada and ended it in Petrograd making exclusive newsreel footage of the Russian Revolution.[82] Thompson's reaction to news that the European war had started was the stuff of which legends are made. "As a newspaper photographer," he recalled in 1918, "I knew that it would be the greatest story in history, and I determined that I was going to cover it." He wired *Leslie's* of his intentions, but when the editors failed to respond immediately—the wire was delayed—he sold what belongings he could, pawned his watch, and with the money thus obtained he purchased a new camera outfit and a steamship ticket to Europe.[83] Shortly thereafter, Edward Alexander Powell, a reporter for the *New York World,* happened upon Thompson in Belgium. His reminiscence of the meeting helped establish Thompson as one of the leading and most colorful figures in American journalism. "Of all the adventurous characters who were drawn to the Continent on the outbreak of war, I doubt if there was a more picturesque figure than a little photographer from Kansas named Donald Thompson. I met him first while paying a

AN UNCREDITED PHOTOGRAPH MADE FOR THE CENTRAL NEWS PHOTO SERVICE SHOWING A WOUNDED SERBIAN SOLDIER BEING CARRIED INTO A RED CROSS DRESSING STATION NEAR THE FRONTLINES. (LIBRARY OF CONGRESS)

UNCREDITED PHOTOGRAPH OF HELEN JOHNS KIRTLAND, PHOTOGRAPHER FOR *LESLIE'S WEEKLY*, EQUIPPED WITH GAS MASK AND HELMET IN A TRENCH IN EASTERN EUROPE, N.D. (LIBRARY OF CONGRESS)

flying visit to Ostend. He blew into the Consulate there wearing an American army shirt, a pair of British officer's riding-breeches, French puttees, and a Highlander's forage cap, and carrying a camera the size of a parlor phonograph." What made this colorful cameraman especially memorable for Powell and others anxious to get to the front was that Thompson "had not only seen war, all military prohibitions to the contrary, but he had actually photographed it."[84]

By his own account, Thompson managed to make his way to various frontline areas, and though often detained or arrested and twice wounded, he maintained a level of mobility that astonished his colleagues. In Russia, for instance, Thompson was on hand to record vicious fighting between factions vying for control of the government in the wake of the overthrow of Czar Nicholas. Florence MacLeod Harper, *Leslie's* reporter in Petrograd, described Thompson's nerve under fire. "It was not always easy to take pictures of the riots, because just as he would establish himself in a good place on some corner, some adherent, either of the Bolsheviki or the Provisional Government, would start a little excitement with the machine guns."

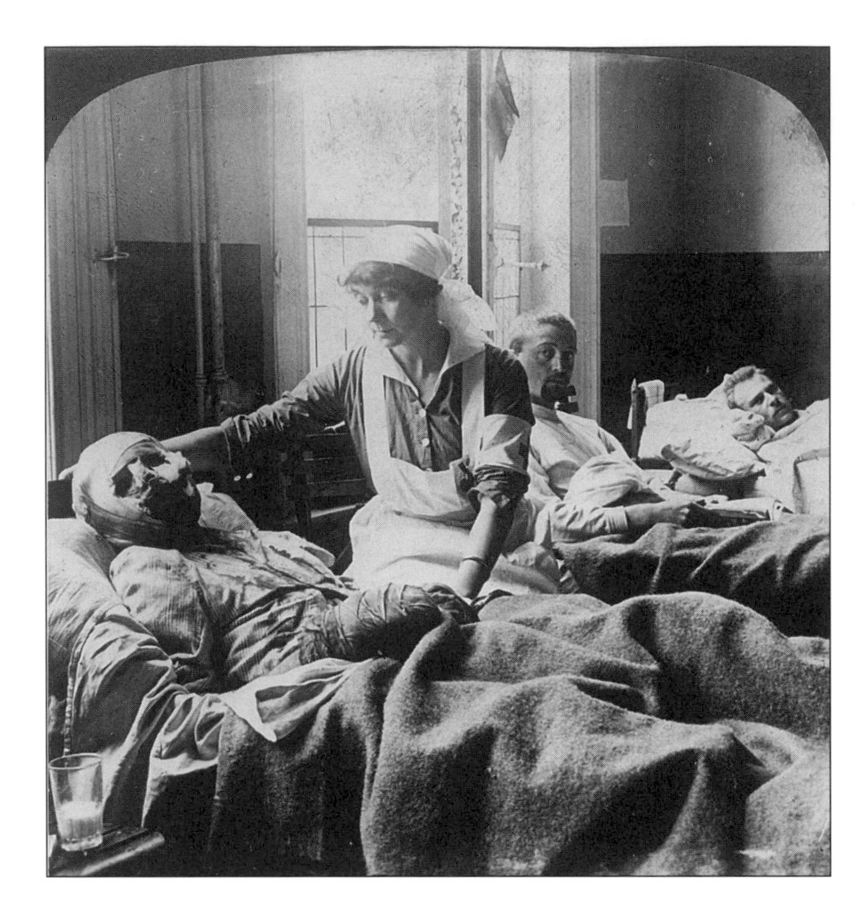

SINGLE IMAGE MADE FROM A STEREOGRAPH BY AN UNIDENTIFIED PHOTOGRAPHER FOR UNDERWOOD AND UNDERWOOD. THE PRINTED CAPTION DESCRIBES THE SCENE AS A "GHASTLY GLIMPSE OF BELGIAN WOUNDED AT [AN] ANTWERP HOSPITAL." (LIBRARY OF CONGRESS)

At such times, Thompson often wisely moved on, but only so that he could find an even better location from which to make pictures. "During these riots," assured Harper, "Mr. Thompson was always to be seen where the crowds were thickest, and where the machine guns were spraying the streets with lead."[85]

Thompson continued to work as a freelance still photographer for *Frank Leslie's Illustrated Newspaper* as well as the *Chicago Tribune,* the *New York World,* and the *Illustrated London News,* but as the war progressed he increasingly turned his attention to making newsreels and films. During the war several of his films were shown in American cities, and as always, his exploits were given considerable play in the press. As some contend, Thompson probably embellished the stories told about him; throughout his career he exhibited a keen instinct for self-promotion.[86] Early in the war, for instance, he claimed to have been captured by Germans, beaten, arrested, released, and finally forced to flee the country just a step or two ahead of the secret police in the company of the comely daughter of a prominent German officer. Although never corroborated, Thompson's daring escape made awfully good reading, and variations of it were published several times in America.[87]

Thompson's escapade cast correspondents in a new and highly favorable light. For years news photographers were demonized for their fondness of sensation and sleaze. In the role of war photographer, however, they seemed more heroic than exploitative, their selfless and courageous actions at the front providing the public with life-and-death information, not fluff. And as these stories of photojournalistic bravado show, photographers had to overcome shot and shell as well as pernicious government policies designed to prevent civilians, or anyone else for that matter, from making frontline activities visible to the general public.

Predictably, some American reporters and photographers in Europe were skeptical about the well-publicized successes of Thompson and a few others. In his memoir of the war years, reporter William Shepherd admonished the thrill-seekers who "rushed from the United States at the outbreak of war, usually traveling on their own money, carrying credentials from some newspaper that was only too glad to have a correspondent in Europe at no expense to itself." Although their letters of introduction and press credentials occasionally enabled them to evade arrest or capture, these adventurers spent most of their time in Europe making "themselves heroes at home by faking stories of their own valiant deeds and great dangers."[88]

AN UNCREDITED PHOTOGRAPH MADE FOR THE CENTRAL NEWS PHOTO SERVICE FOR DISTRIBUTION TO AMERICAN PUBLICATIONS. THE ACCOMPANYING CAPTION READS, "ANOTHER SORT OF WAR RUIN—AFTER SEVERAL DAYS IN THE TRENCHES. NO WARRIOR CARES TO BE CAPTURED AND YET, JUDGING FROM THE CONDITION OF THE WOUNDED GERMAN, . . . WE CAN'T BELIEVE THAT HE IS ENTIRELY DISPLEASED AT HIS FATE." (NATIONAL PHOTO COMPANY COLLECTION, LIBRARY OF CONGRESS)

Photographers, though, could and did offer their own pictures as proof of presence on the frontline. The public's veneration of photographic truth had not dimmed significantly since the day of the daguerreotype, and images that purported to be made at the front were usually accepted as such. We know now, however, that the public was often deceived. Military restrictions led to numerous attempts by both civilian and military photographers to recreate and even fabricate events. One now notorious example is an image by Lieutenant Ivor Castle, who was named Official Canadian Photographer by military authorities in 1916. Ivor's experience as manager of the photography department at the *Daily Mirror* in London served him well during the war; his images were made to order for the pictorial press. Ivor's most famous photograph shows a plucky Canadian soldier supposedly going "over the top" while thumbing his nose at the enemy during the dreadful battle of the Somme in July 1916. The photograph was widely distributed among the Allies, and Ivor's stories regarding the picture added to its allure. "Taking photographs of the men going over the parapet is quite exciting," he wrote in 1917. "Nothing, of course, can be arranged. You sit or crouch in the first-line trench while the enemy do a little strafing, and if you are lucky you get your pictures." Ivor contended that a moment after he took his famous picture the entire unit was mowed down by a German machine gunner.[89]

As several historians point out, Castle's original negatives show that one of the soldiers charging out of the trench still has the breech cover on his rifle, which indicates that the photographs were made during training, not in the thick of the fighting. It now appears that Castle made his picture at the trench-mortar school near St. Pol, France, where Canadian troops were instructed before being fed into the lines. Indeed, it is likely that the jaunty gesture that so moved viewers during the war was actually directed at the photographer or at least made at his suggestion.[90]

Photographers desperate to describe the war but restricted to secure

LT. IVOR CASTLE'S PHOTOGRAPH OF TROOPS "GOING OVER THE TOP" NEAR ST. POL, FRANCE, IN OCTOBER 1916. CASTLE, OFFICIAL PHOTOGRAPHER WITH THE CANADIAN ARMY, CLAIMED TO HAVE MADE THE PICTURE DURING AN ASSAULT AGAINST GERMAN TRENCHES, BUT IT WAS MORE LIKELY MADE DURING A TRAINING EXERCISE FAR FROM THE FRONTLINES. (STILL PICTURES BRANCH, NATIONAL ARCHIVES)

areas far behind the lines did bend the truth; most of them felt they had no choice. Their editors back home demanded photographs, and so they did what they could, using diplomacy and military connections to construct realistic and believable situations. According to the editors of the *Photographic Journal of America* in 1917, a befriended general might thus "be induced to trot out a battalion or so and stage an attack or shoot off a few four-inch guns. He may even, if properly approached, send his army out of a city already taken and let the camera record the triumphal entry for the benefit of the public." The resulting photographs should not be cursorily dismissed as fiction, wrote the editors, since "they represent true conditions, and merely have the advantage of being taken under favorable circumstances."[91]

A certain nonchalance in regard to outright fabrication and theatrical reenactments of events was magnified by an unofficial code of silence regarding the military's strict rules. Since the merest hint of public dissatisfaction or criticism could mean permanent blacklisting, members of the press corps in Europe kept frustrations and complaints to themselves for the duration. After all, war correspondents, as Charles Edward Montague noted, lived in the world of the general staff, not that of the ordinary foot soldier. "The Staff was both their friend and their censor. How could they show it up when it failed?" he asked. "One of the first rules of field censorship was that from war correspondents 'there must be no criticism of authority or command'; how could they disobey that?"[92] They did not.

Shortly before America finally entered the war in the spring of 1917, the military insisted that they be given absolute control over the press in the coming conflict, even if such rigid supervision seemed to belie principles of free speech and press. In his capacity as chief army censor,

Douglas MacArthur argued that during wartime "the army and navy are the only agencies of the Government by which it can obtain its desired ends." As a result, he said, military organizations "become paramount and every utility and influence within the country should be brought to their aid."[93] George Creel, a newspaperman and ardent supporter of President Wilson, was one of a number of influential journalists to argue for a more open system. In his autobiography, Creel recalled how "admirals and generals pressed forward with the demand for a hard and fast censorship law that would have put the press in leg irons and handcuffs." Apparently, Wilson was initially inclined to accede to the wishes of the high command. But Creel believed that absolute control of the press by the military was "criminally stupid and bound to work untold harm," and he prepared a lengthy brief that "set forth the dangers in detail," and sent it to the president.[94]

Such criticisms by Creel and others persuaded Wilson to modify the military's proposal. On April 14, 1917, just days after the United States

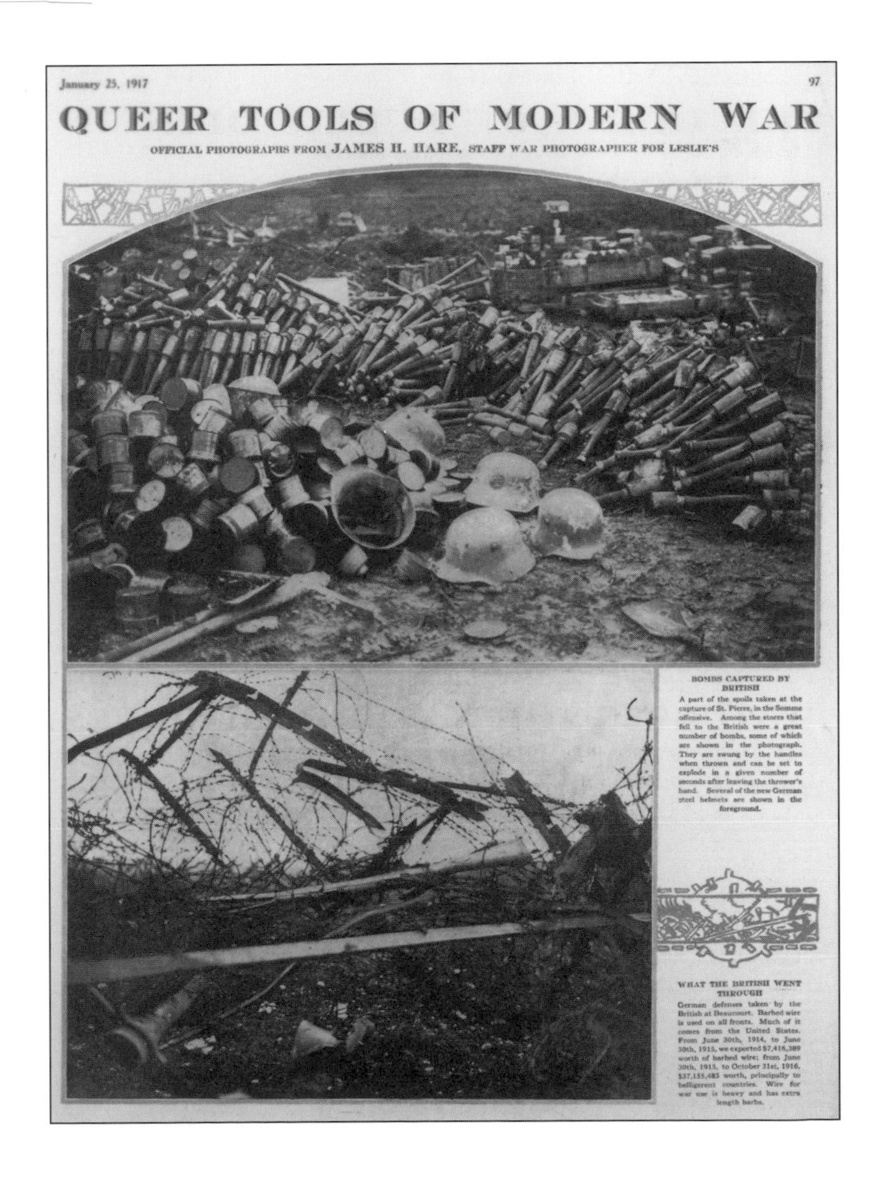

January 25, 1917 97

QUEER TOOLS OF MODERN WAR

OFFICIAL PHOTOGRAPHS FROM JAMES H. HARE, STAFF WAR PHOTOGRAPHER FOR LESLIE'S

BOMBS CAPTURED BY BRITISH

A part of the spoils taken at the capture of St. Pierre, in the Somme offensive. Among the stores that fell to the British were a great number of bombs, some of which are shown in the photograph. They are swung by the handles when thrown and can be set to explode in a given number of seconds after leaving the thrower's hand. Several of the new German steel helmets are shown in the foreground.

WHAT THE BRITISH WENT THROUGH

German defenses taken by the British at Beaucourt. Barbed wire is used on all fronts. Much of it comes from the United States. From June 30th, 1914, to June 30th, 1915, we exported $7,416,389 worth of barbed wire; from June 30th, 1915, to October 31st, 1916, $37,135,485 worth, principally to belligerent countries. Wire for war use is heavy and has extra length barbs.

PHOTOGRAPHS MADE BY JIMMY HARE AND PUBLISHED BY *LESLIE'S* SHOWING GERMAN EQUIPMENT AND HAND GRENADES CAPTURED BY BRITISH FORCES DURING THE SOMME BATTLES AS WELL AS GERMAN BARBED-WIRE ENTANGLEMENTS MEANT TO DELAY THEIR ASSAULT. (LIBRARY OF CONGRESS)

declared war on Germany, Wilson established by executive order the Committee on Public Information (CPI), which would function partly as a filter for information relating to the war and partly as a vast governmental public relations agency. Not surprisingly, George Creel was named its director; in most respects, the new committee incorporated his suggestions to the president.

Throughout the war, one of the most important functions of the committee was to control the production and dissemination of still pictures by military and civilian photographers. Originally, oversight was the province of the Division of Pictures; after March 1918, however, the Bureau of War Photographs in the Division of Films took over the picture division. Lawrence Rubell, a well-connected businessman from Chicago, directed the bureau, which saw to the distribution of photographs made by military (chiefly Signal Corps) photographers as well as those by civilians.

Despite the government's clear intention to regulate the visual record of the war, Creel and others within the government defended the benevolence of their institution, and proclaimed that they not only valued freedom of the press, but actually protected it. "Despite general opinion," Creel wrote in January 1918, "censorship plays but a small part in the work of the committee." To put it mildly, not everyone agreed. In response to a flurry of criticism, mostly from the press, Creel explained that while supportive of free expression, there "is a difference between free speech and seditious speech."[95] There were justifiable laws against the latter, and the CPI was mandated to ensure they were followed. CPI officials argued that their purpose was neither to promote a single point of view nor give absolute control to the military. "Aside from the disclosure of military secrets of importance, aside from any protest that is liable to weaken the

UNCREDITED IMAGE OF AN AMERICAN TANK IN ACTION DURING THE ST. MIHIEL OFFENSIVE IN 1918, MADE FOR THE NATIONAL PHOTO COMPANY AND COPYRIGHTED BY THE DIVISION OF PICTURES OF THE COMMITTEE ON PUBLIC INFORMATION. (NATIONAL PHOTO COMPANY COLLECTION, LIBRARY OF CONGRESS)

PHOTOGRAPH CREDITED TO PAUL THOMPSON SHOWING THE ACTOR DOUGLAS FAIRBANKS SR. SPEAKING ON BEHALF OF THE THIRD LIBERTY LOAN AT THE SUB-TREASURY BUILDING IN NEW YORK CITY, APRIL 1918. FAIRBANKS AND OTHER PROMINENT AMERICANS SUPPORTED THE GOVERNMENT'S EFFORTS TO STRENGTHEN MORALE AND PUBLIC SUPPORT FOR THE WAR. (RECORDS OF THE WAR DEPARTMENT GENERAL AND SPECIAL STAFFS, NATIONAL ARCHIVES)

will of the country to continue this war, or that may interfere with the prosecution of this war," wrote Creel in the *Annals of the American Academy of Political and Social Science,* "we stand for the freest discussion that any people in the world ever had." As historian Stephen Vaughn rightly contends, however, Creel and his coworkers in Washington mounted an extensive and extraordinarily effective propaganda campaign on behalf of the Allied war effort and the Wilson Administration. "We shall not discharge our full duty to the national defense until we have reached every community in the United States by written or spoken word or motion picture," Creel and his associate chairman, Edgar G. Sisson, wrote on January 7, 1918. Given widespread forces of dissension and disbelief, it was imperative the federal government reach and convince every person in the country "that this war is a war of self defense, and that it has got to be master of his every thought and action."[96]

Although perhaps well-intentioned, Creel and his committee institutionalized the government's near total control of moving and still images of the war. At the request of the military, practically all official photographs of frontline activities were made exclusively by Signal Corps personnel, many of whom were commanded by Major Bert Underwood of stereo card fame. Signal Corps pictures were carefully sifted by censors who culled any deemed the least bit problematic. Until mid-1918, work produced in Europe was screened at the Paris office of the CPI, where Joe T. Marshall, a captain of cavalry, acted as chief military censor. In addition to its work as a clearing house for pictures, the Bureau of War Photographs also investigated all applications for photographic credentials, with veto power residing in Military and Naval Intelligence.[97]

An elaborate distribution system for war pictures, those made by Signal Corps photographers as well as by civilians, was established. Film taken in American sectors was sent to the Signal Corps for censoring. According to one directive, after copies were made for the military and the CPI, approved originals were returned to the photographer, usually within four days. Photographers working for the press, agencies such as the Red Cross and the YMCA, nonmilitary branches of government, and the Signal Corps followed the same routine. All film was passed through the Signal Corps and the Committee on Public Information before distribution to the public. Domestic newspapers and magazines agreed to run only those photographs that had been officially cleared and stamped "Passed by the Committee on Public Information, Washington"; photographs that somehow evaded the censors, such as those made in the trenches by soldiers with Kodaks, remained private for the duration.[98]

AN UNCREDITED AND POSSIBLY RETOUCHED PHOTOGRAPH THAT WAS DISTRIBUTED TO NEWSPAPERS IN THE UNITED STATES BY THE CENTRAL NEWS PHOTO SERVICE. "EQUIPT FOR THE TRENCHES. A FRENCH SERGEANT AND HIS MASCOT, SNAPPED WHILE ON THEIR WAY TO THE FRONT LINE." (LIBRARY OF CONGRESS)

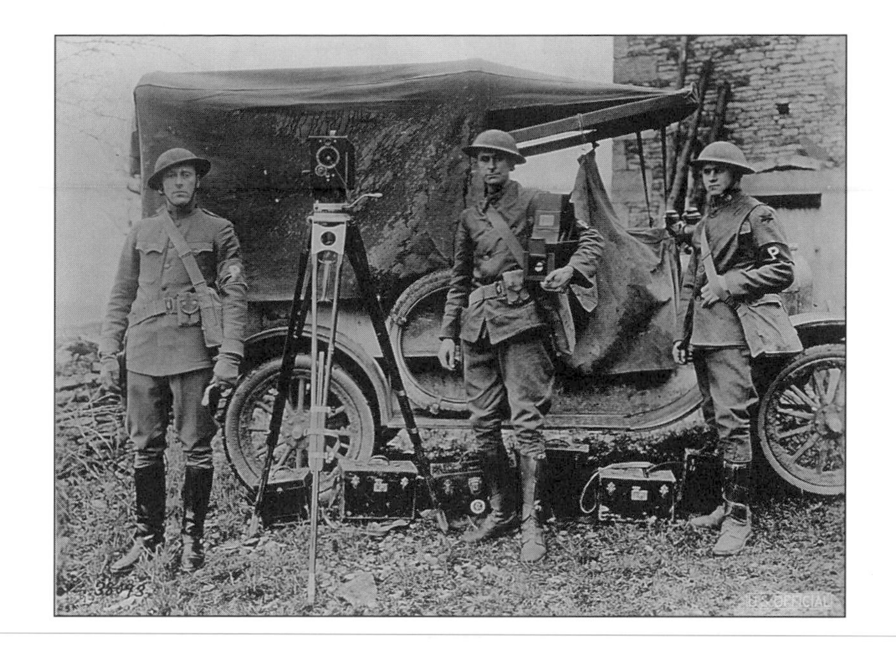

A U.S. SIGNAL CORPS PHOTOGRAPH SHOWING 1ST SGT. J. C. ZIMMERMAN PREPARING FOR WORK NEAR ETALANTE, CÔTE D'OR, FRANCE, JANUARY 9, 1919. (LIBRARY OF CONGRESS)

At the suggestion of Kendall Banning, formerly editor of *System* magazine, the picture division of the CPI invited photojournalists to organize in order to best represent their interests with the committee. The result was a decision in July 1917 to form an association that would "provide equitable opportunities and privileges for the large and small syndicates, photographers, and dealers alike." Founding members included George Bain, D. Z. Murphy from the Central News Company, George Wilkinson representing both the Paul Thompson and Harris and Ewing syndicates, and C. R. Abbott of Underwood and Underwood.[99] The association saw to it that approved Signal Corps pictures received the widest possible distribution. Since civilian coverage of the military was restricted almost to the point of nonexistence, requests by newspapers, magazines, and especially syndicates for Signal Corps photographs steadily mounted during the war. Eventually the corps established a laboratory at Columbia University in New York City that made prints available to the press for as little as ten cents each.

In spite of the demand, however, both military and CPI authorities refused to disseminate images that might somehow damage the war effort by undermining public confidence and support. Signal Corps photographers were trained to avoid scenes that could upset the folks back home, and forbidden subjects were not limited to scenes of carnage. For instance, while the CPI produced films and stills depicting black soldiers during the war, they were intended to be shown or distributed exclusively to black audiences, and whenever possible, the army made sure the person behind the camera was black as well. Thus, Private James S. Campbell, a self-taught African American photographer from Virginia, was commissioned by the government to photograph black soldiers in training at camps across the country.[100] The visual record of blacks during the war is modest even

PHOTOGRAPH BY SGT. J. J. MARSHALL OF THE SIGNAL CORPS SHOWING AMERICAN SOLDIERS WOUNDED DURING FIGHTING IN THE MEUSE VALLEY BEING TREATED IN A DAMAGED CHURCH, SEPTEMBER 26, 1918. (LIBRARY OF CONGRESS)

by CPI and Signal Corps standards since censors excised pictures showing camaraderie between black and white soldiers or between black and white civilians.

Traveling in groups usually consisting of one newsreel and one still photographer, a private to carry equipment and film, and a driver, some six hundred Signal Corps units traveled through combat and rear areas, making photographs that could be used by the military. Whatever their backgrounds or previous experiences in photography or journalism, Signal Corps personnel were soldiers first. Edward Steichen, easily the most famous veteran of Signal Corps operations during the war, recalled that the pictures made under his direction served to inform the military, not the public. He was in charge of a unit consisting of fifty-five officers and more than a thousand enlisted men whose purpose was to supply aerial photographs of German trenches and artillery batteries.[101] He had no illusions about the value of the pictures he made under the direction of General Billy Mitchell during the Second Battle of the Marne, though to the end of his days he abhorred humanity's penchant for making war.

> I had never had to come face to face with another man and shoot him and see him crumple and fall, yet I could not deny to myself having played a role in the slaughter. I had never been conscious of anything but the job we had to do: photograph enemy territory and enemy actions, record enemy movements and gun emplacements, pinpoint the targets for our own artillery. The work had been full of organizational and technical difficulties. We had had to improvise all along the way with inadequate equipment and materials and inadequately trained personnel. But the photographs we made provided information that, conveyed to our artillery, enabled them to destroy their targets and kill.[102]

An article published in the *Photographic Journal of America* just after the war recalled that hundreds of "camera men were engaged in propaganda, in artillery photography, in the hospitals, in laboratories, on news assignments."[103] The images they made constituted the public's principal visual link to the war, but it was neither wholly accurate nor timely. By restricting access and controlling the final product, the government made sure that the public continued to believe in the righteousness of the cause and the utter depravity of the enemy. Images showing the horrors of trench warfare or the terrible human costs it incurred were suppressed since such pictures might cause a diminution of patriotic fervor. The result, as historian Susan Moeller points out, is that most of "the photographs that were allowed to pass the censor were mundane and uninspired."[104]

Signal Corps personnel photographed a variety of subjects, including battle scenes, but such pictures were nearly always considered too troublesome to be seen by the public during the war. Lieutenant E. R. Trabold, a still photographer in the Signal Corps, risked his life to obtain views during the American assault at Cantigny in May 1918. He photographed men in action, and others who were wounded or killed during the ferocious fighting, but an article he wrote on the Cantigny campaign was not accompanied by any of his photographs. "I cannot illustrate this . . . with the pictures that I would like to," he wrote in September 1919, "as all pictures are the property of the Government and have to be censored; but later on, I am assured, I will be given any pictures I wish to use, and then you will see some real war pictures that will interest everyone, and then you will realize what the war photographer really did do."[105]

Eventually Trabold may have obtained copies of some of his own images; after the war some censored photographs gradually made their way into the public domain. In addition, snapshots made by ordinary soldiers armed with Kodaks and other simple cameras began surfacing. Many of these mostly anonymous images eventually found their way into pictorial archives and from there into books about the war. But as historian Estelle Jussim notes, few, if any, of the photographs made informally by soldiers in the trenches were published during or immediately after the war.[106] They now may provide eerie, often chilling glimpses of the Great War, but they are views in retrospect.

Military brass decreed that photographs of real war would dampen morale. Rather than risk even the slightest diminution of homefront fervor

PORTRAIT OF "I SCRUBS"—LITTLE KATIE FROM THE WEST 52ND STREET INDUSTRIAL SCHOOL IN NEW YORK CITY, C. 1898, BY REFORM PHOTOGRAPHER JACOB RIIS. (JACOB RIIS COLLECTION, MUSEUM OF THE CITY OF NEW YORK)

# PHOTOJOURNALISM, DOCUMENTARY, AND REFORM

What with one thing and another, and in spite of all obstacles, I got my pictures, and put some of them to practical use at once. I recall a midnight expedition to the Mulberry Bend with the sanitary police that had turned up a couple of characteristic cases of overcrowding. . . . When the report was submitted to the Health Board the next day, it did not make much of an impression—these things rarely do, put in mere words—until my negatives, still dripping from the dark-room, came to reinforce them. From them there was no appeal.

—Jacob August Riis, *The Making of an American*[1]

Printed at the top of the editorial page of the old *New York World* was a statement that enunciated the political philosophy of the publisher and mirrored the reformist impulses of Jacob Riis. Joseph Pulitzer promised that the institution he controlled would "never tolerate injustice or corruption, always fight demagogues of all parties." The paper would be sympathetic to the poor and downtrodden while forever opposing privilege, and above all, it "would never be afraid to attack wrong, whether by predatory plutocracy or predatory poverty."[2] James Wyman Barrett, the last city editor of the paper before its merger with the *New York Telegram* in February 1931, added exploiters, fanatics, and despots to the *World*'s list of inveterate enemies, and bragged that as a public institution the *World* never ran from a fight and "took delight in tearing down idols."[3]

William Randolph Hearst and Edward Wyllis Scripps were just as vocal in defending their newspaper empires from attacks by those they offended. An editorial in the *New York Journal* characterized Hearst's critics as mere lackeys for "conscienceless wealth and corrupt power." Fellow journalists who sneered at the sensational antics of Hearst and company were singled out and derided for palpable cowardice and greed. "It is because the 'yellow' journal stands for the cause of the people," Hearst's editors wrote, "that it is feared and hated by exploiters of the people and systematically maligned by the organs of the exploiters, which assume 'respectability' as a cloak in which to better serve their paymasters."[4] Scripps concurred. "The press of this country," he wrote, "is now, and always has been, so thoroughly dominated by the wealthy few of the country that it cannot be depended upon to give the great masses of the people that correct information concerning political, economic and social subjects." Without such material the public had no way of resisting "the brutal force and chicanery of the ruling and employing class."[5]

As a fondness for pictures and sensational stories were integral elements of the so-called new journalism created by Pulitzer and Hearst, so too was this skeptical stance toward hallowed institutions—both public and private—and the people who ran them. This was a significant change in the nature of the news business. During the expansion of economic enterprises following the Civil War, the nation's business elite reigned supreme, and leaders of commerce and their numerous friends in high places enjoyed mostly cordial relations with members of the fourth estate. The honeymoon ended at the end of the nineteenth century as many newspapers, led by the Pulitzer-Hearst-Scripps triumvirate, began investigating malfeasance and promoting reform at all levels of society. As historian John D. Stevens observes, however, the righteous indignation and reformist ardor of the publishers of yellow newspapers often masked a far more crass determination maximize profits by increasing circulation.

With prodding from publisher Samuel Sidney McClure, magazines followed the editorial lead of the yellows just after the turn of the century. "Capitalists, workingmen, politicians, citizens—all breaking the law, or letting it be broken," McClure wrote in a scathing editorial that inaugurated the era of muckraking in 1903. "Who is left to uphold it?" Lawyers and judges, he said, were hopelessly compromised by greed and misplaced respect for those who could best manipulate the vast, mysterious superstructure of the American legal system. Even churches and colleges succumbed to a prevailing ethic that respected wealth and corporate success more than anything else. "There is no one left," McClure concluded ominously, "none but all of us."[6]

Ray Stannard Baker, one of McClure's most celebrated investigative reporters, credited the yellow press with awakening the public, though he added that most often they "increased the unrest and indignation of the public without providing the soundly based and truthful information necessary for effective action under a democratic system." Muckrakers and documentary photographers would change that. "What the early 'exposers' did

THE CHILDREN'S CRUSADE, A MARCH ON BEHALF OF PRISONERS HELD FOR VARIOUS WAR-LAW VIOLATIONS, C. 1919, BY AN UNNAMED PHOTOGRAPHER WITH THE HARRIS AND EWING SYNDICATE. (HARRIS AND EWING COLLECTION, LIBRARY OF CONGRESS)

UNCREDITED PHOTOGRAPH OF FREDERICK ALFRED WALLIS, U.S. IMMIGRATION COMMISSIONER, WITH RECENT IMMIGRANTS, POSSIBLY AT ELLIS ISLAND, N.Y., 1920. (LIBRARY OF CONGRESS)

was to look at their world, *really* look at it," wrote Baker. "They reported honestly, fully, and above all interestingly what they found."[7] Baker was speaking of the writers with whom he worked, but he might just as well have been referring to photographers.

During the severe depression that followed the Panic of 1893, Baker and other activist reporters revelled in stories that identified with the victims of hard times. Peering with relish at the underside of the Gilded Age, their coverage propelled populist movements such as Joseph Coxey's Commonwealth of Christ onto front pages across the country. Accompanied by his wife and children, including an infant son named Legal Tender, Coxey led a small army of unemployed laborers and farmers from Massilon, Ohio, to Washington, D.C., where he was arrested for trespassing. Sympathetic members of the press wrote extensively about Coxey's march on Washington, which made him at once famous and infamous.

The photographs that accompanied articles by Baker and others were now most often published as halftones, and offered readers seemingly irrefutable visual evidence of official wrongdoing and daunting social problems. The days of laboriously copying each photograph on a steel or wood

PHOTOGRAPH BY INVESTIGATIVE REPORTER RAY STANNARD BAKER OF THE MEMBERS OF COXEY'S ARMY PASSING A LUMBERYARD ON THEIR WAY TO WASHINGTON, D.C., IN 1894 TO PROTEST THE FAILURE OF GOVERNMENT TO DEAL WITH ECONOMIC DEPRESSION. (LIBRARY OF CONGRESS)

STEREOGRAPH COPYRIGHTED BY J. F. JARVIS AND DISTRIBUTED BY UNDERWOOD AND UNDERWOOD OF COXEY'S ARMY APPROACHING WASHINGTON, D.C. (LIBRARY OF CONGRESS)

PHOTOGRAPH BY GEORGE M. BETT OF JACOB COXEY IN JAIL. (LIBRARY OF CONGRESS)

plate were mostly gone; high-speed rotary presses and halftone engravings dominated the magazine business at the turn of the century.[8] Yellow journalism encouraged the use of photographs to inform and excite the public, and during the era of muckraking, photographs published in sympathetic periodicals were a central component of the reform movement. Images made for publication with the expressed intention of promoting social and political change shared certain approaches to technique as well as to subject matter. Such work eventually came to be known as documentary.

The first book-length study of the documentary genre was published in 1947. A compilation of the writings of John Grierson, a British film producer and director of the Empire Marketing Board Film Unit, it was solely concerned with moving pictures. However, Grierson's comments are aptly applied to still photography in general and photojournalism in particular because they help us make sense of this important though often misunderstood term. He noted that the word "documentaire" was coined by the French to describe a kind of nontheatrical travelogue. Eventually, documentary came to denote a broad range of nonfiction films, which made it a most unwieldy description since everything from newsreels to scientific record films were lumped together in a single category that defied easy analysis. "The use of natural material has been regarded as the vital distinction," Grierson notes, but the resulting "array of species is, of course, quite unmanageable."[9]

Confusion over what constitutes documentary continues, which is not surprising given the vast amount of material that is casually labeled as "natural" and thus given the status of documentary. To be sure, there is agreement on a few points, the most important being the necessity of accu-

IMAGE BY AN UNIDENTIFIED PHOTOGRAPHER FOR THE GEORGE GRANTHAM BAIN NEWS SERVICE SHOWING A HANDICAPPED AND HOMELESS MAN IN NEW YORK CITY. (GEORGE GRANTHAM BAIN COLLECTION, LIBRARY OF CONGRESS)

racy: documentaries are supposed to depict real life, without artifice, manipulation, or theatrics. "Here is an art based on photographs," writes Grierson, "in which one factor is always, or nearly always, a thing observed."[10] Consensus on the need to produce images of things as they are breaks down when considering the other major function of the documentary photographer: interpretation. Here, the objectivity of the lens gives way to opinion, and the raw visual data collected on film is molded into argument and narrative. The documentary photographer does not work dispassionately, wrote historian Beaumont Newhall in 1938. "He will put into his camera something of the emotion which he feels toward the problem, for he realizes that this is the most effective way to teach the public he is addressing."[11] In the end, as the editors of *Minicam* magazine wrote in the 1950s, documentary studies are as much a mirror of "the singular point of view of the photographer as they may be [of] the scene itself."[12] This curious combination of photographic objectivity with interpretation and argument is a principal source of confusion and misunderstanding.

The situation is muddled by those who contend that documentary work is, or should be, objective, factual, and utterly candid. Such an argument may be more strategic than anything else, as film historian Erik Barnouw notes, designed primarily to answer those who disparage documentary as propaganda, but it does little to enhance our understanding. Like all photographers, the documentarian makes choices that affect the final image. Selection of camera, lens, film, angle of view, available or artificial light, moment of exposure, and composition are among the myriad personal, subjective decisions made by the documentary worker. Often, documentary images are posed, especially when the photographer uses large-format equipment. Motive and interpretation are simply unavoidable. As Barnouw writes, in documentary someone "feels there is something about the topic that needs clarification, and that if one can document aspects of it—the whole truth is a legal fiction—the work will yield something useful in comprehension, agreement, or action."[13]

Accurate description is just the beginning in documentary; the purpose of the photographer and the uses made of the images are equally important. Grierson said as much in an article for *Sight and Sound* magazine in 1933. He admitted being uninterested in the formal aspects of cinema; it was the possibility of educating and especially persuading an audience that intrigued him. "I look on cinema as a pulpit and use it as a propagandist." Film is an ideal medium for reaching large numbers of people, he said, for it "is capable of direct description, simple analysis and commanding conclusion, and may, by its tempo'd and imagistic powers, be made easily persuasive."[14] For Grierson and other early documentary filmmakers, as well as for those using still cameras, the possibility of reaching a mass audience with compelling images was the crux of the matter. Perhaps inevitably, the uses made of documentary images gave the genre a distinctive political character. Documentary evidence came to be understood to consist of material that spoke to human and social problems needing not only understanding, but correction as well.

In journalism the interpretive function of documentary photographs is most often underscored by words; appended to the images are captions, perhaps even entire articles that include information about the subject as well as the opinions and reactions of the photographer, reporters, editors, publishers, and sponsoring organizations. As historian Maren Stange rightly points out, the documentary mode consists not of the photograph alone, but also what she calls its "rhetorical framework."[15] Words, shaped into argument and debate, provide essential nuance and meaning. Moreover, unlike the photographs themselves, written texts are not static. New interpretations and arrangements of words and photographs may substantially alter the initial presentation.

Beyond the requirement of verisimilitude and some interpretive purpose, the rules and principles of documentary allow considerable leeway. There is, however, an important distinction to be made between documentary images and ordinary spot-news and feature photography. Whereas single news photographs may describe with perfect accuracy certain tangible places, events, and people, documentary images are usually part of larger, more complex projects. As Grierson put it, "Here we pass from the plain (or fancy) description of natural material, to arrangements, rearrangements, and creative shapings of it."[16] Moreover, in simple news photography the purpose is nearly always primarily descriptive; the interpretive function, so vital to documentary, is often omitted altogether or suppressed.

Ironically, Jacob Riis, who is often cited by historians as the first true documentarian, was by his own admission "no good at all as a photographer." He made his living primarily as a writer, a journalist whose colorful stories for newspapers such as the *New York Tribune* and the *Evening Sun* described, among other things, squalid conditions in the crowded immigrant neighborhoods on the southern tip of Manhattan Island in New York City. He knew those places from personal experience. In 1870 Riis came to America from his native Denmark, and for years he eked out a meager living wandering among the unemployed and dispossessed in New York and New Jersey. When at last he began to find some success in the world of newspapers, mostly as a police reporter, he vowed to use journalism as a vehicle for reform. "It seemed to me that a reporter's was the highest and noblest of all callings; no one could sift wrong from right as he, and punish the wrong," he wrote in his autobiography. "The power of fact is the mightiest lever of this or of any day. The reporter has his hand upon it, and it is his grievous fault if he does not use it well."[17] Riis's reformist impulses coincided with a growing commitment on the part of newspaper and magazine publishers to question authority and attack official mischief.

Riis and others in the waning years of the nineteenth century considered journalism to be an engine of reform, an ideal way to reach and persuade the public about the need for fundamental social and political change. Charles Loring Brace, who spent several decades working on behalf of the Children's Aid Society of New York, described how he cultivated the press in order to further the reform movement after the Civil War. Articles, editorials, essays, and letters "were poured forth incessantly for years through the daily and weekly press of New York," he wrote, "until the public became thoroughly imbued with our ideas and a sense of the evils which we sought to reform." Brace kept in close touch with his friends in the press, and even worked part-time as an editor, so that his story might be told.[18]

Like Brace, Riis used journalism not merely to inform, but to excite and activate. Eschewing the role of purely objective observer, Riis was instead passionately committed to change. His dedication to reform was hardly unique. Prompted by sensational exposés run in "yellow" news-

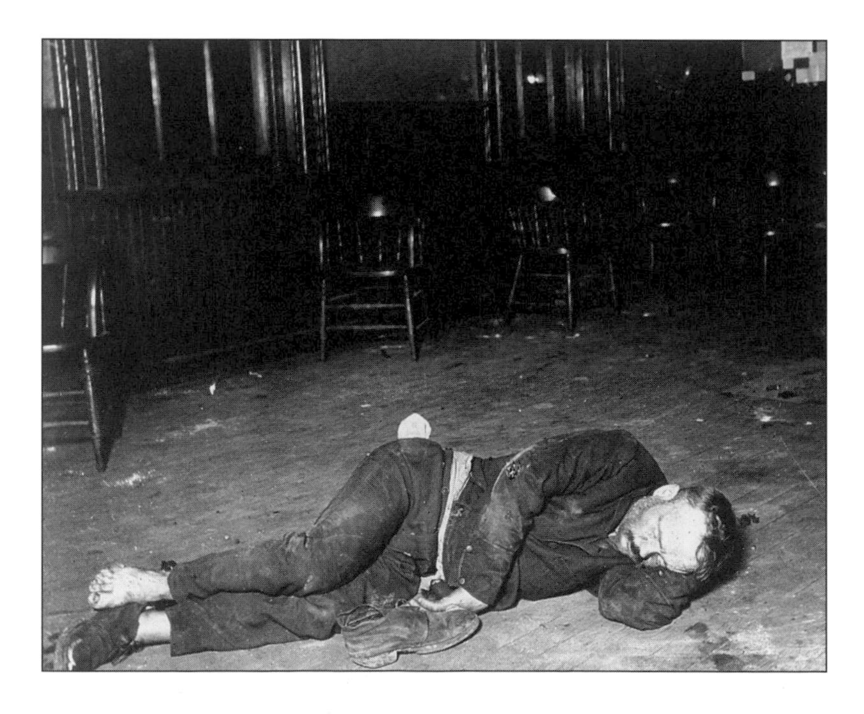

JACOB RIIS PHOTOGRAPHED THIS MAN, WHO WAS DEATHLY ILL WITH TYPHUS, IN A POLICE LODGING ROOM IN ORDER TO MAKE THE CASE AGAINST SUCH PLACES. (LIBRARY OF CONGRESS)

A PHOTOGRAPH BY JACOB RIIS OF MOUNTAIN EAGLE, A NATIVE AMERICAN, AND HIS FAMILY, C. 1898. THE PRINT SHOWS THAT THE ORIGINAL GLASS PLATE WAS EITHER BROKEN OR CRACKED. (JACOB RIIS COLLECTION, MUSEUM OF THE CITY OF NEW YORK)

papers and muckraking magazines, stories critical of the status quo began appearing even in mainstream publications as authors such as Riis, Upton Sinclair, Ida Tarbell, Ray Stannard Baker, and Lincoln Steffens examined the underside of American culture. Photographs were often an essential part of their stories. Armed with new, lightweight equipment, fast film, and plenty of magnesium powder for night work, photographers and writers with cameras began collecting pictures of aspects of American society and culture that until then received scant attention from the nation's press.

Riis approached photography like an enthusiastic amateur, though he was certainly not as unskilled as he pretended to be. The medium was miraculous, he often said, but he was clumsy and found the complicated technical aspects of photography elusive. Nevertheless, he made photographs, and hired others to make photographs for him, because he was convinced that images would buttress his written and oral arguments and evoke strong emotional responses from viewers. Gritty and unblinkingly realistic, they were perfect ammunition to use in his long battle against urban poverty and injustice. "To be precise, then, I began taking pictures by proxy. It was upon my midnight trips with the sanitary police that the wish kept cropping up in me that there was some way of putting before the people what I saw there. A drawing might have done it, but I cannot draw, never could."[19]

At first he could not photograph, either. However, a brief article on the benefits and ease of flash-powder photography convinced him that night pictures were possible, and he enlisted the aid of two skilled amateurs, Dr. Henry G. Piffard and Richard Hoe Lawrence, to accompany him into the slums. When his friends wearied of the long hours, Riis hired pro-

THE MONTGOMERY GUARDS, A GROWLER GANG IN ONE OF THE TOUGH IMMIGRANT NEIGHBORHOODS OF NEW YORK CITY, C. 1898. (JACOB RIIS COLLECTION, MUSEUM OF THE CITY OF NEW YORK)

fessionals, but the results were, at best, mixed. An employee of the *New York Sun* by the name of Collins failed to work fast enough to suit Riis. He next turned to a local studio photographer, probably A. D. Fisk, but things went awry almost immediately, partly because of the professional's reluctance to make some of the pictures ordered by Riis. Fisk claimed, for instance, that photographing orphans at their prayers in the Five Points House of Industry was a sacrilege. A much more serious conflict arose when Fisk attempted to sell the photographs on his own. The professional was paid for his time and efforts, and as far as Riis was concerned the prints as well as every single negative belonged to the employer. "The spectacle of a man prevented by religious scruples from photographing children at prayers, while plotting at the same time to rob his employer," Riis recalled with bitterness, "has been a kind of chart to me that has piloted me through more than one quagmire of queer human nature."[20] Although Riis usually acknowledged the work of his amateur friends, neither of the professionals was ever given credit for the pictures they made.

In 1890, when Riis published *How the Other Half Lives: Studies Among the Tenements of New York*, the word documentary was not yet used to describe the kinds of pictures in the book. The first edition included thirty-nine pictures, most of which were reproduced as halftones. Although not entirely without precedent, the work was innovative in its approach and in the effective use of photographs as evidence. A review in the *Chicago Times* described the book as "a gallery of pictures, each one reeking with a horror of its own kind, of the slums of New York, written by an author who has personally been through them all, has studied them historically and sociologically, has looked at them with the eyes of those who occupy them as well as his own, and now writes of them in simpler terms but with often startling effect."[21]

The use of photographs on behalf of social or political change was not novel. William Henry Jackson's views of the West helped persuade Congress to begin to create a system of national parks, and daguerreotypes, tintypes, and cartes de visite of former slaves fanned abolitionist fires in the years before the Civil War. A more direct precursor was the serialized publication in 1877 of *Street Life in London* by Adolphe Smith, a journalist, and John Thomson, a photographer best known for travel photographs of China and Cambodia. As historian Peter Bacon Hales contends, Smith's approach to the poor of London is compromised by timidity and perhaps, too, a certain fondness for the pernicious social philosophy of Herbert Spencer.[22] However, although Thomson's photographs, each exquisitely reproduced by the woodburytype process, now seem somewhat stiff and contrived, they were intended to be viewed as a genuine and sympathetic attempt to describe the poor of London. For those not accustomed to dealing seriously with poverty, homelessness, and chronic unemployment, the images provided startling and unsettling glimpses of life in London.

What distinguishes Riis's work from that of Thomson is neither his choice of subject matter nor the use of words and photographs to depict certain groups of needy people. Both photographers used cameras and film to describe urban poverty and its consequences, and they intended their pictures to be printed with words and disseminated to a mass audience. Both, in short, may now be regarded as documentary photographers. Rather, the difference lies in the chief objective of the work. Thomson and Smith sought simply to reveal that which was hidden; their's was an observation of places and people that were widely considered to be much less than respectable. In a prefatory statement, the authors noted that the "unquestionable accuracy" of the photographs "will enable us to present true types of the London Poor and shield us from the accusation of either underrating or exaggerating individual peculiarities of appearance."[23] Whatever protests and calls for reform they included in the text were muted.

Riis, on the other hand, was far more concerned with promoting reform than describing anything or anyone. Aesthetics, technique, style, and method were useful only insofar as they could sharpen his central argument. "To win the battle with the slum," he wrote in 1902, "we must not begin by despising politics. We have been doing that too long. The politics of the slum are apt to be like the slum itself, dirty. Then they must be cleaned. It is what the fight is about. Politics are the weapon. We must learn to use it so as to cut straight and sure."[24]

For Riis there was never any doubt about either the meaning or purpose of his pictures. They provided irrefutable corroboration for his attack against the landlords and builders of tenements whose selfishness and greed sentenced "the other half" to lives of unending misery and despair. "I have aimed to tell the truth as I saw it. If this book shall have borne ever so feeble a hand in garnering a harvest of justice, it has served its purpose." Riis was, then, more reformer than educator, and from the beginning he intended that his words and pictures serve as catalysts for significant change. He sought to stir the public conscience. Most important, he would persuade those who constructed, maintained, and profited from slum housing to see the errors of their ways. "Neither legislation nor charity can cover the ground. The greed of capital that wrought the evil must itself undo it, as far as it can now be undone. Homes must be built for the working masses by those who employ their labor; tenements must cease to be 'good property' in the old, heartless sense."[25]

In time, the type of documentary work represented by Jacob Riis—collections of words and pictures designed to promote social and political reform—came to be known as social documentary to differentiate it from its less polemical parent, documentary. What distinguishes the two forms is purpose and use. Documentary seeks primarily to educate and inform, while social documentary has an additional agenda, one steeped in politics and reform movements. Both kinds of documentary, the political and the nonpolitical, usually found their way onto the pages of American magazines and newspapers. Reaching a mass audience for the purpose of teaching, preaching, or persuading is vital in documentary photography and the printed page offers an especially effective forum for the work, whatever the intention of the photographer, publisher, or sponsoring organization.

Of course, the news page is not the only way to reach the public, as Riis himself demonstrated. Although his pictures appeared in several publications, he had other venues and uses in mind. The photographs made during those early nighttime forays into the slums were first printed as crude wood engravings in the *Sun* in February 1888. A little more than a year later, in December 1889, *Scribner's Magazine* published the pictures to accompany a nineteen-page story. The following year the book was published. During this entire time and for many years afterward, Riis lectured widely, and often used the pictures in the form of lantern slides—glass-plate positives projected onto a screen—to entertain and persuade his audiences. Given the ephemerality of such public performances little remains now except for the pictures themselves. Americans at the turn of the century, however, may have experienced the work in a variety of formats, for Riis constructed a veritable publicity blitz on behalf of urban reform. "Last year I had the occasion to address a convention at the national Capital, on certain phases of city poverty and suffering . . . ," he wrote in 1892. Throughout the lecture he "made use of the magic lantern to enforce some of the lessons presented."[26] "How the Other Half Lives" was often seen in the form of a kind of traveling revival meeting, complete with choir, sermon, and prayers. After his speaking tour through the principal cities of Indiana in 1910, for instance, one enthusiastic convert wrote that "he is the sole subject of conversation—the town is carried away, and the surrounding towns are awake." Riis seemed the social gospel personified. "God grant to spare him yet a long time to preach his wonderful gospel of service to the oppressed and the weak."[27]

"Flashes from the Slum," the article accompanying his pictures in the

646 *HOW THE OTHER HALF LIVES.*

In the Home of an Italian Rag-picker, Jersey Street.

From their perch up among the rafters Mrs. Gallagher's blind boarders might hear, did they listen, the tramp of the policeman always on duty in Gotham Court, half a stone's throw away. His beat, though it takes in but a small portion of a single block, is quite as lively as most larger patrol-rounds. There are few streets in the city where the crowd is as dense. A single big tenement, cut in halves lengthwise by a dividing wall with barred openings on the stairs, so that the tenants on either side may see but cannot get at each other, makes the "Court." Alleys, one wider by a couple of feet than the other, whence the distinction Single and Double Alley, skirt the barracks on either side. There are rooms for one hundred and forty-two families in the Court, which, with the ordinary New York average of four and a half to the family, gives a larger population than that of many a thriving country town that spreads itself over a square mile of land. It is claimed that this number has recently been reduced. The cosmopolitan character of lower New York, as well as the constant need of the policeman and the use of the iron bars, were well illustrated by the statement of the agent at one of my visits, that there were one hundred Irish, thirty-eight Italian, and two German families in the Court. It was an eminently Irish suggestion that the two German families were to blame for the necessity of police surveillance; but a Chinaman whom I questioned as he hurried past the iron gate of the alley was evidently of a different opinion, though he prudently hesitated to express it. The whole building is a fair instance of the bad after-thought of the age that followed immediately upon the adoption of the tenement as a means of solving the problems presented by the sudden rapid growth of the city; just how bad the last great cholera epidemic taught the community, when the death-

repair the worst of its old tenements. The process apparently destroyed the home-feeling of the alley, for many of its blind tenants moved away and have not returned since.

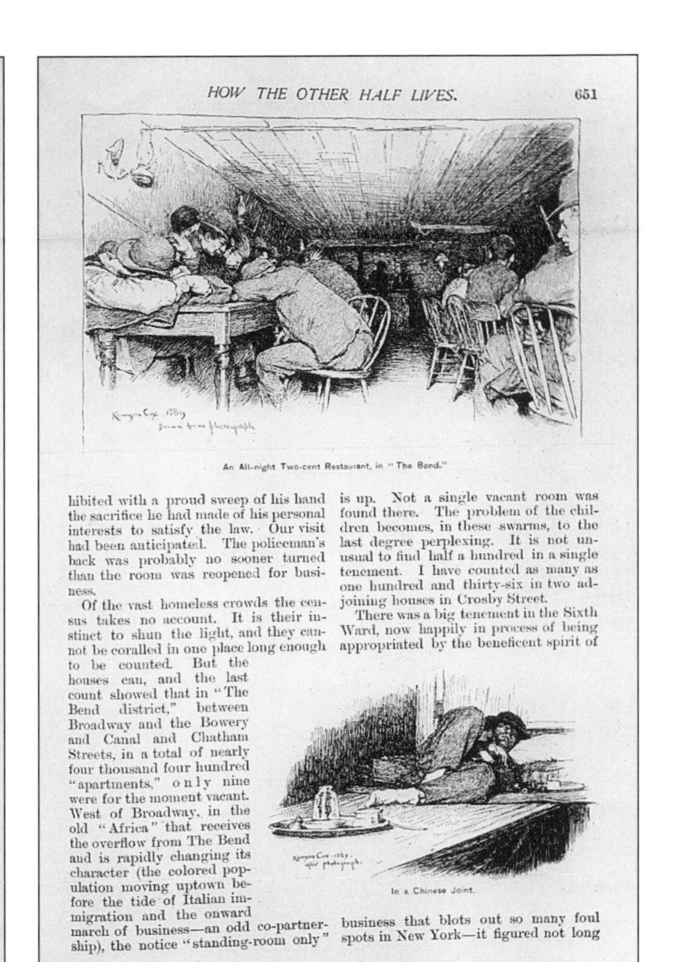

*HOW THE OTHER HALF LIVES.* 651

An All-night Two-cent Restaurant, in "The Bend."

hibited with a proud sweep of his hand the sacrifice he had made of his personal interests to satisfy the law. Our visit had been anticipated. The policeman's back was probably no sooner turned than the room was reopened for business.

Of the vast homeless crowds the census takes no account. It is their instinct to shun the light, and they cannot be coralled in one place long enough to be counted. But the houses can, and the last count showed that in "The Bend district," between Broadway and the Bowery and Canal and Chatham Streets, in a total of nearly four thousand four hundred "apartments," only nine were for the moment vacant. West of Broadway, in the old "Africa" that receives the overflow from The Bend and is rapidly changing its character (the colored population moving uptown before the tide of Italian immigration and the onward march of business—an odd co-partnership), the notice "standing-room only" is up. Not a single vacant room was found there. The problem of the children becomes, in these swarms, to the last degree perplexing. It is not unusual to find half a hundred in a single tenement. I have counted as many as one hundred and thirty-six in two adjoining houses in Crosby Street.

There was a big tenement in the Sixth Ward, now happily in process of being appropriated by the beneficent spirit of business that blots out so many foul spots in New York—it figured not long

In a Chinese Joint.

ABOVE LEFT: AN ENGRAVING BY KENYON CLARK FROM A PHOTOGRAPH BY JACOB RIIS OF AN ITALIAN IMMIGRANT AND HER BABY AT HER "HOME" ON JERSEY STREET IN NEW YORK CITY. ABOVE RIGHT: ENGRAVINGS BY KENYON CLARK FROM PHOTOGRAPHS BY JACOB RIIS TO ILLUSTRATE URBAN POVERTY. PUBLISHED BY *SCRIBNER'S MAGAZINE*, DECEMBER 1889, TO ILLUSTRATE "HOW THE OTHER HALF LIVES." (OTTO RICHTER LIBRARY, UNIVERSITY OF MIAMI)

*New York Sun*, breathlessly describes Riis's original purpose and methods. The object was not only the taking of interesting pictures, but "the collection of a series of views for magic lantern slides, showing, as no mere description could, the misery and vice that he had noticed in his ten years of experience." Riis was certain that besides the inherent human interest of such studies, his words and pictures "would call attention to the needs of the situation, and suggest the direction in which much good might be done." To encourage New Yorkers to clean up their own city, and especially to provide decent housing and suitable activities for poor children, Riis "threw himself with tireless energy into his pursuit of pictures of Gotham's crime and misery by night and day to make a foundation for a lecture called 'The Other Half; How It Lives and Dies in New York,' to give at church and Sunday school exhibitions, and the like."[28]

Although he presented his images as slices of real life, precise and utterly unbiased "flashes from the slums," Riis never intended his work to be viewed dispassionately. Certainly the words that accompanied his slide lectures and various articles and books were anything but objective. "I have no quarrel with the man who would do things by system and in order," he wrote in *The Battle with the Slum*, "but the man who would

AN UNCREDITED PHOTOGRAPH MADE FOR THE KEYSTONE VIEW COMPANY OF *(FROM LEFT AND RIGHT)* JACOB RIIS AND HIS FRIENDS THEODORE ROOSEVELT AND BISHOP VINCENT AT CHAUTAUQUA, N.Y. (CALIFORNIA MUSEUM OF PHOTOGRAPHY AT THE UNIVERSITY OF CALIFORNIA, RIVERSIDE)

reduce men and women and children to mere items in his infallible system and classify and sub-classify them until they are as dried up as his theories, that man will I fight till I die." To mobilize his audience, Riis combined photographs with emotionally charged rhetoric and plenty of evangelical fervor, culled, no doubt, from his work as a deacon in a Long Island church. He believed to the end that "one throb of a human heart"[29] was worth a whole book full of desiccated facts, and photographs—properly presented—might very well trigger such a response.

To ensure the maximum effect for his message, Riis cultivated the support of politicians, bureaucrats, the clergy, and fellow journalists. In fact, an early association with Theodore Roosevelt, when he was head of the Police Commission of New York City, developed into a kind of mutual admiration society. "As president of the Police Board I was also a member of the Health Board," Roosevelt recalled. "In both positions I felt that with Jacob Riis's guidance I would be able to put a goodly number of his principles into actual effect." Convinced that he and Riis "looked at life and its problems from substantially the same standpoint," Roosevelt emphasized that "our beliefs as to the methods necessary to realize them, were alike."[30] Both were especially astute about the publicity value of pictures on the printed page. Not surprisingly, over the years the bond between them strengthened; Riis was a frequent guest at the Roosevelt White House, a trusted advisor, and in 1904 he published a book that chronicled their long and enduring friendship. For his part, Roosevelt supported Riis's documentary work in both word and deed, as he did later for Edward Sheriff Curtis, the chronicler of North American native cultures.

Riis understood how photographs could be used as an adjunct of journalism, and his lessons were not lost on Roosevelt. Most important, he understood that the photographs themselves were less important than the uses made of them. For Riis the purpose was never to create art, nor to compile scenes to be viewed calmly in some comfortable Victorian parlor. Carefully combined with words—in lectures or on the printed page—the pictures Riis made were a clarion call to reform, steeped in politics, and imbued with his intense convictions and beliefs. His success led inevitably to other attempts to use photographs to persuade. The growing number of illustrated newspapers, magazines, and books that promoted reform at the turn of the century assured access to a mass audience.

"It is my purpose, at this time, to take you with me on a tour of observation," wrote Albert Banks, a Protestant minister active in Boston's urban reform movement in the 1890s. Using photographs made by W. H. Partridge, whose previous work included handsome landscapes and panoramas of the Boston highlands, and drawings by Sears Gallagher, Banks took his readers on a documentary word-and-picture tour through Boston's tenement districts. "As well-lighted streets are better than policemen to ensure safety and good order, so I believe that the best possible service I can render the public is to turn on the light, and tell, as plainly and simply as I can, the story of what I have seen and heard and smelled in the white slave-quarters, which are a disgrace to our fair city."[31]

The willingness of some editors and publishers to print stories dealing with the problems of the inner city encouraged more work. As we have seen, in the early 1890s several photographers in San Francisco ventured into immigrant neighborhoods. Their purpose was twofold: to illustrate the exotic lifestyles and living conditions of Chinese immigrants, and especially to provide proof of what they considered to be the nefarious fondness of the Chinese for opium. Like Riis in his midnight excursions into police lodgings, makeshift alleyway hovels, and dank basement saloons, the Californians spoke of their mission in military terms. And in the illustrated articles they produced there is an unmistakable aura of racism, as there was occasionally in the writings of other urban reformers.

"It was what I may call a photographic invasion," wrote Henry W. Canfield of his experience in the opium dens. Armed with "a good camera and plenty of glaring, blinding magnesium," Canfield, photographer Isaiah W. Taber, and several others—some of whom were armed—joined forces in a "most peculiar battle." The pictures, like Riis's, were presented as entirely unposed, candid views, made in the dead of night and without permission. They were proof, publicity, and sensation all rolled into a neat package, and not surprisingly they were widely published. That was the idea from the beginning. "The leader of the party became interested in the work of the missions," Canfield wrote, "and determined to join forces with them, though on an independent track. He believed that publicity would accomplish more good than perhaps anything else; and so he began work on that basis."[32]

The publication of *How the Other Half Lives* undoubtedly stimulated interest in both the problems and possibilities of urban life, but few were as devoted to the idea of reform and fundamental change as Riis. In fact, although the new photographers of the urban scene spoke of the vital educational aspects of their work, many of their articles and lectures reveal the obnoxious nativist sentiment and crude stereotyping characteristic of American culture at the turn of the century. Visual travelogues through the slums often disparaged or poked fun at the poor, especially those of color and foreign origin. At times the emphasis was clearly more on entertainment than providing a unique educational experience or provoking some social reform. Thus were the methods of documentary used to subvert or discredit the reformist impulse.

In 1897 New York philanthropist and missionary Helen Campbell published *Darkness and Daylight; or, Lights and Shadows of New York Life*, a voluminous and heavily illustrated study of poverty in the city. With an introduction by Lyman Abbott, celebrated pastor of Manhattan's Plymouth Church, and long essays by journalist Thomas W. Knox and police superintendent Thomas Byrnes, the book was designed as a primer for those with little or no understanding of or sympathy for those who lived and died in the inner city. In a prefatory statement the publisher stressed the importance of photography in the book, citing the efforts of Riis, Frederick Vil-

PHOTOGRAPH BY F. L. HOWE ILLUSTRATING THE VIRULENT RACISM THAT PERVADED TURN-OF-THE-CENTURY AMERICAN CULTURE. BLACKS AND OTHER MINORITIES WERE OFTEN DERIDED AND RIDICULED IN MAINSTREAM PUBLICATIONS. PUBLISHED IN THE *ILLUSTRATED AMERICAN*, SEPTEMBER 4, 1897. (LIBRARY OF CONGRESS)

STEEL ENGRAVING MADE FROM A PHOTOGRAPH OF NEWSBOYS BY OSCAR G. MASON, STAFF PHOTOGRAPHER AT BELLEVUE HOSPITAL IN NEW YORK CITY. PUBLISHED IN *DARKNESS AND DAYLIGHT*, 1897. (PRIVATE COLLECTION)

mar, E. Warren, and especially of Oscar G. Mason, staff photographer at Bellevue Hospital.[33] All contributed images for the book from their files, though Mason alone worked on assignment, eventually furnishing most of the images from which the full-page engravings were drawn.

"The dark side of life is presented without any attempt to tone it down, and foul places are shown just as they exist," enthused the publisher. "It is said that figures do not lie. Neither does the camera. In looking on these pages the reader is brought face to face with real life as it is in New York; *not* AS IT WAS, but AS IT IS TO-DAY. Exactly as the reader sees these pictures, just so were the scenes presented to the camera's merciless and unfailing eye at the moment when the action depicted took place."[34] In words remarkably similar to those used with other visual explorations of the city, the preface extolled the absolute fidelity of photographs. Ironically, though, not a single photograph or halftone was used in the book. Only engravings based on photographs graced the pages of *Darkness and Daylight*, and the captions omitted the names of the photographers. The pictures thus lose most of their power to persuade. Notwithstanding the hyperbole of the preface, the illustrations in *Darkness and Daylight* have the look of common Victorian genre scenes, their potential as realistic human documents fatally compromised by those bent on presenting a more picturesque view of the poor.

Campbell's book ultimately may have more in common with Thomson and Smith's *Street Life in London* than with the work of Jacob Riis. She means to show the better half how things are downtown, but although sympathetic to the plight of the poor, she includes few calls for municipal action or social reform. Rather, the emphasis throughout is on the power of volunteerism and good works. "Very considerable social reconstruction is necessary before modern society can be truly called Christian," Abbott writes in the introduction. "But to discuss the socialistic questions involved would require space far beyond the limits of such an introduction as this, and I therefore confine myself to a consideration of those remedies which may be put in operation without any radical reconstruction of social order or organization."[35]

Campbell and her fellow contributors offered only tentative and half-hearted calls for political or social change, but there is no denying their empathy for the poor. "Hopeless as the outlook often seems," Campbell writes, "salvation for the future of the masses" is possible if some way is found to save and rehabilitate the wretched children who prowl through the

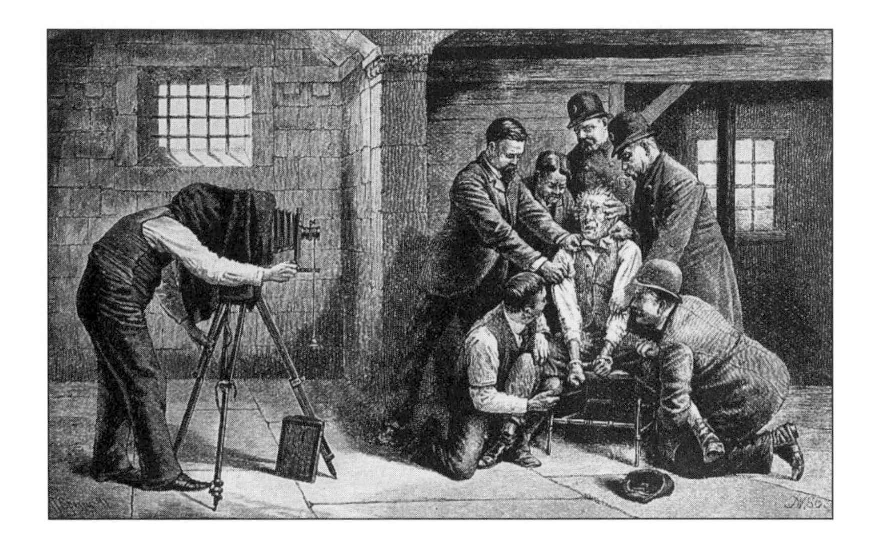

ENGRAVING, POSSIBLY FROM A PHOTOGRAPH BY OSCAR G. MASON, OF A MAN "POSING" FOR A POLICE STATION'S ROGUE'S GALLERY. PUBLISHED IN *DARKNESS AND DAYLIGHT*, 1897. (PRIVATE COLLECTION)

NOVEMBER 27, 1897. THE ILLUSTRATED AMERICAN. 683

THE BUSY POOR OF HESTER STREET, NEW YORK. (*See page 681.*)

1. Italian fruit vendors and their customers of all languages. 2. A typical Hebrew fish stand. 3. How the Jews observe the Christian holiday; thousands of Hebrew carts with fish at a penny a pound.

A PICTURE PAGE PUBLISHED IN THE *ILLUSTRATED AMERICAN*, NOVEMBER 27, 1897, CONSISTING OF CANDID STREET SCENES MADE BY JIMMY HARE ON HESTER STREET IN NEW YORK CITY TO ILLUSTRATE AN ARTICLE BY JAMES REALF ON ITALIAN AND JEWISH IMMIGRANTS. (LIBRARY OF CONGRESS)

PHOTOGRAPH BY JESSIE TARBOX BEALS OF AN UMBRELLA MENDER IN NEW YORK CITY, ABOUT 1905. THE HANDWRITTEN CAPTION ON THE BACK OF THE PRINT READS, "THE JEWISH UMBRELLA MENDER WHO LIVES IN PELL STREET, AND IS ONE OF THE BEST KNOWN CHARACTERS OF CHINATOWN. HE SPEAKS CHINESE, WITH A MARKED HEBREW ACCENT. THE RESULT IS FUNNY, EVEN TO EARS WHICH KNOW NEITHER LANGUAGE. THE CHINESE GATHER AROUND HIM WHEN HE TALKS, AND LAUGH HEARTILY. THEY ARE FAR FROM BEING THE INSCRUTABLE, STOICAL RACE WHICH THEY ARE SO OFTEN PAINTED. AND THEIR SENSE OF HUMOR IS KEEN." (WARREN AND MARGOT COVILLE PHOTOGRAPHIC COLLECTION, BLOOMFIELD HILLS, MICH.)

slums. She praises the work of charitable organizations such as the Society for the Prevention of Cruelty to Children and various church-run shelters, as well as those who would provide slum children with training that would "force their restless hands and mischievous minds to occupations that may ensure an honest living."[36]

Of course, not everyone agreed that the poor were either wretched or in need of special help. An article in the *Illustrated American* by James Realf Jr., accompanied by Jimmy Hare's photographs, described the same Mulberry Street neighborhood made infamous by Riis, but the message was much less sympathetic. The author noted that the polyglot crush of people living in the area were not the least bit unhappy with their lot, having escaped far more loathsome conditions in eastern and southern Europe. In this view Jewish and Italian immigrants reveled in their comparative luxury. "Nowhere in the vast, three-millioned city may one behold so many hawk-eyes and hook-noses . . . ," Realf wrote, and nowhere "so many children and young women, pretty and well-nigh bewitching, in spite of ill-fitting clothes and tawdry ornaments." For Realf and perhaps Hare as well, the people of Mulberry Street were a long way from being abject, hopeless, or—by implication—helpless. "Ceaseless battle for bread on all sides," Realf concluded, "but such a sunny temper on the surface as charms the beholder; for even the aged vendors have, as a rule, a halo of jollity about their poverty and uncomeliness, thus unconsciously helping to point a fine and valuable moral."[37] The message (and moral) here is plain: the poor but happy denizens of Mulberry Street needed no special help from government or private agency.

Stories dealing with aspects of urban blight appeared regularly in the press in the early years of the twentieth century, but not all nascent documentary work described life in the cities. In 1908, for instance, Edmond S. Meany, professor of history at the University of Washington, wrote about his friend Edward S. Curtis for the illustrated magazine *World's Work*. Curtis was then less than halfway through his effort to document the tribes of North America west of the Mississippi River, a monumental project that took him nearly thirty years to complete. For Meany what made Curtis stand out from the army of anthropologists, ethnologists, archaeologists, and artists who were then prowling through the reservations in search of authentic native lore was the depth of his knowledge of and sympathy for tribal people. Curtis was neither ten o'clock nor summertime scholar, but one "so close that he seems a part of their life."[38]

HUNTING INDIANS WITH A CAMERA 10007

ancient Sioux customs. But Red Hawk found it impossible to restrict the invitations; instead of twenty, 300 gathered for the feast, and among them were chiefs equal in rank to Red Hawk. They felt that they must make their importance felt. Chief Slow Bull had brought his council tepee, decorated with buffalo-tails and with a horse's tail floating from the peak. It had come down to him from his father, and his father's father, with traditions of war-parties and the chase. Into this tepee Curtis

IN THE LAND OF THE NAVAJO

was invited for a council. After his speech, Iron Crow, one of the chiefs, replied that to make all perfectly happy would take more beeves than Mr. Curtis had provided. He was reassured, and the council broke up with many "Hows" and much handshaking. But, as the first procession formed in the morning, Slow Bull raised his voice in that wild, matchless oratory of the Indian and brought the procession to a sudden halt. He, too, wished to be placated with more beef. Then a careless teamster nearly ruined the whole enterprise by throwing off one of the sugar-bags with the oats. After it had been rescued, the feast was finished without offense to any-one's dignity. Then, with true Indian caprice, they decided that they must rest and smoke for the rest of the day. Again the plan seemed on the verge of failure. Red Hawk had lost control.

Mr. Curtis quietly folded up his camera, as if he had not traveled many weary miles just to get these pictures. There was no fault-finding, no impatience; but, with infinite tact, he discussed affairs with some of the leading spirits. During the night a reaction in sentiment set in. In the morning the warriors, led by Red Hawk and Slow Bull, rode into camp. Their hearts were happy, they said, and they wished to help their white friend. Old rites were reënacted, old battles re-fought, old stories retold; and Mr. Curtis's pen and camera recorded it all.

TAKING PICTURES UNDER FIRE

At other times, in the Southwest, even after the chiefs had agreed to the picture-taking, crowds would collect in front of the camera. He had to leave one village by night without

PHOTOGRAPH OF NAVAJOS BY EDWARD SHERIFF CURTIS, PUBLISHED IN *WORLD'S WORK* MAGAZINE IN MARCH 1908 TO ILLUSTRATE AN ARTICLE BY CURTIS'S FRIEND, EDMUND S. MEANY. (OTTO RICHTER LIBRARY, UNIVERSITY OF MIAMI)

The Seattle Sunday Times.

A SEATTLE MAN'S TRIUMPH

ED. CURTIS MAKES PHOTOGRAPHS OF SECRET RITES OF NAVAJOES—SCIENTISTS FROM SMITHSONIAN INSTITUTION SAID THIS COULD NOT BE DONE

EDWARD S. CURTIS

SEE NEXT PAGE

COVER PAGE OF THE MAGAZINE SECTION OF THE *SEATTLE SUNDAY TIMES,* MAY 22, 1904, SHOWING PHOTOGRAPHS OF NAVAJOS BY EDWARD S. CURTIS AS WELL AS A PORTRAIT OF CURTIS BY AN UNIDENTIFIED PHOTOGRAPHER. (SPECIAL COLLECTIONS DIVISION, UNIVERSITY OF WASHINGTON LIBRARIES, SEATTLE)

Theodore Roosevelt uttered similar sentiments in the foreword to Curtis's twenty-volume study, *The North American Indian,* a documentary work combining oral histories, scholarly essays, tribal summaries, linguistic analyses, and handsome photogravures. The former Rough Rider's approbation is ironic: long an ardent proponent of Manifest Destiny and Euro-American racial superiority, he now saw the value of preserving Native American cultures, if only on paper. Curtis "has lived on intimate terms with many different tribes of the mountains and plains," Roosevelt wrote in October 1906. "He knows them as they hunt, as they travel, as they go about their various avocations on the march and in the camp." His pictures captured the spirit as well as the facts of native life, something few white men managed to do. "He is an artist who works out of doors and not in the closet . . . ," the president continued, and the publication of his research and pictures provide "a real and great service . . . not only to our own people, but to the world of scholarship everywhere."[39]

Curtis met Roosevelt for the first time in June 1904 while on assignment to make portraits of the Roosevelt children at the family home in Oyster Bay, New York.[40] Curtis showed the president some of his work, and the two struck up a friendship of sorts. Until that time Curtis had provided most of the funds for his Indian work from commissions from his highly regarded studio in Seattle and the sale of prints, but he was now out of money. In December 1904 he persuaded Roosevelt to compose a general letter of support and took it with him to New York. There he sought and received the backing of industrialist and financier J. Pierpont Morgan. Eventually Morgan contributed nearly a quarter of the funds necessary to complete and publish the work.

SELF-PORTRAIT BY EDWARD S. CURTIS, MADE IN 1899. (NATIONAL PORTRAIT GALLERY, SMITHSONIAN INSTITUTION)

Like Riis, Curtis used a variety of media to promote his ideas on behalf of what he called the "vanishing race." From the beginning, though, his purpose was more limited than that of Riis, for he sought simply to document native cultures, not foment public support for particular social or political reforms. Curtis wrote and supplied photographs for magazine and newspaper articles, published two brief "photo-dramas" in book form, and lectured widely, using lantern slides of his images to entertain and educate. In 1911 he produced what he called a "picture musicale," which combined hand-colored slides, snippets of motion picture film, and a score by H. F. Gilbert based on recordings of native songs made on Edison's magical wax cylinders. He hoped to tour the country with the show, giving at least nine performances a week, but despite brief critical and popular success in Seattle, New York City, and Brooklyn, this curious amalgam of operetta and illustrated lecture dissolved, a victim of rancor among the underpaid orchestra members and a sea of red ink.[41] In 1914 Curtis produced a motion picture, *In the Land of the Head Hunters,* which purported to describe the lives of native people in the far northwest. At the time he hoped to raise funds for further work among the tribes, so he designed the film (and a book with the same title) to appeal to a mass audience. Nonetheless, the combination of realistic photographs of the Kwakiutl people of Puget Sound with a narrative based on what Curtis called the "declamatory style of the tribal bards" was not successful. The film opened and played briefly in Seattle, but received little popular or critical support.[42]

Curtis always intended that his pictures be seen in the company of words. In March 1905 ethnologist and author George Bird Grinnell wrote in *Scribner's Magazine* that Curtis "realizes the work's scientific value, and, not content with making these beautiful and faithful records of the old-time life, . . . feels that pictures alone are not enough." This was not art simply for the sake of art, but art in the cause of knowledge and understanding. Grinnell, who first met Curtis on railroad mogul Edward Harriman's Alaska expedition in 1899, noted that Curtis set out to gather from each tribe "all that he can that relates to its customs, beliefs, and ceremonials, and is thus accumulating information of great value in itself, but of still greater value as a supplement to his pictures."[43]

In addition to his various publishing enterprises, Curtis cultivated support within the fine-art movement in photography, and his images were exhibited widely. Whereas Riis confined his efforts to the world of journalism, presenting his pictures as the unvarnished truth, Curtis freely admitted the aesthetic underpinnings of his pictures. In the "General Introduction" to *The North American Indian*, he described his purpose as both scientific and artistic. His aim was to systematically "picture all fea-

PHOTOGRAPH AND ARTICLE BY EDWARD S. CURTIS, PUBLISHED IN *SCRIBNER'S MAGAZINE*, JUNE 6, 1906. (OTTO RICHTER LIBRARY, UNIVERSITY OF MIAMI)

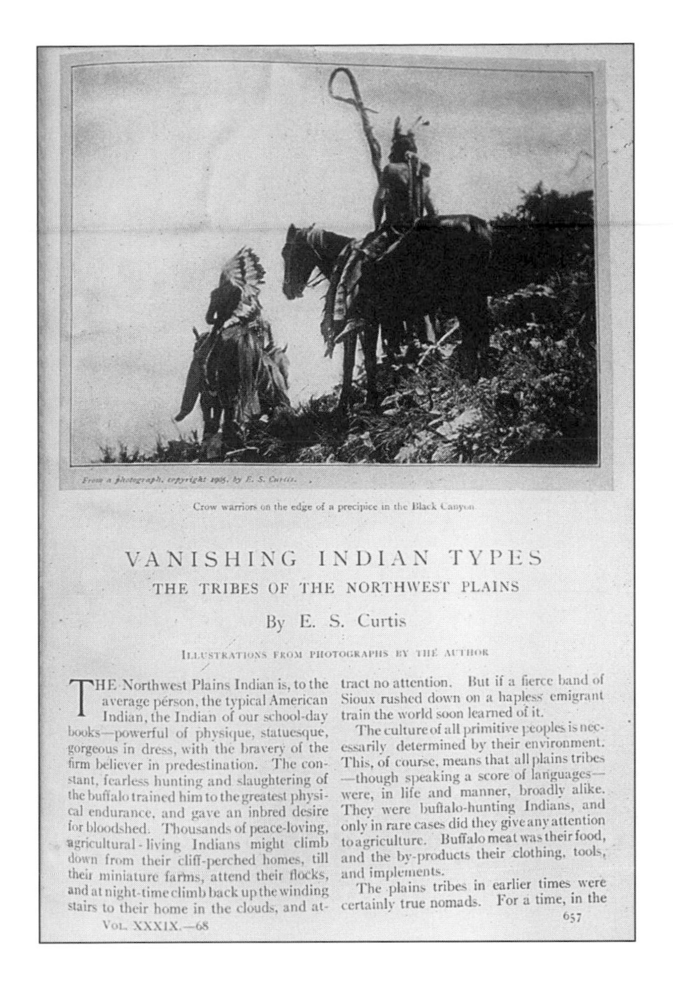

*From a photograph, copyright 1905, by E. S. Curtis.*

Crow warriors on the edge of a precipice in the Black Canyon

VANISHING INDIAN TYPES

THE TRIBES OF THE NORTHWEST PLAINS

By E. S. Curtis

ILLUSTRATIONS FROM PHOTOGRAPHS BY THE AUTHOR

THE Northwest Plains Indian is, to the average person, the typical American Indian, the Indian of our school-day books—powerful of physique, statuesque, gorgeous in dress, with the bravery of the firm believer in predestination. The constant, fearless hunting and slaughtering of the buffalo trained him to the greatest physical endurance, and gave an inbred desire for bloodshed. Thousands of peace-loving, agricultural-living Indians might climb down from their cliff-perched homes, till their miniature farms, attend their flocks, and at night-time climb back up the winding stairs to their home in the clouds, and attract no attention. But if a fierce band of Sioux rushed down on a hapless emigrant train the world soon learned of it.

The culture of all primitive peoples is necessarily determined by their environment. This, of course, means that all plains tribes—though speaking a score of languages—were, in life and manner, broadly alike. They were buffalo-hunting Indians, and only in rare cases did they give any attention to agriculture. Buffalo meat was their food, and the by-products their clothing, tools, and implements.

The plains tribes in earlier times were certainly true nomads. For a time, in the

VOL. XXXIX.—68 657

tures of the Indian life and environment . . . ," but his was no rigid, unfeeling compilation. The fact that Native Americans and the western landscape "lend themselves to artistic treatment has not been lost sight of," he wrote, "for in this country one may treat limitless subjects of an aesthetic character without in any way doing injustice to scientific accuracy or neglecting the homelier phases of aboriginal life."[44]

Curtis's purpose was always to provide a truthful visual record of Native American life, of cultures that seemed to him to be on the verge of disappearing without a trace. There is sentimentality and nostalgia in his grand endeavor, and it is clear now that he occasionally went to great lengths to ensure his pictures had the look and feel of olden times. We know, for instance, that he routinely posed his subjects, and supplied some of them with "authentic" clothing, implements, and other trappings of tribal cultures. Moreover, it seems that a few of the photographs included in his collection were made by his assistants, though crediting the employer instead of the camera operator was a common (yet unfortunate) practice at the time.[45]

Ultimately, the work of Edward Curtis defies neat categorization. By his own admission he sought to infuse his pictures with elements of art, and he employed low camera angles, limited depth of field, and plenty of darkroom manipulation to produce images that fit easily into the pictorialist tradition.[46] At the same time, he clearly intended to provide his own and future generations with accurate descriptions of traditional Native American cultures, not as he found them in the first decades of the twentieth century, but as they were in the days before their disastrous contact with white men. The pictures were accompanied by reams of written material carefully documenting tribal languages, customs, folklore, and history. "To begin with," he said in one of his many public addresses, "for every hour given to photography two must be given to the word picture part of this record of the vanishing Indian."[47] Magazines and newspapers used his photographs, and they were seen as well in the form of lantern slides. He tried from the beginning to be both scientist and artist, and as a result his career took unexpected twists and turns, moving from the staid and comfortable world of his studio to that of the roving artist, documentarian, ethnographer, and entertainer.

That Curtis produced vastly different kinds of work during his lifetime is not surprising, though it makes any definitive assessment difficult. As the possibilities of photography expanded in the twentieth century, offering practitioners a variety of outlets for their work, the eclectic approach became more common. Throughout her distinguished career, for instance, Frances Benjamin Johnston produced all kinds of work, from news pictures for the syndicates and photographic essays for illustrated magazines to studio portraits of the social elite and formal architectural studies. Along the way Johnston produced some documentary work, but except for her consistent and passionate feminism she remained aloof from reform politics and crusades. From the outset she viewed photography primarily as a business, not a means of effecting social or political change.[48]

Johnston's photographs that are most often cited as documentary describe schools established after the Civil War for the purpose of providing mostly vocational training for former slaves and Native American children. In 1868 Samuel Chapman Armstrong, military governor of ten coastal counties in Virginia, established the Hampton Institute to afford young blacks, many of them recently mustered out of the Union army, practical instruction in the manual trades. At the urging of United States Army Captain Richard Henry Pratt, Native Americans were added to the Hampton student body in 1878. Pratt established the Carlisle Indian School in Pennsylvania a year later. The emphasis at both institutions was on discipline, manual labor, and Christian piety. Johnston's documentation of these schools, and of Booker T. Washington's Tuskegee Institute, provided comforting visual evidence of acculturation, an affirmative photographic portrait of the fabled melting pot in action.[49]

At the behest of Reverend Hollis Burke Frissel, Armstrong's successor at Hampton, Johnston came to the school in December 1899 and made more than 150 large-format views of campus buildings and students. According to the editors of Hampton's in-house journal, the *Southern Workman and Hampton School Record,* the photographs would "contrast the new life among the Negroes and Indians with the old, and then show

UNCREDITED PHOTOGRAPH OF BOOKER T. WASHINGTON SPEAKING IN LOUISIANA, MADE DURING HIS LAST TOUR OF THE DEEP SOUTH ON DECEMBER 8, 1915. (LIBRARY OF CONGRESS)

THE CLASSIC PHOTOGRAPH BY FRANCES BENJAMIN JOHNSTON OF A CIVICS CLASS AT THE HAMPTON INSTITUTE IN 1899. (LIBRARY OF CONGRESS)

how Hampton has helped to produce this change."[50] Initially, the images were displayed at the Paris Universal Exposition of 1900, constituting a major segment of an exhibit on black life at the American Pavilion; thereafter, Johnston marketed them to several publications.

Despite the interest of some publishers in stories revealing what was wrong with American society at the turn of the century, Johnston remained steadfastly loyal to those in power and steered clear of stories that might enmesh her in some nasty political quarrel. Early in 1892, however, she journeyed to Pennsylvania for *Demorest's Family Magazine* to write about and photograph the coal industry. Conditions in the mines and squalid company towns were already the subject of numerous exposés, but Johnston's article defended the owners. "I made no socialistic studies, and asked for no labor statistics," she admitted, "but it struck me that the miner and his condition had been painted, perhaps, a little blacker than even the coal-dirt warranted." As for notoriously low wages, she noted that since miners were paid according to the amount of mineral they produced, "their income depends to a certain extent upon their individual effort." The mining population ultimately seemed to her to be more quaint than needy. All those "Huns, Poles, Greeks, and other European peasantry" who drifted into the coal towns, desperate for work, "live on next to nothing, and, clinging to their foreign tongue and manners, build up the queer colonies like 'Shantytown,' which savor . . . of old-world picturesqueness."[51]

Johnston's rosy assessment of conditions in the Pennsylvania mines, however reassuring for owners and operators, was lost in a deluge of documentary material generated by both public and private sources that told a far different story. In 1900 the census confirmed that more than 18 percent of American children between the ages of ten and fifteen worked for their living. In the coalfields of Pennsylvania, thousands of children as young as twelve worked full time and for a pittance. During a ruinous strike among anthracite coal miners in 1902, comprehensive news coverage revealed the extent of child labor in the mines and generally characterized their working conditions as brutal and exploitative.[52] Two years later, Dr. Felix Adler, founder of the Ethical Culture Society and its progressive school in New York City, established the National Child Labor Committee (NCLC), an organization designed to reform the employment practices of American industries. The NCLC and its now legendary staff photographer, Lewis Wickes Hine, used a variety of methods to reach the public, though from the beginning periodicals were the most effective vehicle for their reformist message.

Except for a somewhat self-effacing manner, there was nothing tentative about Hine's approach to the work he did for the NCLC and other liberal and progressive organizations. Deeply committed to the cause, he made photographs to educate Americans and promote fundamental changes in the law. "It was toward visual education that he deliberately turned, with his 5 × 7 camera, his rectilinear lens and his 'barrel of flashlight powder . . . ,'" recalled journalist and critic Elizabeth McCausland, Hine's friend and loyal supporter. "With Hine the sociological objective was paramount; the esthetic attributes seem to have occurred almost casually. At least, no particular attention was paid to them by the enthusiastic public which studied the photographs absorbedly for their social implications." From the beginning of Hine's career as what she called a "social photographer," he made sure that "meaning and purpose came first, the art after."[53]

Hine's photographs made on behalf of organizations such as the NCLC and American Red Cross were published in magazines, brochures, and pamphlets, and they were displayed as lantern slides and in exhibitions. Whenever possible he distributed the same images to a variety of

AS PART OF HIS CAMPAIGN AGAINST CHILD LABOR, LEWIS HINE PHOTOGRAPHED THESE PAPERBOYS SELLING THE *WASHINGTON POST* LATE AT NIGHT. (LIBRARY OF CONGRESS)

outlets. Thus, in 1920 he exhibited a series of portraits of workers at New York's Civic Club. According to an article in the *New York Evening Post,* Hine also intended to show the pictures in the form of lantern slides in a series of lectures at factories and other places of work. "The intention," according to the *Post*'s reporter, "is not to make technical studies, but to develop photographic surveys of the human phase of industry, with its bearing on the whole social problem of labor relationships."[54] Hine's images were invariably presented with text that supplied additional bits of information and commentary; the result was more argument than passive illustration. His working methods included meticulous planning, and often entailed some subtle subterfuge to gain access to the factories, mines, and agricultural areas where people, especially children, worked. He traveled extensively on behalf of various progressive organizations and produced thousands of "straight" prints that were subsequently published—usually in magazines. Critics of the NCLC's reform agenda dismissed the pictures and the text that accompanied them as biased and exaggerated, and in his defense Hine, like Riis before him and many documentary photographers since, insisted that he simply and without artifice recorded what was before the camera. "Most significant," he explained to McCausland shortly before his death in 1940, "was one thing that made me extra careful about getting data 100% pure when possible. Because the proponents of the use of children for work sought to discredit the data, and *especially* the photographer, we used—I was compelled to use—the utmost care in making them fireproof."[55]

Hine's approach to his subjects differed dramatically from the soft-focus poses and gauzy atmospheres favored by pictorialists. The plain people he photographed often stared directly back into the lens, establishing an immediate visceral connection between themselves and the viewer. His pictures were meant to be seen not as character studies but as vivid social

LEWIS HINE PHOTOGRAPHED THIS BOY SELLING CELERY LATE AT NIGHT IN NEW YORK CITY FOR THE NATIONAL CHILD LABOR COMMITTEE. (LIBRARY OF CONGRESS)

YOUNG BLACK WORKERS OUTSIDE A GLASS FACTORY IN ALEXANDRIA, VA., PHOTOGRAPHED BY LEWIS HINE FOR THE NATIONAL CHILD LABOR COMMITTEE. (LIBRARY OF CONGRESS)

documents, and captions underlined the message contained in the image. "Two really significant aspects of my work have been recognized," Hine wrote in 1924 to Paul Underwood Kellogg, his friend and editor of *Survey Graphic* magazine. "The acceptance of the common man in contrast to the white collar stuff and the value of realistic photography which has for some time replaced the fuzzy impressionism of the day."[56]

The straightforward approach adopted by Hine, and his disavowal of pictorialist methods, belies the aesthetic sophistication of his work. However much he and other social documentary photographers defended their images as utterly direct and even artless, there is undeniable evidence to the contrary. Early in his career, even before he left his job as a full-time teacher of geography to be the NCLC's first staff photographer, Hine summarized his philosophy for the *Photographic Times*. Rather than distancing his work from the world of art, he said instead that the principal aim of the artist ought to be "to have something to relate and to know how to select the right things to reproduce that story by accenting the important parts and minimizing the effects of the unimportant factors." For Hine matters of pure aesthetics, though hardly irrelevant, counted less than the intended social or political message. In 1933 he wrote to his friend Florence Kellogg of his "conviction that the design, registered in the human face thro years of life and work, is more vital for purposes of permanent record, tho it is more subtle perhaps, than the geometric pattern of lights and shadows that passes in the taking, and serves (so often) as mere photographic jazz."[57] Ironically, while his use of the press as a vehicle to distribute his pictures undoubtedly enhanced their political effectiveness, the immediate artistic influence of the images was almost certainly diminished. As historian and curator Edward Earle rightly contends, pictures reproduced in the popular press "enter a new realm—one which devalues them as aesthetic objects."[58] Their power to persuade the public is greatly enhanced by

SOUTHERNERS OF TOMORROW

PHOTOGRAPHS BY LEWIS W. HINE
FOR THE NATIONAL CHILD LABOR COMMITTEE

YOUNG CIGAR MAKERS, TAMPA, FLORIDA.

The problems which cloud a camera's lens and which must be faced by the educators, the physicians and the business men of the Southern States if the intelligence, physique, and industrial efficiency of the next generation is to meet the standards which the leaders of the New South set for it

PAGE ONE OF A PHOTOGRAPHIC ESSAY BY LEWIS HINE DESCRIBING THE HIGH SOCIAL COSTS OF CHILD LABOR IN THE SOUTHERN STATES. PUBLISHED IN THE *SURVEY*, OCTOBER 2, 1909. (OTTO RICHTER LIBRARY, UNIVERSITY OF MIAMI)

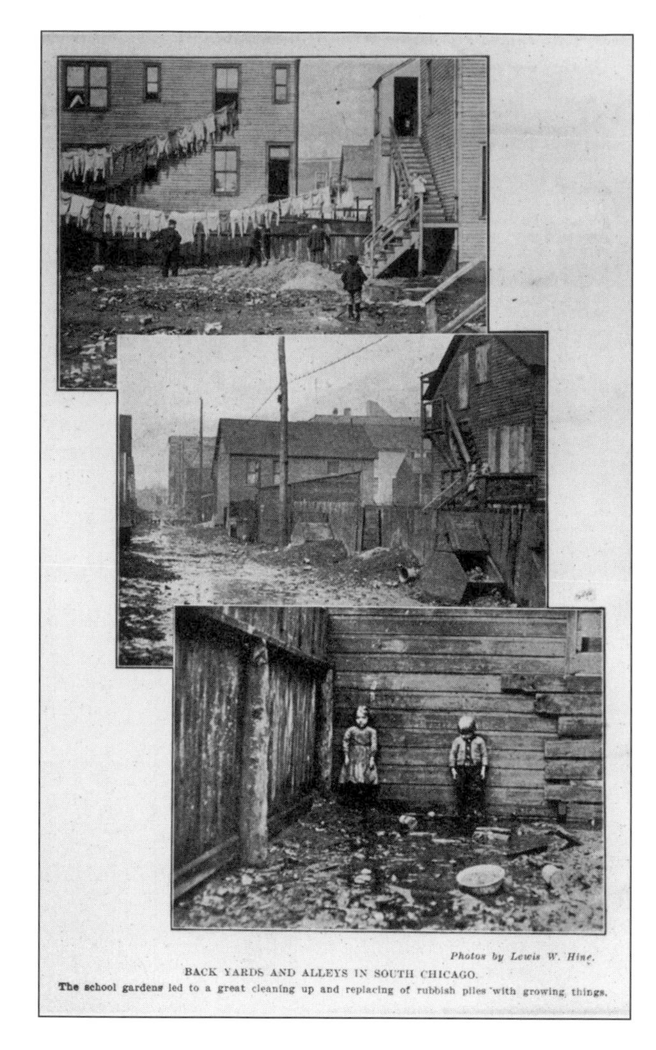
Photos by Lewis W. Hine.

BACK YARDS AND ALLEYS IN SOUTH CHICAGO.

The school gardens led to a great cleaning up and replacing of rubbish piles with growing things.

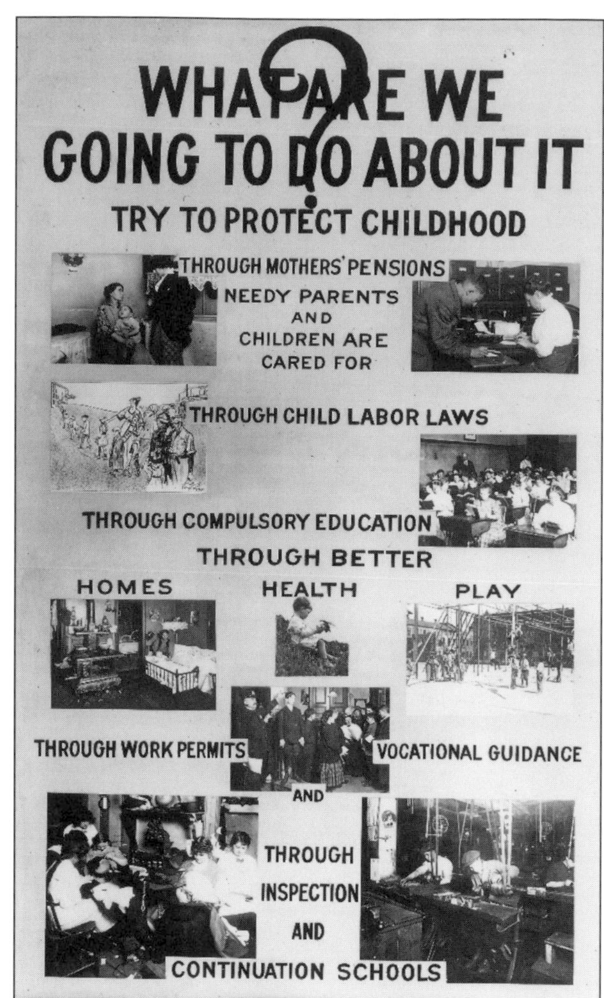


ABOVE LEFT: PHOTOGRAPHS BY LEWIS HINE OF GARBAGE-STREWN ALLEYS AND BACKYARDS IN CHICAGO ILLUSTRATING AN ARTICLE CALLING FOR THE PLANTING OF URBAN GARDENS. PUBLISHED IN THE *SURVEY,* SEPTEMBER 1910. (OTTO RICHTER LIBRARY, UNIVERSITY OF MIAMI)

ABOVE RIGHT: A POSTER PRINTED AND DISTRIBUTED BY THE NATIONAL CHILD LABOR COMMITTEE WITH PHOTOGRAPHS BY LEWIS HINE, N.D. (LIBRARY OF CONGRESS)

publication, but their value as objects of connoisseurship wanes.

The artist in Hine adjusted depth of field to provide more or less back and foreground detail, used flash powder to illuminate interiors and dark city streets, and carefully posed each subject. By so doing he sought not to alter what he confronted, but to clarify and enhance its meaning. He assured Elizabeth McCausland that the "photo-data" he collected over the years was accurate, with "no retouching or fakery of any kind." The pictures were mostly meant to be seen on the printed page, as essential elements of word and picture stories describing various social phenomena. Hine biographer Daile Kaplan notes that the pictures he produced, though prized now by curators and collectors, originated in the worlds of journalism and reform politics in the early 1900s. Moreover, his innovative coupling of words and several related pictures presaged the rise of the photographic essay in *Life, Look,* and other large-format magazines in the mid-1930s.[59]

Despite years of experimentation and the steady evolution of ideas and methods of reproducing photographs on the printed page, editors, pub-

LEWIS HINE'S DOCUMENTARY STUDY OF A YOUNG WORKER IN A TEXTILE MILL IN NORTH POWNAL, VT. HINE SUPPLIED THE FOLLOWING INFORMATION WITH THE PRINT: "ADDIE LAIRD, 12 YEARS OLD. SPINNER IN A COTTON MILL. GIRLS IN MILL SAY SHE IS 10 YEARS OLD." (RECORDS OF THE CHILDREN'S BUREAU, LIBRARY OF CONGRESS)

lishers, and photographers still had a lot to learn about combining words and pictures effectively. Hine, who depended for his living in large measure on assignments from and sales to illustrated magazines, helped pave the way to modern photojournalistic practice. He insisted, for instance, that his images be credited at a time when photographic illustrations in newspapers and magazines were routinely published with no mention of the photographer. Hine's images on the covers of the *Survey,* as well as those used in essays and in ads to promote the magazine, prominently displayed his name.

Even more important (and ultimately problematic), Hine insisted that he retain control of his own negatives. He did so in part because he relied so heavily on sales of pictures from his files. Although some editors and art directors bridled at the thought of running pictures made originally for someone else, Hine argued strongly that their reluctance was misplaced. In a letter to Paul Kellogg written shortly before Christmas in 1923, Hine encouraged his old friend to make use of what he called his "on-hand material." He offered to open his files to Kellogg's staff at *Survey Graphic,* providing they did not waste too much of his time, and added that Kellogg ought to waive his "over-emphasis on the virginity of such material." A good picture, he said in closing, "should not depend too much upon the one element of novelty."[60]

Hine also worked hard to influence art directors and editors who had the final say over matters of layout and design; he did not simply turn his work over to them and hope for the best. Though not always successful, Hine made his wishes known. In November 1921, after examining a large number of his images for use as a picture story, Paul Kellogg agreed that Hine's files constituted "a real treasure trove." But he disagreed about the number of images that could be fashioned into a single story. "I know that all your geese are swans. Not only in your own eyes, but in reality," wrote the editor, "yet, none the less, you can put too many swans on a page."[61]

It may be that Hine's activist approach ultimately gained him as many enemies as friends in the business. By the mid-1920s he acquired a reputation for being difficult and inflexible. Notwithstanding the valuable years of work on behalf of immigrants, children, workers, and others, Hine was

PHOTOGRAPH BY LEWIS HINE FOR THE NATIONAL CHILD LABOR COMMITTEE OF MARSHALL KNOX, 10 YEARS OLD, SELLING MAGAZINES ON MAIN STREET IN ROCHESTER, N.Y., IN THE WINTER OF 1910. (LIBRARY OF CONGRESS)

judged by some editors to be too much trouble. Assignments and sales from the files were increasingly hard to come by, especially after the stock market collapse in October 1929. Even before the crash, Hine was forced to put his home near New York City up for sale and move further north to the small rural community of Hastings-on-Hudson.

Hine's last major assignment came in 1930, when things were at their bleakest. The job was to document the construction of the fabulous Empire State Building, rising over Manhattan in spite of the nation's slide into economic depression. Hine hoped the new images of men at work—a positive, uplifting documentary project—would lead to additional assignments and some measure of financial security. When the federal government established its own documentary program under the leadership of Roy Emerson Stryker, prospects for the future must have seemed pretty good. After all, Hine had helped to guide and formulate Stryker's approach to documentary photography at Columbia University in the early 1920s during the time that Stryker worked with Professors Rexford Guy Tugwell and Thomas Munro on their textbook, *American Economic Life and the Means of Its Improvement*.[62]

When assignments failed to materialize after completion of the Empire State work, Hine looked to Washington, and Stryker, for help. "The Hine fortunes are at an all-time low and if they do not change in the near future . . . the Home Owners Loan Corp. will have to foreclose on the place and we will wander forth to greener pastures," Hine wrote to Stryker in Washington on June 21, 1938. "I'm telling you this to see if you see any way of taking advantage of the situation to get some of the service you said you wanted to do," Hine continued. "I shall probably have to work, for a time, for anything I can get." Hine's plaintive request was one of several he had made to Stryker since 1935, shortly after President Franklin Roosevelt signed the executive order establishing the Resettlement Administration (RA).

Stryker could not or would not help. Some suggest that the photographer's age and especially his reluctance to relinquish control of his negatives were the deciding factors, but we know that occasionally Stryker's budget was, in fact, cut to the bone. During the winter of 1937–38, for instance, he had but two photographers on staff—Arthur Rothstein and Russell Lee. In any event, though outwardly supportive of his long career as a documentary photographer, Stryker refused to hire Hine, even on a part-time basis. "As things are now," Stryker wrote late in 1935, "I do not believe that you can expect anything to open up where we could use your services." The problem, Stryker said, was money, not Hine's ability to do the work; he insisted that although he and others in the government wanted very much to work out some kind of an arrangement, an extremely tight budget simply would not permit it. Perhaps in the spring "our finances might make it possible for us to work out some proposition with you."[63] But it did not happen that spring, nor any time thereafter, and Hine died, penniless and largely forgotten, in November 1940.

The photographs produced by the small number of men and women

COVER OF A BROCHURE PRINTED AND DISTRIBUTED BY THE FARM SECURITY ADMINISTRATION, C. 1939. THE PHOTOGRAPHER WAS NOT CREDITED. (UNIVERSITY OF LOUISVILLE PHOTOGRAPHIC ARCHIVES, LOUISVILLE, KY.)

Stryker did hire to document America during the Great Depression are now well known, as is the history of the photography project itself. Many of the images made under the auspices of the RA and its better-known successor in the federal bureaucracy, the Farm Security Administration (FSA), are now properly regarded as national treasures. Not surprisingly, they are frequently and lovingly displayed in museums and galleries. Some have been reproduced so many times in newspapers, magazines, and books that they are firmly fixed in the nation's collective memory, and prints of the most famous are made from second- and third-generation negatives. Neither the evolution of Stryker's project nor the work of his staff photographers is at issue here. Unfortunately, however, the iconic status of some of the photographs tends to obscure the complexity of the FSA collection, as well as its place in the history of photojournalism.

Stryker's orientation to photography was undoubtedly influenced by the work of Hine and other social documentary photographers who used the medium primarily as a means of communication. Stryker's main job as chief of the Historical Section of the RA and FSA was to collect and disseminate photographs and other materials that effectively described conditions in distressed agricultural regions. "We had to help make a country conscious of the Dust Bowl, the migrants, the sharecroppers, and the difficulties that had beset the country," he explained in 1960. "That was enough to challenge our whole staff."[64] Stryker was right. In the 1930s both the people and the press were divided on the nature of the economic situation as well as the means needed to improve it, and Stryker's first and most important task was political: to persuade the disbelievers. He elected to do so primarily with photographs that were exhibited, published in numerous government handouts and brochures, and distributed for free to publishers and editors willing to use them.

Stryker's function was not unlike that of George Creel in 1917, though the latter's duties certainly extended far beyond the collection and distribution of pictures. Both men were outspoken liberals, hired to convince Americans that the plans and policies adopted by the federal government in times of crisis were appropriate and effective. Both relied heavily on the press to funnel their written and pictorial messages to the public. And as one might expect, both objected vehemently to accusations of exaggeration, political bias, and crude self-interest. The cruelest cut of all was the suggestion that Creel's Committee on Public Information or Stryker's FSA photography project were just propaganda units erected at taxpayer expense for the purpose of flooding the country with false or misleading information.

"We fought indifference and disaffection in the United States and we fought falsehood abroad," wrote Creel in 1919. He and President Wilson believed the inexorable spread of war combined with confusion and uncertainty at home justified a massive and unprecedented federal effort to explain and persuade. To those who complained that the committee's work was more political than anything else, Creel explained that the CPI's output was not anything like the misleading propaganda emanating from the enemy. "We strove for the maintenance of our own morale by every process of stimulation. Our work was educational and informative only, for we had such confidence in our case as to feel that only fair presentation of its facts was needed."[65]

Stryker's rationale for the Historical Section photographs mirrored the language in Creel's 1919 report. The official purpose of the Informational Division, which housed Stryker's Historical Section, was to explain and educate. In 1949 Stryker recalled in a letter to Wallace Richards at the Carnegie Museum in Pittsburgh that the "candor and honesty" of the images made them useful to government publicity bureaus during wartime, but that was not their primary function. Rather, the photographs were meant to help "make the public aware of national problems" and to help urban voters understand that the agency's rural programs were necessary and effective.[66] From the beginning, newspapers and magazines played a vital role in bringing this message to the people. "We began with the press in mind," he told Richards, "and before we knew it had magazines, book publishers, universities, museums, libraries, writers, sociologists, economists, geographers, historians, slide-film producers, research departments from Hollywood to Washington, all eager after pictures."

The documentary approach in photography, with its reliance on straightforward technique and accuracy, as well as its underlying reformist arguments, was perfectly suited to the publicity needs of the New Deal. And the growing appetite of the daily and periodical press for pictures, especially those illustrating hard times in the far-distant countryside, ensured that the images would reach the public. "It didn't take long to realize that photographs of the immigrants, the sharecroppers were a useful tool for the Information people," Stryker told historian Robert Doherty in 1962. "My sense of P.R. . . . grew rapidly. And we were succeeding with our pictures of the immigrants and sharecroppers to a surprising degree."[67]

The overtly political uses made of Resettlement Administration and Farm Security Administration photographs engendered criticism during the life of the project that continues to this day. There is, for instance, skepticism regarding statements by Stryker and others that the overriding purpose of the photographs was to inform, and that the images were objective and thus free from nefarious political motives. Education of the public was undoubtedly an important goal, and Stryker did indeed insist that his photographers tell the truth as they saw it. But there is considerably more to the story.

Like the work of Hine and other social reformers, FSA photographs present facts as well as sentiment and opinion. The combination of the mechanical accuracy of the camera with the photographer's personal response to the subject is unavoidable. So, too, therefore, is the connection between documentary and ideology. "The propagandist note is not just an occupational risk of editorial documentary; it is inevitable if there is any depth to one's interpretation," wrote John Grierson in 1949. "It is at this point that documentary begins to . . . become a vital force in contemporary education."[68] Dorothea Lange, one of the most celebrated FSA photographers, said in 1968 that a documentary image is not simply factual. "It is a photograph which carries the full meaning and significance of the episode or the circumstances or the situation that can only be revealed—because you can't really capture it—by this other quality." Like any artist, she said, the documentary photographer expresses feelings, but there is also the necessity to accurately describe people and things, to say "what is it really."[69]

Naturally, the uses made of the pictures were sometimes political; but more often the photographs were meant to compellingly describe people that—like Riis's "other half"—remained little understood and unappreciated. Moreover, as the project evolved, Stryker encouraged his staff to look hard at all aspects of American culture, not just those dealing with endemic rural poverty. Indeed, if as some suggest Roy Stryker had a hidden agenda, it was this: to create a vast visual encyclopedia of America, not some pictorial monument to Roosevelt's New Deal and the American liberal tradition.

Still, the accusation of an inherently sinister political function would not go away. Even within the agency there were misgivings. Shortly before he accepted a position as senior information specialist in the RA, Walker Evans drafted a memorandum outlining his qualms concerning official photography. "Never make photographic statements for the government or do photographic chores for gov or anyone in gov, no matter how powerful,"

PHOTOGRAPH BY BEN SHAHN FOR A FARM SECURITY ADMINISTRATION BROCHURE EXPLAINING GOVERNMENT PROGRAMS TO AID TENANT FARMERS, N.D. (PHOTOGRAPHIC ARCHIVES, UNIVERSITY OF LOUISVILLE, LOUISVILLE, KY.)

he wrote. Such work inevitably jeopardizes the purity of the artist. His job at the Resettlement Administration must be to record, not propagandize. "The value and, if you like, even the propaganda value for the government lies in the record itself which in the long run will prove an intelligent and farsighted thing to have done. NO POLITICS whatever."[70] Later, long after he left Stryker's employ, Evans continued to dispute his role in the government. "I didn't like the label that I unconsciously earned of being a social protest artist," he wrote in 1974. "I never took it upon myself to change the world."[71]

Much to Evans' enduring disgust, the politics of reform was rarely entirely absent from the work of the Historical Section. Lack of consensus about the agricultural crisis ensured plenty of debate in Washington and elsewhere. Henry Wallace, Franklin Roosevelt's first secretary of agriculture, noted the public's lack of enthusiasm for radical change in agricultural policies and planning, and stressed the need for positive publicity. "Practically the entire population dislikes our basic program of controlling farm production," he wrote in *America Must Choose*, "and they will do away with it unless we can reach the common intelligence and show the need of continuing to plan."[72]

"Showing the need" for various government programs became a major preoccupation of New Deal administrators like Wallace, Tugwell, and Stryker, at least in part because of the absence of such stories and reporting in the press early in the Depression. According to Irving Brant, editor at the *St. Louis Star and Times*, following the stock market crash many newspapers ignored or even denied altogether the existence of the deepening economic crisis. "From the beginning of the business decline," he wrote in a 1933 article in *Editor and Publisher*, "there has been an extensive belief that if newspapers would stop publishing anything about unemployment, bankruptcies, bank closings or the level of steel ingot production, the effect would be magical."[73] The photographs Stryker made available to the press were part of the administration's effort to convince publishers and the public that the crisis was real.

The work of Stryker and his staff on behalf of the rural poor was mirrored by a small group of documentary photographers in New York City calling themselves the Photo League. The group was organized in 1936 to promote social documentary work and provide classroom space and rudimentary darkroom facilities for photographers. "Photography has a tremendous social value," wrote one league member in the August 1938 issue of *Photo Notes*, the group's intermittent newsletter. "Upon the photographer rests the responsibility and duty of recording a true image of the world as it is today."[74]

At the league's small office in Manhattan, guest speakers such as Roy Stryker, Dorothea Lange, Berenice Abbott, and *Life* photographers Eliot Elisophon, Margaret Bourke-White, and W. Eugene Smith, urged aspiring photographers to make and publish pictures that could help improve the lives of the poor and downtrodden. The work of Lewis Hine, an early league member, was offered as proof that photographs could indeed change the world. Hine's longtime friend and supporter, Elizabeth McCausland, lectured on the meaning and purpose of the league's brand of documentary photography. "To state truth, naked, unadorned, is the basic objective of photography. . . . But it follows that in order to reach the audience without which the truth is meaningless the truth must be stated clearly and intelligibly."[75]

Eventually the political activism of league members attracted both the attention and enmity of the federal government. The FBI investigated the group in the late 1940s, and in 1947 Harry Truman's attorney general, Tom C. Clark, included the Photo League in a list of 79 organizations and 11 schools that were either "totalitarian, fascist, communist, or subversive."[76] Membership declined, and the group finally disbanded altogether in 1951, a victim of their own success at combining politics and photography.

Stryker also mixed politics with images, but to the very end he maintained the innocence and purity of the FSA. Despite his strenuous denials of a political agenda, however, it is now clear that RA and FSA photographs ultimately did for the rural poor what Hine's images of working children did for the NCLC. By making them available to a mass audience, especially via the printed page, Stryker began to change the public's perception of rural poverty. In numerous letters to his roving band of photographers, he indicated the need for certain images and stressed the importance of publicizing the agency's programs. "Isolated schoolhouses and roads serving a limited number of people are very expensive items for the taxpayers of any county to maintain," Stryker told Arthur Rothstein in May 1936. "This offers one of the best arguments for Resettlement, particularly so when one or two families living in an isolated region necessitate the maintenance of roads and schoolhouses. We need pictures to illustrate this situation."[77] A few months earlier, he sent a similar request to Dorothea Lange in California. "Would you, in the next few days, take for us some good slum pictures in the San Francisco area." The collection in Washington was apparently perceived by some to be unbalanced, and the letter hints at an underlying political motive. "We need to vary the diet in some of our exhibits here by showing some western poverty instead of all south and east. . . . Do not forget," he added, probably unnecessarily, "that we need some rural slums type of thing, as well as the urban."[78]

Assignments were created that could illustrate aspects of farm programs planned or administered by the government as well as fit the pictorial needs of the press. "Regarding the tenancy pictures," Stryker wrote Lange in June 1937, "I would suggest that you take both black and white, but place the emphasis on the white tenants, since we know that these will receive much wider use."[79] In the end Stryker not only kept alive the idea of creating a photographic survey of American culture, he ensured as well that the images received the maximum public exposure. Thus, in 1941 Stryker exulted that an exhibition of FSA photographs at the Museum of Science and Technology in New York City would surely generate abundant press coverage. "This is going to be a very good thing for us and we are going to get publicity in every paper in New York, and also get a lot of attention from the various photographic clubs," he wrote to Russell Lee. "The big exhibit will have FSA plastered all over it."[80]

That was exactly the point. It was never enough just to document, to capture America artistically and lovingly on film. As Lange noted in 1968, many of the images she and her colleagues produced for the government were destined for the printed page, their purpose to inform Americans about the Depression and the good works of the Roosevelt Administration.[81] The FSA photography project sustained and supported New Deal programs, and in the course of creating a grand visual history of American culture, it also strengthened the indelible link between documentary still photography and photojournalism.

PHOTOGRAPH BY JUN FUJITA OF THE *CHICAGO DAILY NEWS* OF NATIONAL GUARDSMEN ON DUTY IN CHICAGO IN THE WAKE OF VIOLENT RACE RIOTS IN 1919. (CHICAGO HISTORICAL SOCIETY)

CHAPTER FOUR

# TABLOIDS, MAGAZINES, AND THE ART OF PHOTOJOURNALISM

The art of news photography is much more than the pressing of a cable release, the adjusting of scales and shutters and the sighting of an object through a viewfinder. It is the ability of the news cameraman to go beyond the mechanics of exact procedure, and feel, sense and record the story with the vividness of the news gatherer.

—A. J. Ezickson, *Get That Picture!*[1]

The methods and uses of photojournalism changed dramatically during the 1920s and early 1930s, due in no small part to the influence of those working in the documentary tradition. Long-term projects designed to educate and persuade had little in common with sensational news-mongering and ambulance chasing, activities widely thought to be inescapable elements of daily press work. Although photojournalism was and still is considered in some circles to be the exclusive province of boorish spot-news photographers intent on capturing the likenesses of camera-shy personalities or gruesome scenes of mayhem and disaster, documentary work published in magazines and newspapers gave evidence of a much more complex profession.

Still, the view of the press photographer as an everlastingly scandal-happy drone persisted in the phenomenal success of a new kind of illustrated newspaper, the tabloid. Designed and written to appeal to the urban working classes, it seemed to validate those who foretold the demise of traditional journalism. The new newspaper was smaller and much easier to handle than traditional broadsheets, especially for those who read the paper while hanging on to a strap in a crowded subway car or bus on the way to or from work. And it was crammed with photographs. Halftones filled almost all the front and back pages, leaving space only for the masthead, bold headlines, and brief captions. The center pages consisted of yet more pictures, and photographs were run with text on most other pages.

The first successful American tabloid, the *New York Illustrated Daily News,* began publishing on June 23, 1919. British publishing mogul Lord Northcliffe showed the way. His *Daily Mirror* in London, first published as a newspaper for women in 1903, then as the world's first illustrated tabloid a year later, amassed a huge number of readers and American publishers eager to improve circulation took note. An early editorial in the *Daily News* enumerated the philosophy of its principal creator, Chicago newspaper baron Joseph Medill Patterson, who learned about tabloid publishing when he met with Northcliffe while on holiday in England. "We shall give you every day the best and newest pictures of the interesting things that are happening in the world. Nothing that is not interesting is news. The story that is told by a picture can be grasped instantly."[2] That, of course, was the crucial problem for those who composed and vigorously defended the rules and regulations of proper discourse.

"In the last war there were regiments of poor stunted devils, syphilitic, tubercular, crooked in body, incapable of anything but menial work and the kind of fighting where hopeless endurance counts," wrote an unnamed critic in the *Saturday Review of Literature* in 1927. According to this writer, these pathetic humanoids, "the grandchildren of the factory slaves," were the audience to which crass tabloid publishers catered. Herein is the classic critique of tabloidism. It argues that such papers

WILLIAM VANDERBILT, PUBLISHER OF THE *ILLUSTRATED DAILY TAB*, A TABLOID PUBLISHED BRIEFLY IN 1926 TO TAKE ADVANTAGE OF THE BUILDING BOOM IN MIAMI, EXAMINES THE PAPER'S FIRST EDITION WITH HIS WIFE. WHEN THE HOUSING MARKET COLLAPSED LATE IN THE YEAR, SO DID THE *TAB*. (HISTORICAL MUSEUM OF SOUTHERN FLORIDA)

TABGRAVURE PICTURE SECTION

Illustrated Daily Tab

TABGRAVURE PICTURE SECTION

UNCREDITED COVER PHOTOGRAPH OF A NAVY BLIMP OVER MIAMI, PUBLISHED IN VANDERBILT'S *DAILY TAB*, 1926. (HISTORICAL MUSEUM OF SOUTHERN FLORIDA)

exploit people with neither intelligence nor sophistication, cynically using crude writing and lurid illustrations to appeal to their most base instincts. Most worrisome was their popularity; within a few years the *Daily News* was the most widely read paper in New York, and others—some much more scurrilous—populated newsstands in cities all across the country. "What will the grandchildren of the tabloid readers be like?" asked the critic. Though perhaps physically and economically healthy, they would surely be intellectually, emotionally, and morally stunted: "Soiled minds, rotten before they are ripe."[3]

There is an eerie resemblance between this overwrought diatribe and the vitriol that greeted the rise of the yellow press in the 1890s. Once again abundant use of pictorial material is presented as conclusive proof both of declining literary standards and a nefarious plan to exploit hopelessly naive and illiterate people. "The photograph is easier to read," wrote critic Silas Bent in 1926. He compared tabloids to jazz, noting disdainfully that both were popular with primitives. "The tabloids appeal to those who find pictures within their grasp," he sneered. "Picture-features are a throw back to the intelligence which communicated by means of ideographs, before the alphabet was invented. They are comprehensible to the most numerous audience, the lowest mental common denominator. They enter the consciousness over the lowest threshold."[4] In fact, several studies show that tabloids appealed mostly to the middle class. Critic and historian Simon Michael Bessie noted in 1969 that the *New York Daily News* sold about 80 percent of its papers in middle-class neighborhoods, and actually did better among the well-to-do than the very poor who often could not afford the price of even the cheapest papers.[5]

In terms of design and orientation, tabloids were a logical extension of American daily journalism, not an entirely new and revolutionary form. James Gordon Bennett's dictum that the purpose of newspapers was to startle, not inform, was merely put to better use, and advances in camera and printing technology ensured an endless supply of interesting and occasionally risqué images. Most important, the tabloid press suited the tenor of the times. Mass media in the postwar decade reveled in spectacle and ballyhoo, and the public gobbled it all up and begged for more. Celebrities and scandals, fads and their devotees, disasters, crimes of passion, and the twisted malevolence of urban gangsters and small-town hoods—all was fodder for press photographers, and tabloids offered ample space for the pictures.

"There had been a war fought and won and the great city of the conquering people was crossed with triumphal arches and vivid with thrown flowers of red, white and rose," wrote F. Scott Fitzgerald, preeminent chronicler of the 1920s. "Never had there been such splendor in the great city, for the victorious war had brought plenty in its train."[6] Fitzgerald was right. Fortunes were made and gleefully displayed—the world made safe for self-indulgence. Photographs captured the frenetic swirl of events that vied for the attention of the public after the war; black-and-white images

VIOLENT CRIME BECAME A STAPLE OF DAILY ILLUSTRATED JOURNALISM IN THE 1920S. NO SINGLE INCIDENT MATCHED THE ST. VALENTINE'S DAY MASSACRE FOR AUDACIOUSNESS AND GORE, AND THE PRESS MADE THE MOST OF IT. THIS IS ONE OF SEVERAL IMAGES MADE OF THE VICTIMS BY JUN FUJITA OF THE *CHICAGO DAILY NEWS*. (CHICAGO HISTORICAL SOCIETY)

Today

At Last They Got Him.
Money Did It, as Usual.
Air Wisdom, and Nonsense.
New Coins for Austria.
BY ARTHUR BRISBANE

Complete Baseball and Race Results

Details in Sports Section

Herald and Examiner

2 CENTS METROPOLITAN EDITION

TUESDAY, JULY 24, 1934

# HUNT DILLINGER HOARD; NELSON ESCAPES TRAP!

PUBLIC ENEMY NO. 1 PAYS HIS DEBT

'NO MERCY!' U. S. EDICT IN GANG MOP-UP

Mail Robber's Wife, Informant, Promised Leniency; Physician in Case Is Sought

America's greatest drama, its smashing first-act curtain leaving John Dillinger dead, after the most sensational outlaw career of modern times, was unfolding an amazing prospect of events to come last night.

What development was coming next was guarded with the utmost secrecy by Melvin H. Purvis of the Chicago branch of the Department of Justice, but it was freely prophesied that one climax was to follow another in rapid, dramatic sequence as the government hastened to smash the remnants of Dillinger's gang.

*Women, Their Weakness, to Be Their Downfall.*

These steps lay ahead, as Purvis and his aids, consulting with Attorney General Homer Cummings, who arrived here late yesterday afternoon from Washington, plotted their course of action:

FIRST—Roundup of the five Dillinger gangsters remaining at liberty, through the same agency that brought the downfall of Dillinger himself.

Turn to Page 3, Column 3.

Heat Will Keep Grip at Least Another Day; Relief Hope Dim

BISHOP'S BODY FOUND IN CREEK

Weary Old Father Dillinger Comes to Claim Son's Body

SCENE OF DEATH MADE A BAZAAR!

THE WEATHER

PAGE ONE LAYOUT OF THE *CHICAGO HERALD AND EXAMINER* WITH AN UNCREDITED PHOTOGRAPH OF THE BULLET-RIDDLED BODY OF JOHN DILLINGER SURROUNDED BY LAW ENFORCEMENT PERSONNEL, JULY 24, 1934. (PRIVATE COLLECTION)

splayed across the front and center pages of tabloids provided daily doses of shock, titillation, and gritty realism. In 1919, for instance, newspaper and magazine readers saw photographs of widespread pitched battles between workers and armed guards, police, and state militia; women marching for the right to vote; virulent race riots in Chicago; and continuing turmoil and unrest over America's experiment with Prohibition. These news photographs constituted a sharp break with the evocative images favored by pictorialists and other fine-art photographers. Moody studies meticulously printed on fine paper had little in common with the in-your-face style of modern press photography.

The growing gulf between the worlds of photojournalism and fine art stemmed in part from the requirements of printers. In a paper read to the January 1897 meeting of the Chicago Trade Press Association, Charles Stadler noted the differences between "a good or artistic photograph" and one that is suitable for reproduction. "A good photograph in the artistic sense . . . has to have certain qualities which render it unsuitable, or less suitable, for reproduction as a halftone. A certain softness is needed, and just in this a good photograph for art purposes differs from a good photograph for halftone reproduction."[7]

There were also conflicting attitudes toward subject matter and camera technique. Charles Henry Caffin, colleague and admirer of Alfred Stieglitz, noted the difference between those committed to artistic expression in photography and all others. "There are two distinct roads in photography," he wrote in 1901, "the utilitarian and the aesthetic; the goal of the one being a record of facts, and of the other an expression of beauty." Most tourists and strictly commercial photographers, as well as those who recorded "war scenes and daily incidents used in illustrated papers," were primarily interested in precision and accuracy, whereas artists sought to depict the beautiful.[8] Writing in Stieglitz's influential journal *Camera Work* two years later, critic Sidney Allan disparaged the production of visual records. "Accuracy is the bane of art. There is no despotism so ghastly, so disastrous in its results." Allan scorned photographers who strove to make factual images of contemporary life. "The love for exactitude is the lowest form of pictorial gratification," he wrote contemptuously, "felt by the child, the savage, and the Philistine—it merely apprehends the likeness between the representation and the object represented."[9] Given the disdain of the art world, it is hardly surprising that the press photographer's fascination with the noisome aspects of modern urban life found few admirers in big-city salons.

Photographers working for tabloids, broadsheets, and magazines in the 1920s were not wholly bereft of artistic impulse, though both the purpose and presentation of their images often differed fundamentally from

"BIG BILL" HAYWOOD LEADS A PROCESSION OF STRIKERS AT LOWELL, MASS., BY AN UNIDENTIFIED PHOTOGRAPHER FOR THE BAIN NEWS SERVICE, 1912. (GEORGE GRANTHAM BAIN COLLECTION, LIBRARY OF CONGRESS)

PHOTOGRAPH BY WILLIAM DINWIDDIE OF SECRETARY OF WAR WILLIAM HOWARD TAFT AND HIS ESCORTS IN YOKOHAMA, JAPAN, NOT LONG AFTER LEAVING THE PHILIPPINES IN 1905. TAFT'S OBSERVATIONS OF FILIPINO CULTURE AND CUSTOMS WERE LATER PUBLISHED BY *NATIONAL GEOGRAPHIC MAGAZINE.* (NATIONAL PORTRAIT GALLERY, SMITHSONIAN INSTITUTION)

those of artists. As historian Judith Mara Gutman rightly notes, "If these photographs were not really art, neither were they without art. . . . These were the photographs that reached into a public." Their main purpose was to satiate the expanding national appetite for news, gossip, and entertainment. "It was more photography, more information, more exciting insight, more of everything that probed fact and artistically shaped that information."[10] Aesthetics were not absent, merely muted. In the rush to make pictures that resonate with a mass audience even though printed in halftone on the flimsiest, cheapest newsprint, photojournalists often seem preoccupied with the mundane and careless of artistic standards, but that appearance misleads.

In fact, as illustrated journalism flourished in the first decades of the twentieth century, purely pictorial and artistic photographs often made their way onto the printed page. Editors and publishers discovered that their readers responded to all kinds of pictures, not just to news views and mugshots, and they made space for feature and pictorial pictures. Photographers such as Aubrey Bodine, who worked at the *Baltimore Sun* from 1927 to 1970, were hired not to make news pictures but to produce a constant stream of pictorial images that could be run in the paper's Sunday rotogravure sections. Bodine's romantic and evocative pictures of life along the Chesapeake Bay provided readers with weekly doses of art and contrasted sharply with the graphic depiction of events supplied by the paper's news photographers. He spent a lifetime working for one of America's leading metropolitan newspapers without making more than a handful of hard-news images and maintaining the highest aesthetic standards for his work. Harold A. Williams, Bodine's biographer and former editor of the *Sun*'s Sunday section, notes that the finest salons in this country and around the world exhibited Bodine's photographs. He thus effectively

Rotogravure MIAMI DAILY NEWS Supplement

MIAMI, FLA., SUNDAY, JANUARY 31, 1932

DADDY'S HOME with lunch. This mother warbler is bringing back the bugs to four hungry little warblers despite the depression. The photographer happened to catch them out on a limb. (Photo by S. A. Grimes.)

ELSIE KNIGHT, of Dayton, Ohio, is shown at the Fleetwood hotel, Miami Beach. Close examination reveals she is holding what some day may be a dog. (Miami Beach News Service.)

MRS. CROSBY NOYES, wife of the Washington Star executive, is on her honeymoon at the Flamingo hotel, Miami Beach. She formerly was Miss Betty Ulmore of Oshkosh, Wis. (Miami Beach News Service.)

SKIING, like the stock market, has its ups and downs. We see a group of fast skiers at Lake Placid, N. Y., losing their feet but keeping their heads on Mirror Lake. (Wide World Photo.)

ERNIE TRIPLETT needs a rudder and wings for his racer. The Pacific coast racing champion, upper right, was injured in this wreck at the Ascot speedway in which these automobiles figured. The photographer caught the beginning of the accident. (Wide World Photo.)

WATER POLO is becoming popular at Miami Beach but it looks like these fair players will have to quit because the ball is sunk. This picture was taken at the Roney Plaza pool. (Photo by Cox.)

THE SUNDAY ROTOGRAVURE SECTION OF THE *MIAMI DAILY NEWS* FOR JANUARY 31, 1932, SHOWING TYPICAL DESIGN AND LAYOUT. PHOTOGRAPHS ARE CREDITED TO S. A. GRIMES *(TOP)*, THE MIAMI BEACH NEWS SERVICE AND WIDE WORLD *(MIDDLE)*, COX *(LOWER LEFT)*, AND WIDE WORLD *(LOWER RIGHT)*. (HISTORICAL MUSEUM OF SOUTHERN FLORIDA)

straddled the worlds of art and journalistic photography, enlarging the dimensions of both.[11]

Photojournalism could also be defended on its own merits. In 1933 H. Crowell Pepper noted that the purpose of photojournalism was less to produce fine pictures than to provide the public with a steady ration of visual stimulation and information. "I have always held a feeling for the 'news' photographer. Humor, pathos, tragedy and love enter into his daily assignments. The views of the great and the lowly, the saint and the sinner, he learns and in his efficient way depicts with his camera."[12] Pepper's gentle assessment was not unprecedented, but those who supported newspaper photography in mainstream publications were definitely in the minority, and practically no one spoke well of the tabloids. Their unapologetic quest for stories and pictures that titillated without actually breaking blue laws offended elites and even gave rise to a kind of journalistic gallows humor.

MEMBERS OF THE SIOUX INDIAN REPUBLICAN CLUB OF THE ROSEBUD RESERVATION ARE ARRAYED IN A STANDARD PHOTO-OPPORTUNITY POSE WITH PRESIDENT CALVIN COOLIDGE IN WASHINGTON, D.C., MARCH 10, 1925. (LIBRARY OF CONGRESS).

UNCREDITED PHOTOGRAPH MADE FOR THE NATIONAL PHOTO COMPANY. THE CAPTION SUPPLIES THE PARTICULARS: "CHARLESTON AT THE CAPITOL. REPRESENTATIVE T.S. MCMILLAN OF CHARLESTON, SOUTH CAROLINA KEEPS TIME WITH THE 'WE MODERNS' AT THE CAPITOL TODAY, AS THEY SHOW THE STEPS ORIGINATING IN HIS HOME TOWN. MISS RUTH BENNETT (ON THE LEFT) AND MISS SYLVIA CLAVINS," N.D. (NATIONAL PHOTO COMPANY COLLECTION, LIBRARY OF CONGRESS)

Will Rogers reported that tabloid readers quickly caught on to the new code: "if they saw a half-page picture of a pretty woman they felt that she was either a murderess or a movie divorcée; if it was a full-page, she might be both."[13]

Rogers had a point. Tabloids were notoriously fixated on crime and sex, in any order. But that was only part of the story. The real problem was with pictures that elbowed words right off the page, relegating them to a minor role as caption or brief explanation. Even worse, some tabloid publishers, eager to increase circulation and profits, encouraged the use of highly manipulated and "re-created" images.

The combination of salacious subject matter and gross fabrication gave rise to the notion that tabloids routinely dispense misinformation and outright lies. Without a doubt, the exuberant pictorial excesses of a particular tabloid, bodybuilder Bernarr Macfadden's infamous *New York Evening Graphic*, first published in September 1924 and called the "Porno Graphic" by its enemies, gave the entire industry a black eye. Through his Physical Culture Publishing Company, headquartered in New York's famed Flatiron Building, Macfadden touted physical fitness in books and periodicals such as *Health and Beauty* and *True Story Magazine*. "We need stronger, more capable men; healthier, superior women," he wrote in 1916. "Force is supreme—the king of all mankind. And it is force that stands back of efficiency, for efficiency . . . means power."[14] Using plenty of pictures of his own well-muscled physique as prime example, Macfadden promoted healing and well-being through energetic exercise, and in the process he made a fortune.

In 1926 Macfadden hired Hungarian-born fashion and portrait photographer Nickolas Muray to make a series of dramatic portraits for his *Physical Culture Magazine*. These were no ordinary portraits. Macfadden wanted pictures of himself, and he preferred to be photographed wearing a kind of modified classical Roman outfit—a pair of gladiator shoes and "tiger skin uppers." Muray showed Macfadden illustrations from a book about Michelangelo, hoping to persuade the publisher to forgo the animal skins and be photographed seemingly nude (he would be wearing a jockstrap). Macfadden agreed.

In an unpublished reminiscence, Muray recalled that Macfadden retired to the dressing room, then came out a few minutes later wearing nothing at all, no animal skins, no gladiator shoes, and no jockstrap, but holding "his hand in front to cover his masculine part." Muray said, "You don't have to be shy, Mr. Macfadden. Just be yourself, as if you were all by yourself, all alone." Macfadden immediately launched into a spirited and exceedingly unphotogenic series of push-ups. Muray finally persuaded him to adopt classical poses, and the portrait session commenced in earnest. Muray made about eighteen large-format negatives. When Macfadden saw the proofs he expressed satisfaction. However, when the photographs were published in *Physical Culture*, Muray was surprised to see that the images had been crudely retouched and that Macfadden once again appeared to be wearing his gladiator shoes and a fancy leopard-skin costume.[15]

Macfadden's cavalier treatment of Muray's original photographs was no anomaly. At the *Evening Graphic* photographs were the mainstay of the news operation, but there was minimal commitment to photographic truth. In an ultimately successful effort to increase circulation, the *Graphic*'s managing editor, Emile H. Gauvreau—formerly of the *Hartford Courant*—along with Ryan Walker and Harry Grogin of the art department, perfected a method of fabricating news pictures that blended artwork, mugshots from the files, and staged photographs into a single image called a "composograph." The process, wrote Gauvreau. allowed the recreation of scenes "without the necessity of photographing them."[16]

When *Graphic* photographers were unable to cover news events, Grogin and the art staff created what they needed in the paper's own studio. Run with considerable fanfare and touted as both exclusive and unprecedented, composographs boosted circulation and added immeasurably to the notoriety of Macfadden's paper and tabloids in general. In the late summer of 1926, for instance, the foremost luminary of American cinema, Rudolph Valentino, was stricken with acute appendicitis and pleurisy in New York City, and the story was front-page news around the world. In the final volume of his grand novel of American culture, *U.S.A.*, John Dos Passos described the scene outside the Polyclinic Hospital in characteristic stream-of-consciousness style. The press was desperate for news and pictures of Valentino, and "grimy fingered newspaper men and photographers stood around bored tired hoteyed smoking too many cigarettes making trips to the nearest speak exchanging wisecracks and deep dope waiting for him to die in time to make the evening papers."[17]

Macfadden's staff at the *Graphic* could not wait. In August, Gauvreau's art department produced an illustration depicting physicians and other medical personnel clustered around the dying superstar during an operation to save his life. After Valentino's death, Gauvreau published a picture showing the actor entering a celestial spirit world where he is greeted by a number of departed celebrities, including operatic tenor Enrico Caruso. To add spice to the pictures, the *Graphic* suggested Valentino had been poisoned, then published an interview with an Italian spiritualist named Nicola Peccharara, who spoke with the dead star and confirmed the story.[18]

Composographs were derided as fakes and outright lies, which they were, but the *Graphic*'s staff was both undeterred and unrepentant. "This is the story of a grotesque, fantastic world of impatient people; a world as large or as small as you want to make it," Gauvreau wrote in 1931. "In this new world, you do not have to wait for exciting things to happen. You can *make* them happen. When these happenings are not exciting enough, you ignore them. If they thrill you, then you call them 'Hot News.'"[19] As long as people kept buying the paper, Macfadden saw no compelling reason to stop printing the illustrations, regardless of the vituperation of critics and fellow journalists. In fact, in an effort to attract yet more readers, composographs were made increasingly lurid. Perhaps inevitably, Macfadden's affinity for the ribald got him and his paper into trouble.

The *Graphic*'s coverage of two sensational divorce cases in 1925 and 1927, provoked especially bitter attacks. The first concerned the attempt by Leonard Kip Rhinelander, heir to a mercantile fortune, to annul his marriage on the grounds that his young wife, Alice, had kept from him the fact that her natural father was black. Rhinelander's own father—stern, brutish, and implacably racist—was said to be the principal instigator of the proceedings. The case had everything: young love, fabulous wealth, sex, and race, and the entire New York press establishment ran stories. But none outdid the *Graphic*.

On November 23, 1925, Alice Rhinelander's attorney, Lee P. Davis, suddenly and without warning requested that his client disrobe in front of the jury in order to show them the obvious darkness of her skin and thereby demonstrate the emptiness of her husband's contention. The judge assented, and Alice was led weeping into the jury room, where she was told to strip to the waist. Those present included the judge, the jury, one lawyer from each side, a stenographer, and the younger Rhinelander. Photographers and reporters were barred. This turn of events confounded the rest of the press corps, but not Gauvreau and Grogin of the *Graphic*. According to Lester Cohen, who supervised the paper's numerous contests, the absence of photographs was problematic but not fatal. Muttering "the hell with photographers," Grogin went to work on a composograph, combining file mugshots with a carefully posed studio photograph.

> He began tearing pictures. He had pictures of Alice, of the Judge, of opposing counsel, of the stolid, forlorn Rhinelander, of Alice's mother, of Kip's lordly father. The pictures were put through a process by which they would come out in proper proportion. Meantime, Harry sent for Agnes McLaughlin, a showgirl, . . . and got her to pose as he imagined Alice Kip Rhinelander would stand before her mother, the lawyers, the judge—and with as little on as possible.[20]

The resulting illustration was duly published and it generated both increased sales and renewed criticism. Eventually, Rhinelander was awarded his precious annulment, and he drifted back into relative obscurity. Alice, however, had achieved celebrity status. When she and her mother sought to escape the unwanted attentions of the press by sailing to Europe after the trial, she was pursued by a small army of avid amateur and professional photographers. According to a report in the *New York Times*, "When she arose in the morning she found a dozen people lying in wait to take pictures," and officers on board received numerous requests from passengers that "they induce the young woman to walk along the deck at a certain time so they could see her and snap a picture."[21]

The *Graphic*'s penchant for vulgarity and the seamy side of modern life led to a concerted effort to reform the press as well as the reading habits of the public. In December 1925, during the height of the Rhinelander furor, the *New York Times* reported that Dr. Mebane Ramsay of the Calvary Presbyterian Church in Staten Island was horrified by the sensationalism of the city's newspapers. "The modern newspaper is . . . a

A "COMPOSOGRAPH," CONSTRUCTED BY HARRY GROGIN AND HIS STAFF FOR THE *NEW YORK EVENING GRAPHIC,* PURPORTEDLY SHOWING ALICE RHINELANDER STRIPPED TO THE WAIST BEFORE JUDGE, JURY, ATTORNEYS, AND HER MOTHER DURING DIVORCE PROCEEDINGS IN NOVEMBER 1925. (LESTER COHEN, *THE NEW YORK EVENING GRAPHIC: THE WORLD'S ZANIEST NEWSPAPER*)

powerful agency for good or evil," Reverend Ramsay intoned, "and in the way it treats such news it strikingly reveals its own character." The newspaper that builds circulation through "an artificial stimulation of the evil passions of its readers through photographs, and the filth of both its news columns and its special features" should be avoided at all costs.[22] Macfadden was unmoved. "Sensationalism is nothing more than a clear, definitive, attractive presentation of the news," he said in 1929, "and is perfectly proper as long as one adheres to the truth."[23] Of course, that was precisely what the *Graphic* failed to do.

The tabloid's visual exploitation of the divorce of Manhattan real estate tycoon Edward West Browning from his child bride, Frances "Peaches" Heenan, caused another flood of criticism in 1927. Finally, John S. Sumner, successor to Anthony Comstock of the New York Society for the Suppression of Vice, persuaded the Tombs Court to arrest Macfadden, Gauvreau, and several other *Graphic* staff members for violating the obscenity provisions of the city's penal code. Sumner argued that the paper's "handling of the Browning separation suit and the pictures featured on the first page were . . . the chief cause of the many complaints."[24] This was an old song for Macfadden. He'd been arrested at the behest of Comstock himself in 1905 and again in 1907 for pictures he published in his physical fitness magazines.

Constant legal turmoil and the threat of a citywide boycott organized by religious leaders began to take a toll. Although the *Graphic*'s circulation seemed healthy, averaging nearly 300,000 from 1926 to mid-1932, businessmen were wary of purchasing advertising space in such a controversial publication. Large department stores, the mainstay of the city's other newspapers, would not buy space; in fact, about the only regular advertisers were dealers in used furniture. The paper was a losing proposition in Macfadden's otherwise profitable empire, and in July 1932 he pulled the plug.[25]

PRESS PHOTOGRAPHERS POSE FOR A COLLEAGUE FROM TIMES WIDE WORLD PHOTOS WHILE WAITING OUTSIDE THE QUEENS COUNTY COURTHOUSE DURING THE APRIL 1927 TRIAL OF RUTH SNYDER FOR THE MURDER OF HER HUSBAND. MRS. SNYDER WAS CONVICTED AND LATER EXECUTED AT SING SING PRISON IN OSSINING, N.Y. (*NEW YORK TIMES*/NYT PICTURES)

AN UNIDENTIFIED PHOTOGRAPHER FOR THE RISE STUDIO IN RAPID CITY, S.D., MADE THIS IMAGE OF PRESIDENT CALVIN COOLIDGE WITH WHITE HOUSE PHOTOGRAPHERS ON A TOUR OF THE WEST. (LIBRARY OF CONGRESS)

The demise of the *Graphic* led to no serious diminution of pictorial journalism. In addition, since Macfadden's paper was a lightning rod for criticism of the press, when it went out of business the entire industry breathed a sigh of relief. Tabloids remained popular and profitable, of course, and their photographs continued to provide the public with eyewitness views of significant events as well as of the purely profane features of modern life. In the wake of the composograph and other excesses, however, tabloids never entirely dispelled the aura of outrageous hype and bunkum that Macfadden and his editors worked so hard to create, and the label of "tabloid journalist" is still both insult and epithet.

Criticism and complaints had little outward effect on the activities and attitudes of press photographers and their newsroom bosses, most of whom felt embattled and unappreciated anyway. In fact, they took pride in

AN UNNAMED PHOTOGRAPHER FOR THE TIMES PHOTO SERVICE CAPTURES RALPH DE PALMA IN CAR NO. 4 CROSSING THE FINISH LINE IN THE SECOND RACE AT SHEEPSHEAD BAY, N.Y., IN WORLD RECORD TIME. DARIO RESTA WAVES FROM THE SECOND-PLACE CAR; RALPH MULFORD WAS THIRD. AUGUST 18, 1918. (*NEW YORK TIMES*/NYT PICTURES)

their ability to function successfully despite a daunting array of obstacles. "Theirs is a valuable service to this generation and to the generations that are to follow," wrote a sympathetic observer in the *Camera* in 1915. "They have dexterity, craftsmanship, courage; some of them have also recklessness, audacity, and a degree of unscrupulousness. But the one word that tells the story . . . is 'gumption.'"[26] As the pictorial needs of newspapers and magazines expanded, so too did the temerity of photographers, who could only succeed by being both persistent and present. "The public must realize that it is hard to avoid the quick-trigger cameraman, and it is far better to succumb graciously," wrote veteran journalist A. J. Ezickson. "The brandished cane or stick, or threat of punishment and reprisal, will never intimidate the news photographer."[27]

"Pictures can lead the reader into the paper as surely as stories can—because of the emotional appeal of good news photographs," wrote one group of experts in 1939. "When a single dramatic shot of a big news story is played boldly on the front page, and the reader is referred to the daily picture page or to an inside page for more, he is practically certain to turn to them."[28] Modern camera equipment made it possible to capture spectacular moments on film, and editors and publishers of newspapers and magazines refined methods of presentation and display.

Photographers in the 1920s and 1930s continued to rely on the venerable Graflex camera, especially when covering sporting events at long range. Armed with 40- or 60-inch "Big Bertha" and "Long Tom" telephoto lenses, photographers made views of action that were once beyond the grasp of even their most enterprising colleagues. For a public already entranced by the swift ebb and flow of organized sport, such pictures had the power to mesmerize. Intimate stop-action photographs dramatized the most ordinary plays; when made of peak moments they were the stuff of which legends are made. Pictures of Mildred "Babe" Didrickson competing at the 1932 Olympics or on the links, of automobiles hurtling down some track, of Joe Louis dispatching yet another contender, added to the allure of sports and attracted avid readers.

In 1920 Andrew J. "Buck" May, photographer for the *Washington Star,* was assigned to cover a game between the Senators and Philadelphia Athletics. That day he made a picture of Washington outfielder Sam Rice sliding into third base, only to be called "out" by the umpire. May's picture, which ran prominently in the next day's paper, clearly showed that Rice beat the tag; the umpire missed the call. The photograph caused an uproar among the fans, and consternation among the umpires. When May arrived to work the next game in the series, chief umpire Tom Connolly summarily ordered him off the field. The photographer, unbowed and undaunted, appealed to the owner of the Senators, Clark Griffith, who allowed him to take his customary position alongside the third-base line. May eventually left the *Star* and joined the staff of the Harris and Ewing agency in Washington. He was one of the founding members of the White House Press Photographers Association.[29]

For midrange and close-up work, and especially for covering spot news, many press photographers preferred the Speed Graphic. Introduced in 1912 by William Folmer's old company, now the Folmer-Schwing division of Eastman Kodak, the Graphic used either 4 × 5- or 5 × 7-inch film,

HEAVYWEIGHT BOXING CHAMPION JOE LOUIS, HIS WIFE, AND THEIR FANS IN HARLEM, N.Y., SEPTEMBER 25, 1935, MADE BY A PHOTOGRAPHER FOR TIMES WIDE WORLD PHOTOS. (*NEW YORK TIMES*/NYT PICTURES)

UNCREDITED PHOTOGRAPH MADE FOR THE HARRIS AND EWING SYNDICATE OF STILL AND NEWSREEL PHOTOGRAPHERS ON THE LAWN OF THE WHITE HOUSE, N.D. (LIBRARY OF CONGRESS)

and replaced the Graflex's tall, leather, focusing hood with a folding wire viewfinder and peep sight. It was fast, relatively lightweight, and easy to use, but bulky by today's standards. Though slightly smaller than the Graflex, Speed Graphics were virtually impossible to conceal. Dickey Chapelle, whose long, distinguished career in photojournalism ended when she was killed in Vietnam, remembered how Speed Graphics affected the way photographers worked in the era before miniature cameras. "It is so big that snap-shooting, or making a picture casually, can't be done." Instead, the photographer must carefully "plan the picture . . . and move to the vantage point from which to shoot" before raising the camera.[30]

For some the conspicuousness of Speed Graphics actually became something of an asset. Since the camera was widely perceived as standard equipment for the industry, brandishing it sometimes opened doors. The legendary and archetypal press photographer Arthur Fellig, better known as Weegee, swore by his trusty Speed Graphic. "If you are puzzled about the kind of camera to buy," he advised young photographers in his most famous book, *Naked City*, "get a Speed Graphic . . . [for] with a camera like that the cops will assume that you belong on the scene and will let you get beyond the police lines."[31]

Weegee's unabashed approach was not infallible, for there were times when it was better, even essential, to be unobtrusive. The photographer laden with equipment, with press card boldly displayed, was far too easy a target for those wishing to avoid the attentions of the press. According to John Chapman, historian of the *New York Daily News,* in the 1920s many news photographers turned to any one of several European cameras that—like detective cameras in the old days—could be more easily concealed. Two German imports using 4 × 6-inch sheet film, the Ica and the Zeiss Corporation's Orix, were especially popular with New York press photographers. The Ica was equipped with a fast lens and leather bellows, and when folded up "it was relatively slender and could be slung from a shoulder strap and concealed under a suit jacket."[32]

Graflexes, Graphics, Icas, and other cameras using sheet film, whether tucked modestly under an arm or brandished like a battering ram, could not produce great volumes of images quickly. Photographers rarely carried more than a few film holders on assignment (each contained two sheets of film). Most often, those working for newspapers sought only to make a few views in time to meet the next deadline. Since editors rarely ran more than one or two images anyway, most newspaper photographers in the 1920s and 1930s saw no need to make additional pictures. It may be

SUFFRAGETTE ROSALIE JONES LEADING A MARCH TO ALBANY, N.Y., ON JANUARY 1, 1914. (GEORGE GRANTHAM BAIN COLLECTION, LIBRARY OF CONGRESS).

WITH AN EYE FOR NEWS AND HISTORY, MIAMI PHOTOGRAPHER GLEASON WAITE ROMER CAPTURED A MORE SINISTER PROCESSION: THE KU KLUX KLAN CONTINGENT MARCHING IN THE "FIESTA OF THE AMERICAN TROPICS" PARADE IN 1926. (ROMER COLLECTION, MIAMI-DADE PUBLIC LIBRARY, DOWNTOWN BRANCH)

difficult to fathom today, when motor-driven cameras spawn endless images at split-second intervals, but the system worked remarkably well.

Louis A. Odille, who joined the staff of the *Pittsburgh Press* in 1928, not long after graduating from the U.S. Navy's photographic school at Anacostia, Maryland, told Jack Price of *Editor and Publisher* that photographic equipment, deadlines, and the vagaries of modern urban and suburban transportation often made it impossible to make more than a handful of images. Odille recalled one assignment in 1934, a five-alarm fire at the Crucible Steel Mill, which was located about seven miles from downtown Pittsburgh. With less than an hour before deadline he had to rush, but on the way out of town his car got a flat tire. Still determined to get to the fire and back *with* pictures, Odille flagged down a passing motorcycle cop, and asked for a lift. He recalled what happened next:

> [The policeman] agreed, but stipulated that I would have to hang on as best I could, the side car being covered with a tarpaulin which he refused to take time to remove. That ride over an unusually rough road, with me hanging precariously to the top of the side car and trying to keep my equipment from falling off was something to remember. However, I got to the fire in short

order, and shot two pictures. Then I jumped into a taxicab and returned to the office in time to make the edition.[33]

Odille sought not to produce an in-depth pictorial narrative of the fire, but to sum up the situation in a few salient images. Impelled by an immovable deadline, and equipped with a camera that slowed the process to a crawl, Odille produced timely photographs despite daunting obstacles. It was a tour de force, but not an uncommon one; news photographers were adept at producing usable pictures despite tight deadlines, and they rarely wasted film.

To be sure, the usual run of assignments lacked the inherent interest and excitement of Odille's five-alarm fire. Most of what passes for news is visually dull, as ordinary and humdrum as the drone of dispassionate functionaries at a local school board meeting or the carefully orchestrated enthusiasm of a groundbreaking ceremony for an industrial park. The trick is always to find some scintilla of human interest in what Jack Price calls "the cosmic ho-hum"; no easy task.[34]

Perhaps understandably, photographers succumbed on occasion to the banality of daily assignments, and their images reflected both lack of interest and effort. Marlen Edwin Pew complained in *Editor and Publisher* in 1933 about the lack of "originality shown in picturing groups of people, arranging them so that they are in neat formation, animated, natural and interesting." Having worked as head of the Press Illustrating Service and the News Bureau of the War Department during World War I, Pew probably considered himself an expert on news photography. But his experience with cameras was minimal; he was more manager than cameraman. In any event, he wrote disgustedly about seeing a photograph of a man with "his shirt sticking out" at a fashionable New York City hotel, and added that society women were often captured "with clothes in sorry disarray, hats on dizzily, skirts skewed around, feet in ridiculous poses."[35] As in the earliest days of the medium, when daguerreotypists defended their work as being perfectly accurate and truthful, photojournalists answered critics like Pew by pointing out that they merely recorded what was in front of the camera. It is not the fault of the person clicking the shutter, they said, that a disheveled potentate photographed for the morning paper looks unkempt.

When time permitted and the subject warranted it, photographers, especially those working for magazines, provided their editors with additional views. Weekly and monthly publications often used several pictures to tell or illustrate a story, and the pace was considerably more relaxed. Still, there were no guarantees, and photographers who returned empty-handed, for whatever reason, might wait a long time for the next assignment. That nearly happened to George Higgins, a well-respected New York portrait photographer, assigned by James A. Quigney of *American Magazine* in 1931 to photograph Thomas Alva Edison at the inventor's home in Menlo Park, New Jersey.

As was his custom, Higgins chatted with Edison for about an hour before unlimbering his equipment. Eventually he made some twenty-four carefully posed pictures on 5 × 7 film. Apparently, Edison enjoyed the com-

A SINGLE-PAGE PHOTOGRAPHIC ESSAY OF WOODROW WILSON CAMPAIGNING DURING THE 1912 ELECTION BY AN UNNAMED PHOTOGRAPHER FOR UNDERWOOD AND UNDERWOOD. PUBLISHED IN *HARPER'S WEEKLY*, SEPTEMBER 28, 1912. (LIBRARY OF CONGRESS)

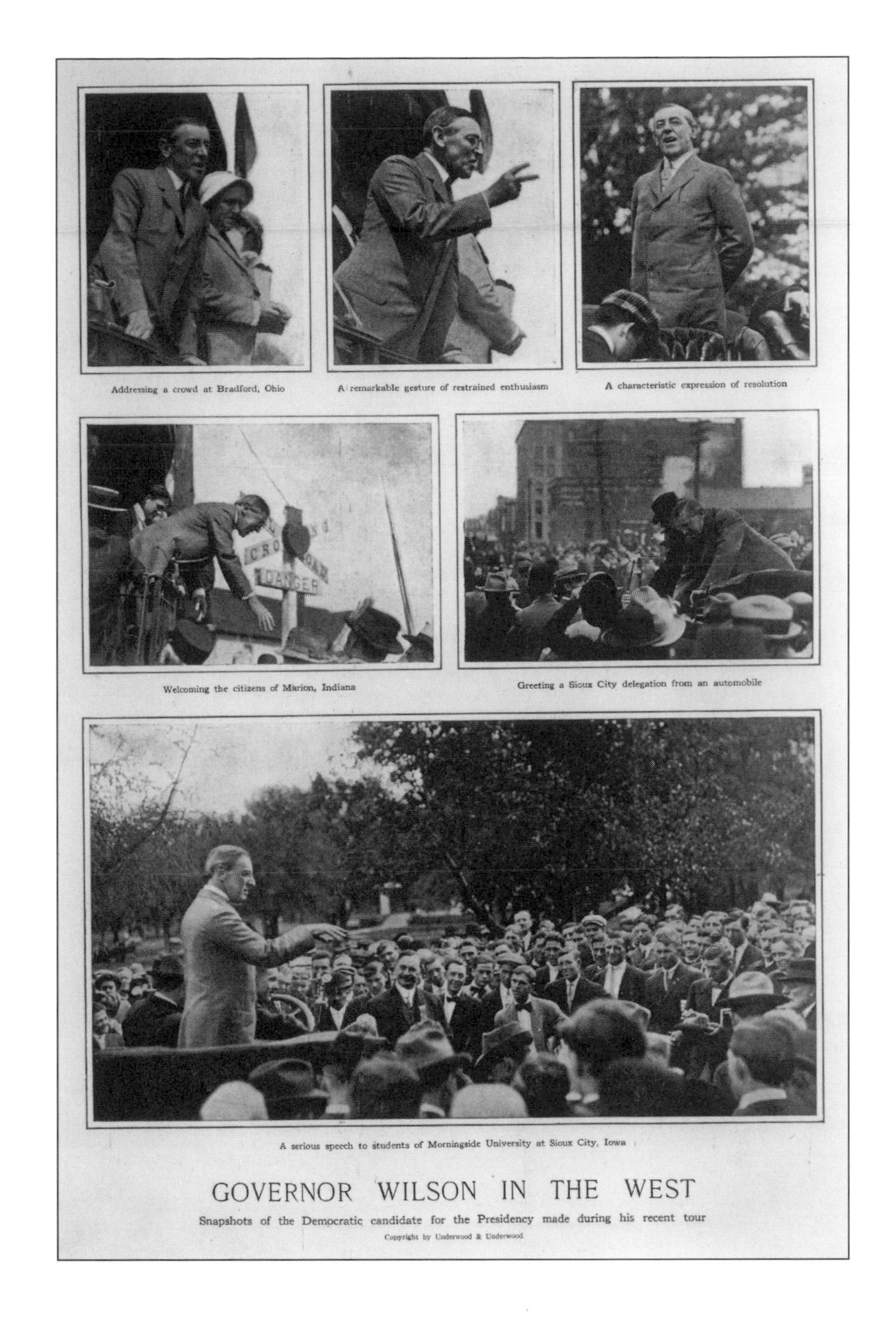

Addressing a crowd at Bradford, Ohio

A remarkable gesture of restrained enthusiasm

A characteristic expression of resolution

Welcoming the citizens of Marion, Indiana

Greeting a Sioux City delegation from an automobile

A serious speech to students of Morningside University at Sioux City, Iowa

GOVERNOR WILSON IN THE WEST

Snapshots of the Democratic candidate for the Presidency made during his recent tour

Copyright by Underwood & Underwood

pany of the photographer, for he invited Higgins to stay for dinner and the night. Early the next day, Higgins hurried back to the city, eager to process his film. There, he discovered that he had made a fundamental error. According to Leo Solomon, Higgins "grabbed a handful of 5 × 7 holders and went into the developing room. Then as he pulled out slides, he almost died. Every holder was empty." Somehow, he brought a stack of unloaded holders to New Jersey. Finally, he found that the last two holders in his camera bag contained film, and he developed and printed the images. *American Magazine* ran one of them, a portrait of Edison at his desk. When the inventor died a short time later, more than a hundred utility companies ordered copies of Higgins' portrait, which may have somewhat eased his chagrin.[36]

EDISON

*"The Greatest American of the Century"*

By

EMIL LUDWIG

I HAVE met many of the greatest living Americans. History has made me familiar with the great Americans of the past. Yet I call Edison the greatest American of the century.

I call him the greatest, not merely because of his thousand-odd inventions, nor because of the incredible changes his genius wrought in our civilization, but because of the exceptional qualities of his human character. He combined the highest characteristics of his nation—the imperishable youthful ardor and fighting spirit; mature patience and persistence in achievement; kindly humor in the face of adversity; and, finally, intense devotion to the labor of turning ideas and theories into the practicable and useful.

To Americans, marveling at the flood of inventive wonders he brought into their hands, he came to be known as "The Wizard." Because, by some strange power, he achieved what other men called impossible, his name has passed almost into fable and legend. But, to the world, Edison remains a beloved human symbol of America.

There might be named numbers of his illustrious contemporaries who equaled or surpassed him in talent, scholarly attainments, and scientific knowledge. He surpassed them by starting where they left off. He took facts and principles as he found them and made them tangibly useful to his fellow men.

Edison's interest in an idea or a theoretical discovery was always measured by the possibilities of its profitable use. Early in life he reached the conclusion that an idea was not worth laboring over unless somebody had use for it. For example, his first patent, when he was twenty-one years old, was for an electrical vote recorder which, through the pressing of a button, gave an exact and speedy count of the vote

THE PICTURE THAT VERY NEARLY DID NOT GET MADE: GEORGE HIGGINS' PORTRAIT OF THOMAS ALVA EDISON FOR THE *AMERICAN MAGAZINE*. (OTTO RICHTER LIBRARY, UNIVERSITY OF MIAMI)

Several important technological developments in the 1920s made it easier to cover events. Flashbulbs and 35-millimeter cameras, occasionally equipped with a new generation of compact telephoto lenses, revolutionized the way pictures were made. Small cameras loaded with fast film allowed photographers to provide detailed and in-depth coverage in place of the traditional single, static large-format view. The introduction in 1935 by the Associated Press of an improved, low-cost, and efficient method of transmitting photographs over telephone lines completed the equation.[37]

Providing their own light source was nothing new for photographers; they had long used sudden, brilliant explosions of magnesium powder to light dark interior spaces. But magnesium was volatile and unpredictable. Moreover, a single magnesium flash produced so much choking smoke that further photographic efforts were either delayed or impossible. The author of one instruction manual for beginning photographers noted that "flash-powder is just exactly as dangerous to handle as gun-powder. It must be kept away from heat. Friction will sometimes ignite it." He cautioned young photographers eager to explore the possibilities of nighttime work to "keep cool, work carefully, and never hold your hands or face over the powder at any time."[38]

The photographic press published numerous cautionary stories of those wounded by unexpected magnesium explosions; losses of fingers, hands, eyes, even a life or two offered proof—as if any were needed—that sloppy procedure could maim or kill. In 1930 William Randolph Hearst learned first-hand about the danger of magnesium powder. He was being photographed by George E. Sheldon, staff photographer with his own San Francisco *Examiner*, when suddenly the powder exploded prematurely. Sheldon was severely burned on his hands (he lost the tips of three fingers). The following day Hearst ordered photographers throughout his chain to stop using flash powder and switch to bulbs.[39]

Invented in Germany in 1929 and introduced to the American market a year later by General Electric, flashbulbs took both the danger and smoke out of artificial-light photography. Photographers immediately became acceptable if not actually welcome guests. "The U.S. Press spent $600,000, employed 726 journalists to write 5,000,000 words about the Republican National Convention at Chicago last week," reported *Time* magazine in 1932. That was a great many words for a convention that offered little in the way of hot news, but the real story was in pictures anyway. "For the first time at a National Convention, photographers with their safe new flashlamps were permitted to ply their trade up and down the aisles."[40]

A Speed Graphic with attached flash unit could be used at all hours and in nearly all lighting situations. "I always use a flash bulb for my pictures which are mostly taken at night," Weegee wrote, stating the obvious. But he added that "on the few occasions where I have made shots by daylight, I still use a flash bulb."[41] Flashbulbs allowed photographers freedom of movement and standardized both exposure and focus; one only had to remember to bring along enough bulbs to get the job done.

Sammy Schulman, a photographer with Hearst's International News Photos syndicate, made coverage of Franklin Roosevelt something of a specialty, and he usually made his pictures with flash. In February 1933 Schulman made two memorable pictures that demonstrated the effectiveness of artificial-light photography. After his successful campaign against Herbert Hoover, Roosevelt went to Florida with a few friends to do some private Gulf Stream fishing aboard Victor Astor's plush *Nourmahal*. In the late afternoon of February 15, Roosevelt was scheduled to go directly from Astor's ship to his train for the trip to Washington for the inauguration; most of the press corps decided to meet him on the train. Not Schulman, who went to Bayfront Park in Miami to make a shot or two of Roosevelt speaking off-the-cuff to a small crowd of supporters. Schulman was especially anxious to test an experimental device that synchronized the ignition of the flash with the opening of the camera shutter. He was thus the only news photographer present when an anarchist named Giuseppe Zangara opened fire with an old-fashioned 32-caliber pistol. He missed Roosevelt, but hit five others, including Anton Cermak, the mayor of Chicago, described by Schulman as "a baggy, hearty old politician with a flair for making friends with newspapermen and a taste for Prohibition beer."[42] Schulman acted instinctively. As Secret Service agent Bob Clark and Miami City Manager L. L. Lee pulled Cermak to his feet, Schulman aimed his camera and clicked the shutter—once. The resulting image showed the mayor being led toward Roosevelt's waiting car, a long smear of blood darkening his shirt just above the beltline. They loaded Cermak into the car, which immediately sped off toward the hospital. Schulman followed,

NOT SO COLD

THE MINNEAPOLIS STAR

CITY

MINNEAPOLIS, MINN., FRIDAY, FEBRUARY 17, 1933

Price Two Cents in Minneapolis

*Would-Be Assassin in Court, Mayor Cermak Better*

AMENDMENT 8 HELD ADOPTED

*First Pictures of Attempted Assassination of President-Elect Roosevelt at Miami*

OFFICIALS WILL BLOCK ZANGARA INSANITY PLEA

Roosevelt Assailant Must Face Charges of Attempted Murder

HEAVY GUARD FOR ROOSEVELT

Wounded Mrs. Gill Still in Critical Condition in Miami Hospital

*Text of Resolution for Repeal of 18th Amendment Adopted by Senate*

House O.K. of Dry Repealer Held Assured

NEW BEER BILLS GIVEN TO SENATE SATISFY OLSON

SIX INDICTED FOR AIDING NEIGHBOR

PATIENTS FORCED TO FLEE HOSPITAL

Watchman Foils Attempt to Fire Long's Residence

SENATE TACKLES IDLE AID BILL

*Husband of Dry Leader Accused of Rum Charge*

CONTRACTOR MAY TESTIFY TUESDAY

DECISION BOOSTS CITY BORROWING LIMIT $2,500,000

Highway Probers Expected to Stand Pat on Plan to Quiz Builders

CLASHES MARK PUBLIC HEARING

SLUMP LAID TO OVER-EXPANSION

Hull, Roosevelt Reach Agreement on Cabinet Post

PAGE ONE PHOTOGRAPHS BY SAMMY SCHULMAN OF FRANKLIN ROOSEVELT IN HIS OPEN CAR IN MIAMI'S BAYFRONT PARK, MAYOR ANTON CERMAK BEING LED TO THE PRESIDENT'S CAR AFTER BEING MORTALLY WOUNDED, AND THE ASSASSIN, GIUSEPPE ZANGARA, POSING OUTSIDE HIS CELL. PUBLISHED IN THE *MINNEAPOLIS STAR*, WITHOUT CREDIT, ON FEBRUARY 17, 1933. (PRIVATE COLLECTION).

hoping for just one more picture. It was not to be; all treatment rooms were off limits to the press.

After being assured by Roosevelt himself that no other photographers would be allowed to make pictures of the stricken mayor, Schulman headed downtown to the Dade County Courthouse, which also housed the jail. The lobby swarmed with reporters and photographers, among them Walter Winchell, the *New York Mirror*'s acerbic gossip columnist, who happened to be vacationing on Miami Beach. Since both Schulman and Winchell worked for Hearst, they teamed up, the ultimate odd couple. With the help of a friendly Miami detective, Schulman persuaded the elevator operator to take them—and only them—to the eighteenth floor where the temporary jail was located. Schulman later described what happened in the narrow corridor outside Zangara's cell:

> After a little time, [Sheriff Dan] Hardie, a big, mussed old minion of the law with baggy white pants and a dark coat, dragged Zangara out of the cell, assisted by a towering cop named Jackson. Jackson had Zangara's gun.
>
> "Get that picture—get it, get it," Winchell yelled at me.
>
> I wanted it to be a full-length shot, but Zangara was stitchless. I saw a shirt on a chair and had Hardie tie it around Zangara like a sarong.
>
> "Point the gun at him," I said to the cop. . . . I set up the picture carefully, while Walter kept prodding me to hurry.
>
> "For Christ's sake, pipe down," I finally asked him. "I've only got one bulb left and I've got to make it good."
>
> "One bulb!" Winchell screamed indignantly.
>
> "What kind of a photographer are you, you dope!"[43]

Schulman calmly made his picture—the last flashbulb worked like a charm—thus collecting his second great scoop of the day. In exchange for the use of their darkroom, he gave one set of prints to the *Miami News*. Acme Photos, a division of the Scripps-Howard organization's News Enterprise Association, got another for providing space on the only plane leaving immediately for New York; and the next morning Hearst's *New York Journal* ran the pictures a few hours ahead of the competition.

Sammy Schulman's Miami story was the visual highlight of his career, and the two pictures he made are rightly considered to be classic news photographs. The image of Tony Cermak staggering toward Roosevelt's car was published in more than two thousand newspapers and magazines here and abroad, almost always without crediting Schulman. Instead, publications credited either the company that employed him, International News Photos, or the News Enterprise Association, which provided transportation for the images to New York. Like pictures of other dramatic and historically significant moments, Schulman's photographs eclipse the work he produced before and after those fateful moments in Miami. But he is neither the first nor last photojournalist to have an entire career reduced to a single picture made in a fraction of a second.

A little more than two decades earlier, on August 9, 1910, two dramatic pictures of the attempted assassination of the reform mayor of New York yielded some small measure of renown for news photographers

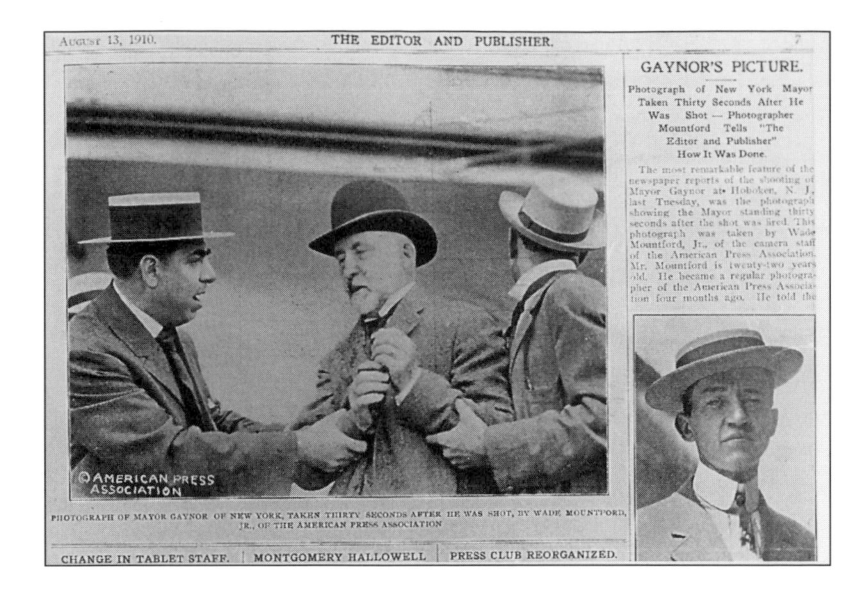

August 13, 1910. THE EDITOR AND PUBLISHER. 7

GAYNOR'S PICTURE.

Photograph of New York Mayor Taken Thirty Seconds After He Was Shot — Photographer Mountford Tells "The Editor and Publisher" How It Was Done.

The most remarkable feature of the newspaper reports of the shooting of Mayor Gaynor at Hoboken, N. J., last Tuesday, was the photograph showing the Mayor standing thirty seconds after the shot was fired. This photograph was taken by Wade Mountford, Jr., of the camera staff of the American Press Association. Mr. Mountford is twenty-two years old. He became a regular photographer of the American Press Association four months ago. He told the

© AMERICAN PRESS ASSOCIATION

PHOTOGRAPH OF MAYOR GAYNOR OF NEW YORK, TAKEN THIRTY SECONDS AFTER HE WAS SHOT, BY WADE MOUNTFORD, JR., OF THE AMERICAN PRESS ASSOCIATION

CHANGE IN TABLET STAFF. | MONTGOMERY HALLOWELL | PRESS CLUB REORGANIZED.

HALFTONE OF WADE MOUNTFORD JR.'S PHOTOGRAPH FOR THE AMERICAN PRESS ASSOCIATION OF WILLIAM GAYNOR, MAYOR OF NEW YORK CITY, JUST AFTER HIS ATTEMPTED ASSASSINATION. MOUNTFORD'S PORTRAIT BY AN UNIDENTIFIED PHOTOGRAPHER IS ON THE RIGHT. *EDITOR AND PUBLISHER*, AUGUST 13, 1910. (OTTO RICHTER LIBRARY, UNIVERSITY OF MIAMI)

William Warnecke of the *New York World* and Wade Mountford Jr. of the American Press Association. Both were in Hoboken, New Jersey, to cover the embarkation of the mayor, William Jay Gaynor, who was sailing to Europe aboard the German liner *Kaiser Wilhelm der Grosse*. J. J. Gallagher, a disgruntled former employee of New York City's Docks Department, joined the group of well-wishers and politicians on board, and just before the ship sailed, he fired three shots, one of which hit Gaynor in the neck.

"I stood about four feet from the Mayor when I saw the man Gallagher draw his gun and fire," recalled Mountford. "Instantly a crowd rushed between me and the assassin and two men grasped the mayor. He staggered away about seven feet. Then, instinctively, I snapped him as he was staggering." Warnecke must have done the same, though from a slightly different angle. In the chaos and confusion of the moment, Mountford looked directly into the eyes of the wounded man. "The Mayor was looking straight at me just before I snapped," Mountford told a reporter for *Editor and Publisher* magazine. "I saw the look in his eyes which said that he didn't want me to take the picture. Then his eyes closed and I snapped the camera. It was my duty, you know."[44]

Over the years many photojournalists have uttered similar words, referring, like Mountford, to a kind of sacred trust, an obligation to produce true pictures of the world's great and small events. The public's right and need to know, they contend, justifies occasional intrusiveness. Naturally, such an argument is easier made when the issue at hand is inherently newsworthy, as in the case of the murder or attempted murder of an important political figure. But critics maintained that photographers in the 1920s and 1930s routinely went too far, that their incessant search for "human interest" led to a new definition of news that has neither physical nor moral boundary. This question "has been growing more urgent ever since the Hearst-Pulitzer press blazed a halftone pathway across Page One," wrote

Silas Bent in 1927. "The photographs which the newspapers regard as best would never be obtained if the camera men were polite enough to ask permission before taking them."[45]

Bent aimed his critique at publishers and their hired photographers who insisted on presenting the public with a flood of pictures decidedly lacking in real news value. The illustrated press clamored for pictures of the rich and famous, for instance, and it seldom mattered what they were doing. Luminaries were fair game at all times, and photographers dogged their every step, heedless of protest. "If you request your subject to accommodate you by posing, you are usually met with a scathing, sarcastic look of silence," wrote photographer Gordon Belmont in *The American Annual of Photography*. "The only course left is that of snapping your party at the first available chance, and with as little obtrusiveness as possible." Belmont suggested using a telephoto lens, which made it possible to obtain usable pictures from thirty or more feet away without attracting the attention or enmity of the subject.[46]

The daily and weekly press in the 1920s avidly sought to delve into aspects of modern life that were traditionally private and hence free from unwanted public scrutiny, and critics like Bent fulminated about loss of innocence and propriety. Yet, for many reporters and photographers, the private activities of those who dominated and controlled American finance, industry, and society were legitimate news stories. For example, like many of his colleagues, Harry Coleman, tireless warrior for Hearst's *New York Journal*, enjoyed documenting the comings and goings of J. Pierpont Morgan, in spite or perhaps because of the financier's legendary antipathy toward news photographers. Morgan was afflicted with an acute skin condition that caused his nose to become grossly inflamed and swollen, and he naturally shunned the camera. Moreover, byzantine dealings with fellow potentates on Wall Street and politicians in New York and Washington, D.C., often necessitated secrecy. But vestiges of the old muckraking spirit persuaded Coleman and a few others to uncover what was hidden and shine a light where none was wanted. Coleman noted that when Morgan spotted him on the street the banker "always ran for his barouche, hiding his livid nose behind a ham-like left palm, but I invariably beat him to the draw." It was a kind of cat-and-mouse game, with the photographer in control. "The crotchety old codger beat the air with wild and vicious swings of his cane," Coleman wrote, "yet [he] never scored a clean hit."[47]

Morgan's desire to be left alone except when he actually wanted press coverage for some pet project is understandable but fundamentally at odds with modern journalistic practice. Photographers working on assignment, especially those employed by newspapers, were encouraged by their editors not to question but to return to the office with usable pictures, preferably before the competition. "When you leave on an assignment, the editor earnestly expects you to come back with a good negative," wrote Thomas Phillips, a news photographer from California. "Nobody else was sent out on that assignment, and the responsibility is entirely on you. There are no retakes in the newspaper game."[48] This immutable doctrine ensures a cer-

UNCREDITED PHOTOGRAPH OF CHARLES LINDBERGH SHORTLY BEFORE MAY 20, 1927, WHEN HE LEFT THE UNITED STATES ON HIS EPOCHAL TRANSATLANTIC FLIGHT ABOARD "THE SPIRIT OF SAINT LOUIS." (LIBRARY OF CONGRESS)

tain amount of friction and even outright hostility between photographers who must return with pictures and subjects who are just as determined to avoid being photographed. No single news story better exemplifies this thorny relationship than photographic coverage of the triumphs and tragedies of Charles Augustus Lindbergh, America's beloved "Lone Eagle."

In the beginning Lindbergh sought out and encouraged the attention of the press and delighted in the public adulation it stimulated. "It was," he wrote many years later, "part of my project." He viewed reporters and photographers as potential allies in making the case for commercial aviation, and he believed (correctly, as it turned out) that celebrity would enhance both his power and financial prospects. He may also have believed that the press was controllable, that he could by dint of his own fierce will and determination restrict coverage to subjects of his choosing. And for a brief time his sudden fame overwhelmed whatever misgivings he had about publicity. "I did not begrudge the time I spent with the press—at first. I answered all the questions I could about my airplane and flight, and tried to laugh off questions that seemed too silly or personal."

Lindbergh's relationship with the fourth estate quickly soured, however, as the press persisted in exploring subjects that had nothing at all to do with flying. Lindbergh happily indulged the public's enthusiasm for flight, but abhorred their evident fascination with his personal relationships and other family matters. Lindbergh was loath to allow even the slightest public scrutiny of his life away from airplanes. Perhaps inevitably, some photographers and reporters stooped to printing fabrication and rumor, thereby earning for the entire press corps Lindbergh's permanent enmity and suspicion.

"Contacts with the press became increasingly distasteful to me," he wrote in *Autobiography of Values*. Interviews and photographs that focused on the superficial and banal did nothing at all to help the nascent aviation industry and made a mockery of his private life. Even worse, composographs and other fictions masqueraded as real news, providing gullible readers with tantalizing—though false—glimpses into matters both personal and confidential. Lindbergh frequently denounced those responsible, but nothing could dampen his own celebrity, the ardor of the public, or the tenacity of the press. On the eve of his long solo flight across the Atlantic on May 20, 1927, Lindbergh already had serious reservations about the media. "At New York, I began to realize how much irresponsibility and license can lurk behind the shining mask called 'freedom of the press.'"[49]

Nothing aggravated Lindbergh more than attention directed solely at his family. Heywood Broun, celebrated columnist for the *New York Evening Telegram,* sympathized but could offer no remedy. Broun noted that Lindbergh's first child would surely enjoy all the benefits of his father's great wealth, courage, and reputation. "But I am already moved with compassion," he added sadly and with dreadful prescience, for "the price he must pay for being a front-page baby."[50] Coverage of Lindbergh's marriage to Anne Morrow and especially of the kidnapping and murder of their son, confirmed his suspicions. For Lindbergh, at times a most reluctant and truculent public figure, the press would always be more antagonist than collaborator.

The crime for which Bruno Richard Hauptmann was tried, convicted, and executed generated an unprecedented media frenzy. Immediately after news of the Lindbergh kidnapping filtered out, photographers fanned out across New Jersey desperately seeking visual scoops and exclusives; supposedly, there was even a break-in at Swazy's funeral home in Trenton, where the boy's body was held before burial. Lindbergh and others denounced press photographers—the most obvious targets—for their ghoulish and cruel behavior, and some of them backed off. On May 12, 1932, the *New York American* sent Sammy Schulman to Trenton to photograph Lindbergh as he identified his son's body at the funeral home. Schulman made a picture of Lindbergh on the way into Swazy's, but he really needed a frontal view. He waited. "When he came out," Schulman wrote, "I put my camera to my eye and looked through my finder at him. Then I put the camera down without making the shot. You know how it is."[51] There are limits to duty.

Lindbergh requested and the national press corps agreed to a temporary moratorium on pictures; the family was allowed to grieve in private. For a while photographers kept their distance. But in late November 1934, Dick Sarno and his editors at the International News Photos syndicate decided that the armistice on photographs had lasted long enough. A report in *News-Week* magazine described how Sarno ended the moratorium. He and the staff at International opted against any overt display that might attract the attention of either the Lindberghs or the authorities. Inside a panel truck parked not far from the Little School for Infants in Englewood, New Jersey, Sarno and an assistant waited anxiously for Anne Lindbergh to emerge with her son, Jon, not yet two years old. When they appeared, walking hand-in-hand down the front path of the school, then along a picket fence, Sarno quietly went to work, using a 35-millimeter camera, probably a Contax affixed with a telephoto lens. "By the time the Lindberghs had disappeared in their waiting automobile, International had half a dozen pictures."[52]

The next day, November 27, 1934, the *New York Mirror* published one of Sarno's images on page one under a banner headline about some sordid double murder, and ran others on an inside page and in the center spread. The cutlines stressed the exclusivity of the images, the pathos of the situa-

THE PHOTOGRAPH BY DICK SARNO FOR INTERNATIONAL NEWS PHOTOS AND THE *NEW YORK DAILY MIRROR* THAT ENDED THE MORATORIUM ON PICTORIAL COVERAGE OF THE LINDBERGH FAMILY AFTER THE KIDNAPPING AND MURDER OF CHARLES JR. ANNE MORROW LINDBERGH IS SHOWN WITH HER SON JON, LEAVING THE LITTLE SCHOOL FOR INFANTS IN ENGLEWOOD, N.J., ON NOVEMBER 28, 1934. (LIBRARY OF CONGRESS)

tion, and the fact that neither Anne Lindbergh nor her son was aware of the camera. No mention was made of International's unilateral decision to end the moratorium. "The little boy was born on August 16, 1932," the caption on page one read, "while his mother still wept over the murder of her first-born." Perhaps to deflect criticisms of Sarno's behavior or methods, the paper also noted that in Anne Lindbergh's car, a "huge police dog growled." Who could blame the photographer from keeping both his presence and intentions secret?

The press simply could not resist Lindbergh and his family. At the trial of Bruno Hauptmann, Lindbergh was besieged when entering or leaving the Flemington courthouse; photographers were everywhere, though only a few pool photographers were permitted inside. "The others—'outside men'—had to get pictures wherever they could," according to one observer. "They found time for tippling. Most of them congregated across Main Street from the courthouse in the Union Hotel's bar, nicknamed 'Nellie's Tap Room' in honor of the black mongrel that attached herself to the press."[53] Newspapers and magazines from around the world clamored for pictures, and when photographs of the trial were either unavailable or visually uninteresting, the swirl of onlookers and entrepreneurs outside could be counted on to provide a suitable photo opportunity.

On February 13, 1935, the jury was scheduled to announce its verdict. In an effort to maintain some small vestige of decorum, presiding judge Thomas W. Trenchard decreed that photographers would not be allowed in the courtroom to record the dramatic moment. Determined to deliver an image of the long trial's penultimate moment at any cost, news photographers met and decided to sneak two of their own, Dick Sarno of the *New York Mirror* and Sam Shere of International News Photos, into court, each armed with a small camera. Shere's view of the proceedings that day was obscured and he could not make a picture. Sarno had better luck. Sandwiched between reporters Damon Runyon and James Kilgallen on the first row of the balcony, Sarno had a perfect view. He wrapped a scarf around his Contax to deaden the sound of the shutter and provide a bit of protective camouflage, then braced it on the balcony railing. When the jury foreman stood to deliver the verdict, Sarno made a single, one-second exposure, then hurried out of court. The exposure was perfect. Because he worked as a pool photographer, copies were made available to other members of the press corps. Sarno's picture ran the next day in newspapers across the country, usually credited only to the agency or syndicate that supplied the picture.

The crush of reporters and photographers at Flemington, each desperate to squeeze the last tidbit of human interest out of the tragedy that befell the Lindberghs, offers a compelling if disconcerting glimpse into a future in which the distinction between what is private and what is public is blurred, even, at times, obliterated. A new generation of small, handheld cameras fitted with fast lenses and high-speed roll film made indoor, available-light photography practically routine, and subjects that were previously forbidden or technically daunting were suddenly fodder for

12 L+✠ THE NEW YORK TIMES, THURSDAY, FEBRUARY 14, 1935.

# Plan to Appeal Announced as Hauptmann Is Sentenced

## HAUPTMANN FOUND GUILTY OF MURDER

By RUSSELL B. PORTER.

Continued From Page One.

acled. His right wrist was handcuffed to the hand of a State trooper, his left to the hand of a deputy sheriff in plain clothes. Previously, they had simply held him by each arm as they led him in and out.

Walking through a crowd inside the rail, Hauptmann looked ahead, his head bowed slightly and his eyes now up and now downcast. His face was very white, and there was even then a look of terror in his eyes like his expression in the very first half hour of his cross-examination, when the Attorney General took him by surprise by showing him his own notebook, in which he had spelled the word "boat" "b-o-a-d," just as it appeared in the final ransom note.

**Mrs. Hauptmann Calm.**

Mrs. Hauptmann came in a moment after her husband. Her expression was emotionless as she took her regular seat at her husband's left, separated from him by two guards. She smiled halfheartedly at him, and he looked at her without smiling. Mr. Fisher talked with Hauptmann, Mr. Reilly with Mrs. Hauptmann. Then man and wife leaned across the guard's knees and talked briefly.

Troopers and detectives virtually surrounded the couple, and a dozen troopers in uniform formed an aisle from the door to the jury box. Through this aisle the jury filed in at 10:35, led by Sheriff Curtiss, Chief Constable Bagstrom, and Charles Walton, foreman of the jury.

The jurors, their demeanor grave, did not look in the direction either of Hauptmann or his wife, who watched them with mute hopefulness, following them with their eyes to the jury box. Mrs. Snyder was biting her lip in an apparent effort to keep from tears. It was obvious that the verdict was guilty.

The jurors took their seats. There

Times Wide World Photo.

THE SCENE IN THE COURT ROOM AS VERDICT WAS RENDERED AGAINST HAUPTMANN.

The jury at the right reporting their findings to Justice Trenchard seated on the bench as Hauptmann and his guards stand at lower left.

as a death mask, his eyes sunken. The jurors were still sitting in their places as the condemned man disappeared from view.

At 10:51 Justice Trenchard excused the jury after thanking them "most sincerely for the service that you have rendered in the performance of this jury duty."

Others in the court room were instructed to keep their seats until the jury left. Led by the Sheriff and the chief constable, the jurors picked up their hats and coats and walked out of the court room single file, down the stairs, out into the street and through an aisle formed by State troopers to the hotel.

At the time the verdict was returned Hunterdon County Court

tremely nervous, pacing up and down his pen, and giving signs of breaking for the first time since his arrest.

At 10:20 P. M. the Attorney General, after receiving word from the Sheriff, faced the court room and called:

"Get those guards out there and close those doors. Lock them, and put a guard at each window."

Chief Assistant Attorney General Joseph Lanagan and others of the prosecution staff entered the room.

The jury box was cleared, a police whistle sounded outside, and the court orderly arranged the bench for the arrival of the judge.

With suppressed excitement, the small crowd in the court room

seating capacity of the trial room was filled.

**Hauptmann's Face Pale.**

Hauptmann came into the room in his habitual manner, his head bowed and his eyes downcast. As he approached his seat in the middle of the row of chairs just inside the rail which cuts off the public part of the court room, he raised his eyes and glanced about the crowded room. There was a half-smile on his countenance. His full round face was very white and his high cheekbones appeared more prominent than ever.

A reporter from the first press row directly behind him leaned over Hauptmann's shoulder, and

case were available to the jurors. Hats and coats of some of the prosecution lawyers, moreover, had to be removed from an adjoining room.

**Jury Retires at 11:21.**

At 11:21, the sheriff announced that the jury room was ready, and Justice Trenchard declared:

"The jury may retire."

Gathering up their hats and coats, the jurors walked across the room in single file, passing between the judge's bench on their right and Hauptmann between his guards on their left. All were grave. Not one looked in the direction of Hauptmann or his wife, although they passed within a few feet of them. Hauptmann was

through the same door which Colonel Lindbergh and Hauptmann had used little more than an hour earlier, Justice Trenchard sat back in his chair waiting for the lawyers to decide on the exceptions they wished to make to his charge.

**Prisoner Refuses Comment.**

Down in the middle of the court room, a reporter leaned over Hauptmann's shoulder from behind and asked what he thought about the judge's charge.

Hauptmann frowned, shook his head and leaned away from his questioner.

"I say nothing," he replied curtly.

The lawyers, who had left the court room, returned, and defense counsel one after the other registered exceptions to the judge's charge in anticipation of an appeal.

At 12:08 P. M. Attorney General Wilentz proposed, by agreement of counsel for both sides, that the court room be cleared of spectators except for newspaper men and others required to be there by their duties, and that it be kept cleared until after the verdict was returned. Justice Trenchard directed that this be done, and it was done, over the protests of many spectators.

Justice Trenchard ordered at 12:09 that Hauptmann be "remanded to the custody of the Sheriff" until the jury returned its verdict, and this was done also. The Sheriff and his men led Hauptmann out of the room in the same fashion as he had entered, one man holding him by each arm. He gave a half-nod and a half-smile to his wife as he walked past her and went through the door to his cell with his head down and his eyes lowered. His New Jersey counsel again spoke to him as he passed them and one patted him on the shoulder, but Mr. Reilly walked off in another direction and did not look at Hauptmann.

**Robbed of $50 in Trial Crowd.**

Special to THE NEW YORK TIMES.

FLEMINGTON, N. J., Feb. 13.—Joseph Herink, 23 years old, a butcher, of 718 Park Avenue, Hoboken, N. J., came here on his half holiday from work today, and his pocket was picked of $50. The money, representing his salary, was stolen by some one in the crowd in

THE POOL PHOTOGRAPH BY DICK SARNO OF THE *NEW YORK DAILY MIRROR* SHOWING THE FOREMAN OF THE JURY AT THE LINDBERGH TRIAL DELIVERING THE VERDICT. THE PHOTO IS CREDITED TO TIMES WIDE WORLD AND WAS PUBLISHED IN THE *NEW YORK TIMES*, FEBRUARY 14, 1935. (OTTO RICHTER LIBRARY, UNIVERSITY OF MIAMI)

the camera. Lindbergh felt some of the effects of the technological revolution and despaired. Photographers, editors, and publishers were more enthusiastic.

"We want pictures of people 'as they are,'" wrote Dr. Paul Wolff, a German portrait and landscape photographer who endlessly extolled the benefits of the Leica camera. This tiny instrument, introduced in 1925 at an industrial fair in Leipzig by Oskar Barnack of the E. Leitz optical company, employed 35-millimeter motion picture film in rolls sufficient to produce thirty-six individual exposures. Wolff maintained that the candid images made possible by the Leica were preferable to those "by would-be portrait photographers which required elaborate lighting tricks and claim to be portraits, although they simply represent a lifeless, conventional 'Sunday edition' of an otherwise lively and natural subject." In the old days, Wolff said, news photographers were forced to wait for just the right moment, knowing they might have but a single chance to make a picture. Flashbulbs or semicontrolled explosions of magnesium dust provided additional light needed to create images. Now, however, "the tense expression has left the face of the reporter who views the events comfortably through the finder and relies upon his little camera with its large film carrying capacity and its constant readiness."[54]

European cameras such as Wolff's vaunted Leica and its principal competitors, the Zeiss company's Contax and the Ermanox, which used glass plates, transformed the look and practice of photojournalism. At the 1932 Democratic Party convention in Chicago, for instance, Sammy Schulman used a new Ermanox to augment more traditional Speed Graphic views. The photographs he made with the little camera caused a sensation. Working without flash he quietly made pictures of "a bevy of homely committeewomen stuffing food in their open mouths, a Senator picking his teeth, a one-toothed Governor picking his nose." He photographed Huey Long whispering into the ear of the publisher of the *Atlanta Constitution*, politicians unable to keep their eyes open during a succession of windy speeches, and Roosevelt exulting with his choice for vice president, John Nance Garner.[55]

Schulman's inspiration as well as his decision to use the Ermanox came from lawyer-turned-photographer Dr. Erich Salomon, whose candid, "slice of life" images were used in magazines in Europe as well as the United States in the late 1920s. "I had seen him in Europe," Schulman recalled, and "studied his equipment and general manner." Salomon's success seemed due in part to his ability to mingle easily with the aristocrats and diplomats who governed Europe. Suave, multilingual, and always immaculately dressed, Salomon's presence at important state functions was neither jarring nor disruptive. He simply did not act like an ordinary press photographer, and the pictures he made did not look like ordinary news photographs.

"Salomon . . . profited from the various talents and abilities which he had acquired over the years: worldly wisdom, a knowledge of languages, and charm," his son remembered. He became skilled at the fine art of photographing without being noticed, "and his legal training provided the criterion of just how much manipulation was consistent with true reportage." Eventually, he decided to ask his subjects to pose only when "circumstances made it inevitable."[56]

Salomon's success in Germany naturally attracted the attention of American publishers. In 1929 Hearst brought Salomon to New York and was so impressed with the pictures he made that he ordered nearly fifty Ermanox cameras for his staff photographers. A little more than a year later, Salomon accompanied French premier Pierre Laval on his state visit to Washington, D.C. With Laval's assistance Salomon persuaded White House officials to allow him to make candid pictures during the premier's meeting with President Hoover in the Lincoln study. The best-known image Salomon made that day captures Laval in animated midgesture while Hoover, sitting in an easy chair under a portrait of George Washington, stares stone-faced at the camera. For John Faber, historian of the National Press Photographers Association, Salomon's work did much more than open the White House to candid photography, though that was no mean feat. Most important, Salomon demonstrated the historical importance of unposed, available-light photography of the people who shape events and make public policy.[57]

In 1932 Salomon was back, this time invited by the Wide World

PHOTOGRAPH BY ERICH SALOMON OF PRESIDENT HERBERT HOOVER AND THE FRENCH PREMIER PIERRE LAVAL AT THE WHITE HOUSE, 1931. (WARREN AND MARGOT COVILLE PHOTOGRAPHIC COLLECTION, BLOOMFIELD HILLS, MICH.)

syndicate to photograph the American political scene, and as in Europe he gained access to events that were closed to other photographers. The head of International News Photo's New York office, Walter Howie, was so annoyed by Salomon's string of exclusives for Wide World that he decided to create a fictional competitor, one "Baron" Schulman. Donning a new pair of striped pants and a wing collar and armed with his tiny Ermanox, Sammy Schulman got into a number of high-level Washington and New York political meetings. "The rest of the boys gave me the horse laugh at my get-up and sputtering French and Italian," he wrote later, "but at least I was trying to keep up with Salomon and Wide World."[58] For a while, at least, the ruse worked.

In spite of the well-publicized successes of small cameras and available-light photography, newspaper editors continued to use photographs sparingly, rarely running more than one with any story, and most photographers stubbornly hung onto their reliable Speed Graphics. Crisp, detailed 4 × 5-inch negatives seemed more substantial than rolls of 35-millimeter film, and newspaper photographers took justifiable pride in their ability to come away from an important event with one or two perfect pictures that told the whole story. For them, clicking away with a 35-millimeter camera seemed like cheating. "At the outset, what we believe is needed in picture coverage of . . . big stories such as disasters, fires, and crimes is a little more thinking and a little less picture snapping," wrote Frank Scherschel and Stanley Kalish of the *Milwaukee Journal*.[59]

Carl Mydans, who worked at the *American Banker*, a business daily in New York City, before joining Roy Stryker's staff at the Resettlement Administration in 1935, was frustrated by widespread resistance to small cameras. Editors and his fellow photographers constantly complained about grain and lack of sharpness, and nearly all of them insisted that small cameras were more toy than anything else. Mydans persevered, however, and found an ally in Stryker. "Carl came in with hundreds of feet of 35-mm film," Stryker recalled. "I had never seen anybody take so many pictures! We had to spread everything out on the floor of the office just to see what he had. It was wonderful!"[60]

As both Stryker and Mydans knew, 35-millimeter cameras added an entirely new element to pictorial reporting. Because of their dependence on certain kinds of pictures, newspapers were slow to adopt the new cameras; however, Leicas and Contaxes were ideally suited to fulfill the pictorial needs of magazines. John Szarkowski, former director of the Department of Photography at the Museum of Modern Art in New York City, explains that photographic equipment ultimately defines both the way pictures look and the content of the news. Most newspaper work in the 1920s and 1930s demanded "one climactic shot that would describe with clarity and simplicity the central facts of a situation," writes Szarkowski. It was not so in the world of magazines. With looser deadlines and considerably more space for visual material, magazine and freelance photographers were encouraged by editors to produce "a fabric of pictures that would tell a relatively complex story."[61] Thirty-five-millimeter cameras were ideally suited to such work.

Of course, Leicas were not the only small cameras on the market; nor were they either automatic or foolproof. George Eastman's company continued to extol the ease of photography and hordes of amateur enthusiasts armed with Kodaks offered proof that clicking the shutter was about all there was to it. This notion persuaded some publishers to provide for the bulk of their pictorial needs by giving reporters simple cameras and purchasing the rest from freelancers. Why hire a photographer, they reasoned, when just about anyone can make a perfectly good picture?[62] This reliance on reporters and other amateurs led to some missed deadlines and technical mishaps, and by the 1920s, professional photographers worked on staff at all but the smallest newspapers and magazines. For the most part, however, their coverage was restricted to the local scene. Agencies and syndicates with contacts around the world supplied pictures of newsworthy events and personalities beyond the reach of the locals. By 1933 there were some fifty photographic news services operating in New York.[63]

The business begun tentatively by George Bain in 1905 continued to grow as the market for pictures expanded. The *New York Times* established Wide World Photos in 1919 to compete with Hearst's International News Photos and Scripps-Howard's News Enterprise Association; the *Chicago Tribune* and the *Daily News* in New York teamed up to create Pacific and Atlantic Photos two years later. The News Photo Service of the Associated Press was established in 1926. Kent Cooper, the AP's general manager, finally convinced his skeptical board of directors that pictures are a legitimate component of the news as well as a potential source for profits. "I visualize the day when we will be sending pictures over our own leased wire system, just as we now send the news," he told the directors in 1926.

Nine years later, on January 1, 1935, AP demonstrated their new transmission system, perfected by engineers of the Bell Telephone Laboratories in New York.[64]

The role of syndicates in popularizing photojournalism can hardly be overstated. Photographs of local news events, once confined to narrow audiences, were now available to a vast network of periodicals. "The run of news is syndicated to papers large and small," wrote Silas Bent in 1927. Photographs, comic strips, written news items, and editorials were gathered together by major metropolitan news organizations and sent to newspapers around the country. As a result, "Syndicated matter has come more and more to be the daily bread of the small-town newspaper."[65] Given the right mix of visual interest and sensational subject matter, photographs of local events now could circle the globe.

During the first weeks of February 1925, the long and ultimately fatal ordeal of Floyd Collins, a cave explorer trapped deep inside a sandstone cavern twelve miles from Cave City, Kentucky, kindled an extraordinary media blitz. More than twenty newspapers sent representatives to cover the story; syndication ensured that their words and pictures reached a national audience. The only real problem was that the hero of the piece was unavailable for either comment or pictures. Wedged in a tiny crevice sixty feet below the surface, his foot caught under a huge fallen boulder, Floyd Collins could neither be seen nor heard. Most of the photographers con-

UNCREDITED PHOTOGRAPH MADE FOR THE BAIN NEWS SERVICE OF A NEW YORK CITY PUBLIC HEALTH WORKER WITH FERRETS THAT WERE RELEASED INTO RAT-INFESTED BUILDINGS AND APARTMENTS, 1920. (GEORGE GRANTHAM BAIN COLLECTION, LIBRARY OF CONGRESS)

UNCREDITED PHOTOGRAPH MADE FOR THE UNDERWOOD NEWS SERVICE, ONE OF THE MANY SYNDICATES COVERING THE TRIAL OF JOHN SCOPES. A TYPED CAPTION ON THE BACK OF THE PRINT SUPPLIES THE CONTEXT: "CLARENCE DARROW, THE LEADING ATTORNEY FOR THE DEFENSE OF JOHN T. SCOPES AT HIS TRIAL IN DAYTON, TENNESSEE, RECEIVED MAIL BY THE SACK FROM ALL PARTS OF THE COUNTRY. THE INTEREST IN THE EVOLUTION TRIAL, NOW GOING ON, IS SO INTENSE, THAT THOUSANDS OF PEOPLE WRITE ADVICE OR CRITICISM TO THE ATTORNEY. HIS TIME IS SO LIMITED THAT MUCH OF THE MAIL IS TAKEN TO THE COURTROOM AND READ THERE DURING THE PROGRESS OF THE TRIAL. JULY 18, 1925." (LIBRARY OF CONGRESS)

tented themselves with pictures of his distraught family and friends and the frenzied efforts of rescuers.

But despite complete lack of access, William Eckenberg of the *New York Times*' Wide World syndicate, and John W. Steger, of the *Chicago Tribune*, produced dramatic pictures showing Collins deep inside the earth. Ironically, the picture Eckenberg produced with help from William Johnson of the *Chicago Tribune*, which became the principal visual record of Collin's entrapment, was not made by them, nor did it depict the actual event. Frustrated by their inability to photograph the doomed man, the photographers tracked down a local farmer who had taken a snapshot of Collins on a previous underground expedition. They bought the photograph for five dollars and sent it to their papers, and from there the picture was circulated to newspapers around the country. The farmer who took the photograph in the first place received neither credit nor any additional money.

Steger's effort was prodigious and risky, but the results were, at best, marginal. On February 16, shortly after learning that Collins had died of exposure and starvation, Steger crawled and wriggled with his camera and flash down into the narrow passage holding Collins' body. He made a single picture in that rocky place, but halation and perhaps improper exposure made the print difficult to read; the dead man was barely visible.[66]

A few years later, in November 1928, another set of pictures propelled a local story onto the national stage. Fred Hansen, one of 199 crewmen aboard the Lambert and Holt Line ship, the *S.S. Vestris*, purchased an inexpensive folding Kodak the day before sailing. When the ship's cargo of agricultural machinery suddenly shifted in heavy seas off Virginia, causing a fatal list, Hansen recorded panicky passengers and fellow crew members filling the lifeboats.

PHOTOGRAPH BY FRED HANSEN, AN AMATEUR PHOTOGRAPHER AND CREWMAN ABOARD THE *S.S. VESTRIS*, WHICH SANK IN HEAVY SEAS OFF THE COAST OF VIRGINIA ON NOVEMBER 12, 1928. THE PHOTOGRAPH WAS PURCHASED AND DISTRIBUTED BY PACIFIC AND ATLANTIC PHOTOS. (LIBRARY OF CONGRESS)

The story might have ended there if not for syndicates. When rescue ships carrying survivors finally reached New York harbor, Martin McEvilly, assignment editor of the *Daily News,* was among those waiting on the docks. He heard about Hansen's photographic efforts from another crew member, and made arrangements for the purchase of the film by the paper's syndicate, Pacific and Atlantic Photos.[67] Hansen's images eclipsed all other efforts—written and photographic—to describe the tragedy, and provided yet more proof of the monetary and publicity value of good news pictures.

To satisfy the needs of their subscribers, syndicates used pictures by staff photographers, professional freelancers, and amateurs like Hansen. Still, the demand increased. "Magazines, Newspapers and Advertisers buy thousands of pictures!" crowed the publisher of an instruction manual for neophyte photojournalists. Promising carefree, at-home instruction with no annoying calls from traveling salesmen, the advertisement assured readers that they could "'cash in' on their cameras in [their] spare time."[68] There is plenty of hyperbole in the ad, as one might expect, but it included at least a kernel of truth, for magazines did indeed need a great many pictures. In a review of another instructional text, the editors of the *Camera* noted a woeful lack of preparation and technical ability among those wishing to break into magazine work. "If our readers could 'sit in' just one day with any one of a thousand magazine editors and see the amount of material which must be rejected because of lack of knowledge of the publisher's requirements, they would quickly realize the necessity of acquiring knowledge of the field to which they would contribute."[69]

In 1915 John O. La Gorce, associate editor of *National Geographic* magazine, asked the readers of the *Camera* to send him their work for possible publication. "We are interested . . . in collections of hand-colored, photographic prints of scenes in various parts of the world, more particularly of types of people in out-of-the-way places or street scenes in towns and cities." This was not *Geographic*'s first foray into illustrated journalism; halftones of black-and-white photographs were first used to illustrate articles in 1890. Since then, collections of pictures depicting cultures and places around the world occupied space once reserved for dense scientific writing. The work of amateurs, some of whom were politically well-connected and therefore useful to the magazine, was published alongside photographs made by scientists, writers, and professional photographers. In April 1905, for instance, the magazine published photographs made in the Philippines during a state visit by secretary of war and future president William Howard Taft, and in July 1907 Edward Sheriff Curtis's images of Native Americans appeared.

The number and quality of pictures steadily increased. In 1910 the magazine published William W. Chapin's hand-colored black-and-white photographs from Korea and China, thereby becoming the first American magazine to run photographs in color. A few years later, in the July 1914 issue, *Geographic* ran another set of pictures from the Orient, hand-tinted studies of Japan by the Geographic Society's foreign secretary, Eliza R. Scidmore. Although the response of the public to the pictures was positive, some board members expressed opposition to running so much visual material in the society's principal publication. In fact, two of them resigned in disgust. Gilbert Hovey Grosvenor, *Geographic*'s editor and a skilled amateur photographer, continued to use pictures, however, secure in the public's enthusiastic response and rising circulation figures.[70] One month after Chapin's article with its thirty-nine hand-tinted photographs appeared, Grosvenor announced that the "series of illustrations published in the November number . . . have proved so popular that a similar series will be published at least twice in 1911."[71]

Led by Grosvenor, the editors of *National Geographic* pushed the boundaries of photojournalism. The magazine was the first in America to build its own black-and-white and color photography labs; the first to publish flash photographs of wild animals at night; the first to publish underwater photographs of fish in natural color. The Autochrome process, introduced to the French Academy of Sciences on May 30, 1904, by August and Louis Lumière, then slowly perfected over the next three years, made photography in natural color possible. After the Lumière brothers

ONE-PAGE LAYOUT IN *NATIONAL GEOGRAPHIC* WITH IMAGES BY DAVID GEORGE MCCURDY, STAFF PHOTOGRAPHER AT ALEXANDER GRAHAM BELL'S LABORATORY, ILLUSTRATING BELL'S ARTICLE ON KITES. BELL IS THE BEARDED MAN IN THE BOTTOM-CENTER OF THE PHOTOGRAPH. (NATIONAL GEOGRAPHIC IMAGE COLLECTION)

PHOTOGRAPH MADE IN WASHINGTON, D.C., BY *NATIONAL GEOGRAPHIC* STAFF PHOTOGRAPHER CLIFTON ADAMS, 1924. (NATIONAL GEOGRAPHIC IMAGE COLLECTION)

began commercial production of autochrome plates in June 1907, *Geographic* became an enthusiastic proponent and eventually ran more of them than any other American publication.

Despite the success of *National Geographic* and the abundant use of color in advertising, illustrated journalism retained its predominantly black-and-white orientation in the 1920s and 1930s. But other changes were in the air. Spurred in part by the public's enthusiastic response to photographs in newspapers, especially those run in Sunday rotogravure sections, several weekly illustrated news digests were established. One of the most interesting of these was *Mid-Week Pictorial,* an expanded rotogravure section first published by the *New York Times* in 1914. Run by George Ochs, brother of the publisher of the *Times, Mid-Week Pictorial* experimented with a variety of word and picture combinations. Though initially a haphazard visual compendium of war photographs from Europe, the magazine did occasionally run more narrative and in-depth picture stories. A month after the war ended, the editors assured their readers that "*Mid-Week Pictorial* will continue to present the official, authentic, documented photographs of all phases of the great war on land, on sea, and in the air, and the world rebuilding to follow."[72]

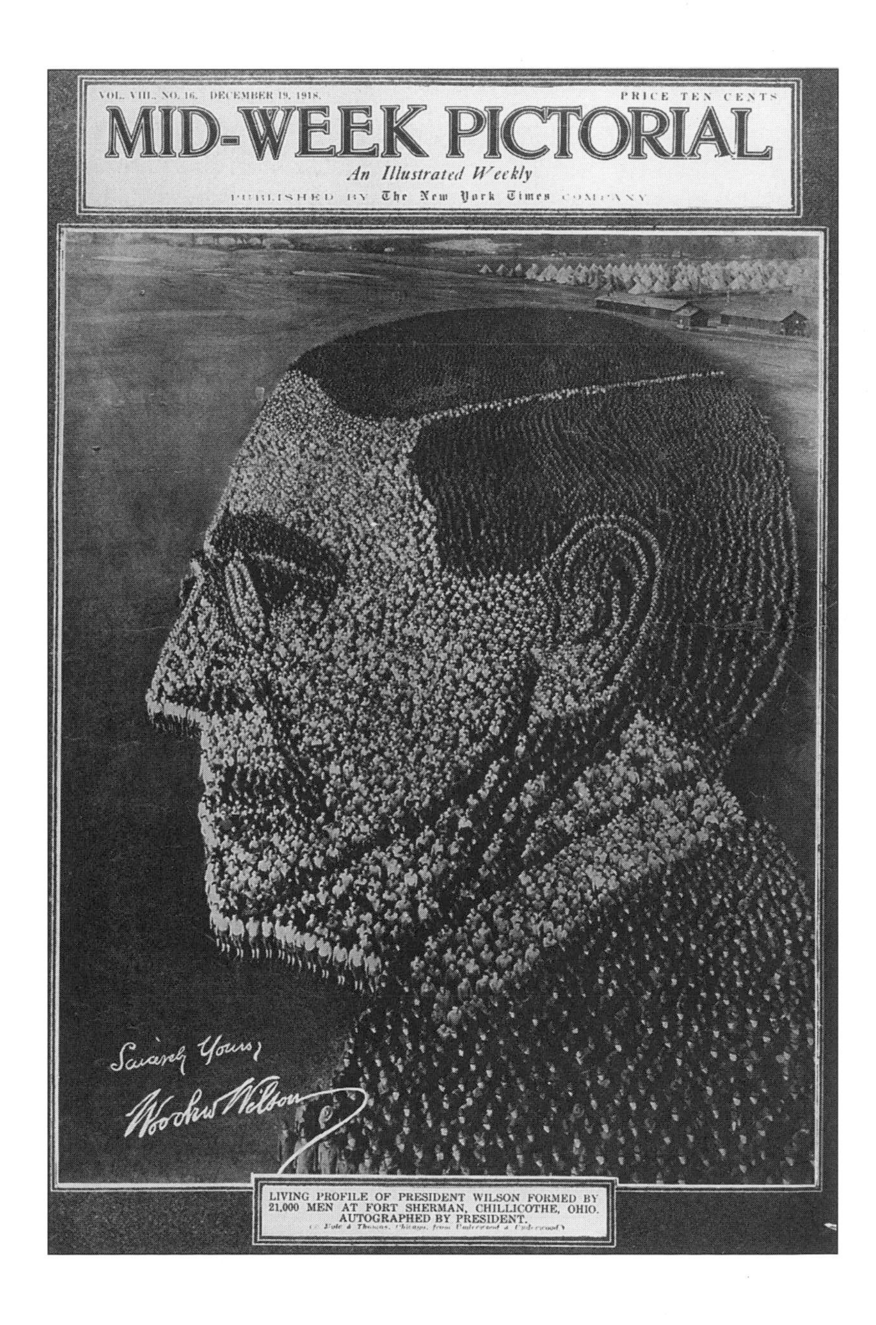


THE DECEMBER 19, 1918, COVER OF *MID-WEEK PICTORIAL* BY CHICAGO PHOTOGRAPHERS MOLE AND THOMAS FOR UNDERWOOD AND UNDERWOOD OF A VAST "LIVING PROFILE" OF PRESIDENT WOODROW WILSON FORMED BY SOLDIERS AT FORT SHERMAN IN CHILLICOTHIE, OHIO. (PRIVATE COLLECTION)

Historian Keith Kenney notes that peace brought with it a slow, steady decline in circulation. Caught somewhere between a news magazine and an ordinary rotogravure section filled with pictorial fluff, the editors of *Mid-Week Pictorial* struggled without success to find an appealing and profitable formula.[73] During the 1920s unrelated feature pictures began to outnumber genuine news images. Legitimate news pieces sometimes competed with celebrity profiles and titillating glimpses of high school and college beauty queens, all of them jumbled together in dense cookie-cutter layouts. Occasional experiments with picture sequences and in-depth pictorial reports, though a portent of things to come in American journalism, did not appreciably alter the downward spiral. In mid-1936 the magazine was sold to Monte Bourjaily, a former executive with the United Features syndicate, but he had no more success than his predecessors at the *New York Times*. On February 10, 1937, Bourjaily shut down operations for good, convinced there was no way to compete with the phenomenal success of Henry Luce's brand new illustrated weekly, *Life*.

*TIME* COVER PHOTOGRAPH OF GEORGE BERNARD SHAW CREDITED TO PAUL THOMPSON. MOST EARLY *TIME* COVERS WERE DRAWN BY ARTISTS, BUT THIS ONE FORETOLD THE MAGAZINE'S FUTURE RELIANCE ON PHOTOGRAPHS. (COPYRIGHT 1923, TIME, INC. REPRINTED BY PERMISSION)

Luce and his partner, Britton Hadden, graduates of Hotchkiss and Yale with modest experience as reporters, unlimited ambition, and a few influential and well-heeled contacts on Wall Street, began working full-time on a weekly illustrated news magazine in February 1922. A year later, on March 3, 1923, the first issue of *Time* magazine hit the newsstands. In a carefully crafted prospectus designed to attract investors, Luce and Hadden summarized their intentions and methods. "From virtually every magazine and newspaper of note in the world, *Time* collects all available information on all subjects of importance and general interest," they wrote. Each week, editors and writers sift through this mountain of material and reduce it to not more than one hundred pithy articles, none over 400 words long. Finally, each piece is fitted into "its logical place in the magazine, according to a FIXED METHOD OF ARRANGEMENT which constitutes a complete ORGANIZATION of all the news."[74]

During its first decade, photographs in *Time* were a secondary concern; the vast majority were stiff head-and-shoulder portraits. The illustrations used on covers were almost as often drawn by artists as made by photographers. Moreover, little attention was paid to the quality of the reproductions. After seeing the first issue, writer and actor Robert Benchley said that the pictures inside appeared to have been engraved on slices of bread.[75] In the 1930s, however, pictorial policy at *Time* and other American magazines began to change. The introduction and success of *News-Week* in 1933 undoubtedly encouraged the competition to reexamine picture usage, for the new magazine touted the importance of its illustrations and used pictures boldly. Some might say too boldly. In a major story on a string of crippling strikes in the Midwest in the fall of 1934, for example, *News-Week* editors used a photograph on the cover that originally was made for an advertising agency, Batten, Barton, Durstin, and Osborne. Valentine Serra's moody portrait of a thuggish, unshaven man leering at the camera, his right fist clenched in a decisive thumbs-down, was dramatic but fictional, a set-up generated in a Chicago studio by a photographer

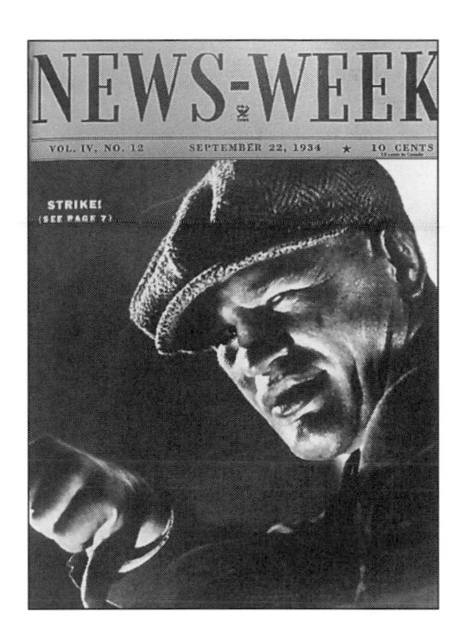

ABOVE LEFT:
PORTRAIT BY CHICAGO PHOTOGRAPHER VALENTINO SERRA, ORIGINALLY MADE FOR BBDO-NY (BATTEN, BARTON, DURSTIN AND OSBORN), AN ADVERTISING AGENCY. THE PHOTOGRAPH MAY HAVE COME TO THE ATTENTION OF *NEWS-WEEK'S* EDITORS DURING AN EXHIBITION OF THE NATIONAL ALLIANCE OF ART AND INDUSTRY AT ROCKEFELLER CENTER IN NEW YORK CITY. 

ABOVE RIGHT:
UNCREDITED PHOTOGRAPH DISTRIBUTED BY KEYSTONE PHOTOS OF POLICE AND SECURITY PERSONNEL IN MINNEAPOLIS AFTER A SERIES OF VIOLENT STRIKES AND WORK STOPPAGES. *NEWS-WEEK*, JULY 28, 1934. 

more accustomed, perhaps, to making pretty pictures of consumer products. In any event, and despite this atypical venture into journalistic make-believe, the portraits and spot-news photographs that *News-Week*'s editors put on their covers and used to illustrate stories dramatized the news and lured subscribers away from *Time*.

By January 1936 *Time*'s assistant managing editor, Daniel Longwell, was convinced that picture policy would have to change in order to maintain the magazine's circulation lead. In a memorandum to Ralph Ingersoll, Luce's chief assistant, Longwell stressed the need for a more liberal policy toward both pictures and photographers. Luce believed that the pictorial needs of *Time* could be met by buying relatively inexpensive wire photos, but Longwell demurred. He pointed out that *News-Week* printed far more pictures than *Time*, and consistently chose more interesting and compelling views. "I'm not criticizing," he wrote critically, "merely pointing out that *Time*'s editors, charming, affable, and exceedingly intelligent, faced with a picture other than a face become insufferable stuffed shirts, start talking about *Time*'s traditions. What the hell is *Time* doing with traditions?"[76]

Longwell's memo undoubtedly prompted some change in picture usage, but in fact Luce was already firmly committed to photography. In 1928 and 1929, during the planning stage for Time, Inc.'s newest publication, *Fortune*, Luce insisted that photographs play a central role. He contacted Margaret Bourke-White, a young photographer whose stunning images of American industry, of steel mills, dynamos, and skyscrapers, were published in magazines, newspaper rotogravure sections, and annual reports across the country, and asked her to come to New York. She was less than enthusiastic. "I very nearly did not go," she wrote in *Portrait of Myself*. "The name Luce meant nothing to me. Of course I knew *Time*. . . . A trip to the public library to look though back files confirmed my impression that the only important use *Time* made of photographs was for the cover, where the portrait of some political personage appeared each week. I was not the least bit interested in photographing political personages."[77] Still, it was a free trip, and Bourke-White decided she had nothing to lose.

The meeting with Luce and Parker Lloyd-Smith, who would shortly become *Fortune*'s managing editor, convinced Bourke-White that photographs in the new magazine would be an equal partner with the printed word. *Fortune*, in short, would not be another *Time*. Rather, Luce and his editors hoped to illustrate their new magazine "with the most dramatic photographs of industry that had ever been taken." What really impressed Bourke-White and made her an enthusiastic member of the staff eight months before the first issue was published on February 1, 1930, was not simply the promise of a national showcase for her pictures—though the prospect of working on a slick, well-financed forum for industrial photography must have seemed almost too good to be true. Equally important was the determination of Luce and his editors to break "away from the practice most magazines had followed . . . of picking up illustrations at random, almost as an accidental sideline." At *Fortune*, Luce said, photographers would examine all aspects of industry, "from the steam shovel to the board of directors," and their images and printed words would be "conscious partners."

Luce was true to his word: *Fortune* did indeed use pictures differently. The photograph, once a device employed to brighten up a page or add a bit of visual corroboration for more important printed words, was now integral and indispensable. On occasion, editors and reporters even accompanied photographers in the field, serving as unpaid assistants and gofers. A few months before the inaugural issue, Luce himself traveled with Bourke-White to Indiana to help work on a complex story describing the industries and workers of South Bend. There, he toted her heavy camera, a 5 × 7 Corona View, and other paraphernalia essential to good industrial work.

During one memorable session inside a foundry, the publisher took an especially active role. Bourke-White had just begun to make pictures of molten steel being poured into sand molds, a technically daunting image requiring steady nerves and an array of 1,000-watt lamps to provide fill light. Suddenly, the huge ladle containing molten metal slipped, and red-hot liquid steel poured out onto the floor. "With a gallantry I have never forgotten," Bourke-White recalled, "Harry Luce dashed forward, grabbed my bulky camera and light stands out of the path of molten metal and swept all the equipment back to safety."[78]

Although *Fortune* magazine appeared for the first time in the midst of the Great Depression, it achieved a circulation of 100,000 by February 1935, at least in part on the strength of a sophisticated and innovative use of pictures. There were reverberations throughout Luce's growing empire. Daniel Longwell's argument for a more central role for photographs at *Time* was bolstered by both the success of Luce's striking new business magazine and the arrival of German-born photographers and editors in the mid-

1930s. Nazi loathing of Jews and the press persuaded some of Europe's most talented journalists to emigrate, and they had an immediate and profound influence on American journalism.

During the late 1920s in Europe, magazines began using photographs not merely as illustration but as the principal components of news and feature stories. Relying on photographers such as Salomon, Alfred Eisenstaedt, Fritz Goro, Tim N. Gidal, and Martin Munkacsi—all of whom made intimate, unposed images with small cameras—editors Stefan Lorant of the *Muncher Illustrierte,* Kurt Korff and Kurt Safranski of the *Berliner Illustrierte Zeitung (BIZ),* and several others experimented with layouts of pictures in complex narrative sequences. Nor were the Germans alone. In England the *Illustrated London News* and *Weekly Illustrated* were filled with picture stories, as were *Vu* and *Pour Vous* in France.

Words accompanying the images in these magazines were, if not incidental, relegated to a secondary role. "The size of the picture," wrote Gidal, "was no longer determined by the number of words. Quite the contrary: the photoreport, dynamic and complete in itself, dictated the length of the text."[79] The formula worked well; at its peak in the early 1930s, *BIZ* had more than two million readers. After Adolf Hitler was named chancellor of the German Reich in January 1933, many of those most actively involved with new methods of photography, layout, and design left Germany and came to the United States. Tragically, however, Erich Salomon was not among them. During the war he was arrested in Holland by the Nazis; he died at Auschwitz in 1944.

At Time, Inc., the influence of German pictorial practice was especially important. At the behest of Henry Luce, Longwell hired Kurt Korff in 1934 to begin working with him and Joseph Thorndike on a new picture magazine aimed at a general audience. As University of Missouri professor C. Zoe Smith has pointed out, Korff's input was decisive. He offered advice on a wide range of matters, from the name of the new publication (keep the title short) to the budget (spend freely since "rumors spread quickly that you pay the best"). Korff urged that Luce hire mostly European-trained photojournalists because they had more experience producing photographic essays. He even helped to fashion a dummy of the magazine, which included feature pictures and a variety of longer photo stories and essays—a portent of things to come at *Life.*[80]

On July 31, 1936, a few months before *Life* began publication, Korff suddenly resigned. Publicly, at least, the reason for his departure was a better offer from a competing company, but there was probably more to the story than that. Although seemingly grateful for his efforts on behalf of *Life,* Longwell refused to give Korff an editorial position. Instead of waiting patiently for the axe to fall, Korff left Time, Inc., and joined his old friend Kurt Safranski as an advisor at Hearst's magazine division. Korff displayed neither animus nor regret in a farewell memorandum to Luce. "I predict a big success. You really are going to create the long expected great American magazine." He was sorry to leave, for he felt a kindred spirit at Time, Inc., a commitment to illustrated journalism that matched his own. But, he

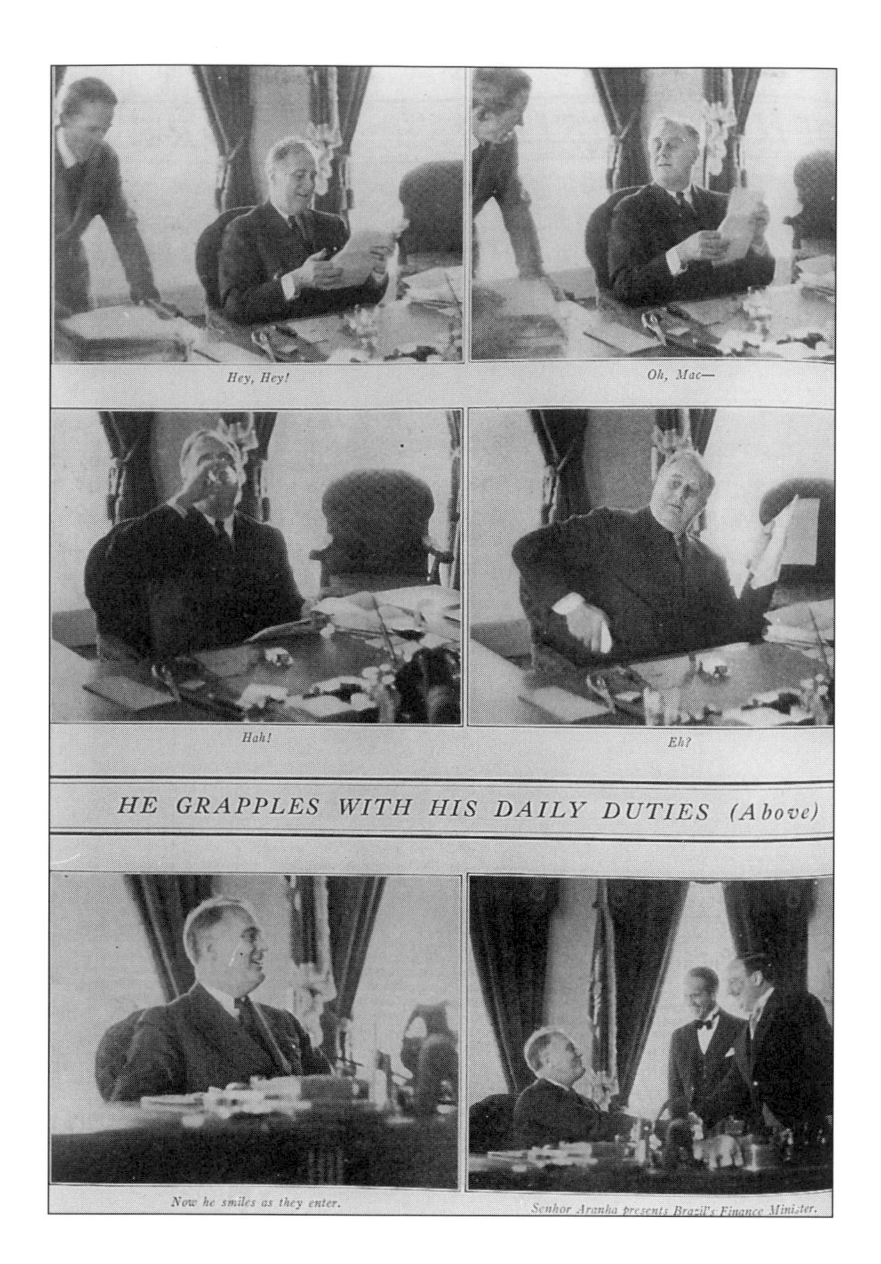


AN EARLY EXPERIMENT WITH THE PHOTOGRAPHIC ESSAY AT *TIME*, A MULTIPAGE LAYOUT ENTITLED "THE PRESIDENT AT WORK" THAT RAN IN THE FEBRUARY 25, 1935, ISSUE. THE IMAGES WERE MADE BY THOMAS D. MCAVOY, WHO BECAME ONE OF THE FIRST PHOTOGRAPHERS HIRED TO WORK ON *LIFE*. (THOMAS MCAVOY/ TIME MAGAZINE, COPYRIGHT 1935, TIME, INC. REPRINTED BY PERMISSION)

added, "Maybe I can help Mr. Hearst in cleaning [up] his picture business a bit. That would be fine."[81]

Luce and his team of young editors were not alone in their plans to launch a large-format picture magazine; on the contrary, in the mid-1930s it was more a matter of which media mogul would be first on the market. Change was in the air, and a new era of magazine photojournalism based on the picture story seemed inevitable. Time, Inc.'s major competition would ultimately come not from another East Coast publishing giant, but from a family-owned newspaper company in Des Moines, Iowa. The date-line may be misleading, for there was absolutely nothing provincial about Gardiner Cowles Jr., called "Mike" by friends and family. In fact, Cowles and Luce were very much alike.

Educated at Philips Exeter Academy and Harvard, Cowles went to work as a full-time reporter at the family's evening newspaper, the *Tribune*, in 1925. Not long afterward he switched to the morning *Register*, where he advanced steadily through editorial positions, from city editor to executive editor to publisher, by 1935. Cowles's decision to venture into the heady world of mass-market magazines stemmed from his observation that readers of the *Register* loved photographs. "I gradually began to appreciate the tremendous but still unrealized potential in photojournalism," he wrote in his autobiography. He had no desire to take pictures himself, but like Luce he understood the enormous appeal of photographs, and beyond that, the likelihood that printed photographs could dramatically increase profits.

For Cowles the decisive impetus to begin planning a magazine came from the work of a doctoral student at the University of Iowa. During the course of his studies, George Gallup developed sampling and polling techniques that precisely measured attitudes and responses, and Cowles hired him to produce a survey of reader attitudes toward both textual and visual material. Gallup found that the stories with the most appeal combined text and related pictures. Words alone could not compete with words and pictures together.[82] Thereafter, Cowles greatly expanded picture usage in the *Register* and *Tribune*, and early in 1936 he began working on a general-interest picture magazine tentatively called *Look*. Gallup went on to found the American Institute of Public Opinion.

Cowles heard rumors that Luce was one of several American publishers eyeing the magazine market, and since they were friends he suggested a meeting. Cowles brought along a dummy of his magazine, as did Luce and Roy Larsen, Time, Inc.'s general manager. At that point, early in 1936, it appeared that the publications were aimed at different markets. "*LIFE* planned to cover the news while we saw *LOOK* as feature-oriented," Cowles recalled. Even more important, Luce seemed determined to reach the affluent and well-educated, whereas Cowles aimed his magazine at "a more downscale audience, the sort of people who read New York's *Daily News*."[83] Luce encouraged Cowles to proceed, and even invested in his new magazine.

The subsequent history and cultural impact of *Life* and *Look* have been painstakingly examined by historians, media analysts, and biographers. Luce introduced his magazine first, on November 23, 1936; *Look's* first issue was dated February 1937, though it actually hit the newsstands almost a month earlier. Though similar and intensely competitive, the magazines were never mirror images of each other. There were differences in style, content, layout, and especially in editorial policy. But Cowles and Luce did share an abiding belief in the power of photographs to reach a mass audience. *Life's* prospectus may have said it best, however old-fashioned some of the language:

> To see life; to see the world; to eye-witness great events; to watch the faces of the poor and the gestures of the proud; to see strange things—machines, armies, multitudes, shadows in the jungle and on the moon; to see man's work—his paintings, towers and discoveries; to see things thousands of miles

PHOTOGRAPH BY SAM SHERE FOR INTERNATIONAL NEWS PHOTOS OF THE *HINDENBURG* DISASTER AT LAKEHURST, N.J., MAY 6, 1937. (INTERNATIONAL MUSEUM OF PHOTOGRAPHY AND FILM AT GEORGE EASTMAN HOUSE).

> away, things hidden behind walls and within rooms, things dangerous to come to; the women men love and many children; to see and take pleasure in seeing; to see and be amazed; to see and be instructed.[84]

At *Life* and *Look* photographers were at the center of the enterprise. Some of them even achieved celebrity status, ultimately garnering almost as much attention as their glittery subjects. Well-paid, highly respected, and almost always properly credited for their work, magazine photographers seemed a definite cut above their peers in the grimy world of daily newspapers. On occasion, however, even newspaper photographers got their due. On May 6, 1937, the fiery crash of the zeppelin *Hindenburg,* pride of the German aviation industry, provided some twenty ordinary press and newsreel photographers and at least one amateur with an extraordinary and unprecedented opportunity to record a disaster as it happened. Photographers there to cover a routine landing saw and photographed the giant airship as it burst into flames and crashed tail-first into the tarmac at the Naval Air Station at Lakehurst, New Jersey.

This was not the first time that the *Hindenburg* played a significant role in the history of photojournalism. A year earlier several American news companies contracted with the *Hindenburg* to bring the first photographs of the Berlin Olympic games to America. But according to A. J. Ezickson, one syndicate outdid its competitors by arranging to have a package of film attached to a parachute and thrown overboard when the ship first swung over the hangers at Lakehurst. A customs official was there to check on and approve the contents, and the film was then rushed to the syndicate's lab in New York City. Since the dirigible spent the next six hours hovering over the airfield, unable to land because of unfavorable winds, the syndicate achieved a notable scoop over its rivals.[85]

Nothing like that occurred the next May. Instead, the gaggle of photographers and newsreel operators waited patiently as the ship slowly approached the mooring platform. Suddenly, and without warning, a small explosion near the tail blossomed into a huge, mushroom-shaped fireball. Murry Becker of the Associated Press, Sam Shere of the International News Service, Charles Hoff of the *Daily News* in New York, Bill Springfield of Acme, and Gus Pasquerella from the *Philadelphia Bulletin* all came away with dramatic images showing the dirigible engulfed in flames. Working with Speed Graphics, they exposed sheet after sheet of film, until all that was left to photograph was a blackened and twisted steel skeleton. After it was over, reporters and photographers "were still white-faced and shaken by the startling conflagration of burning hydrogen, the crash of metal and the inhuman screams of the bon ton people who only a few seconds before had been waving gaily from the windows of the ship."[86] Like

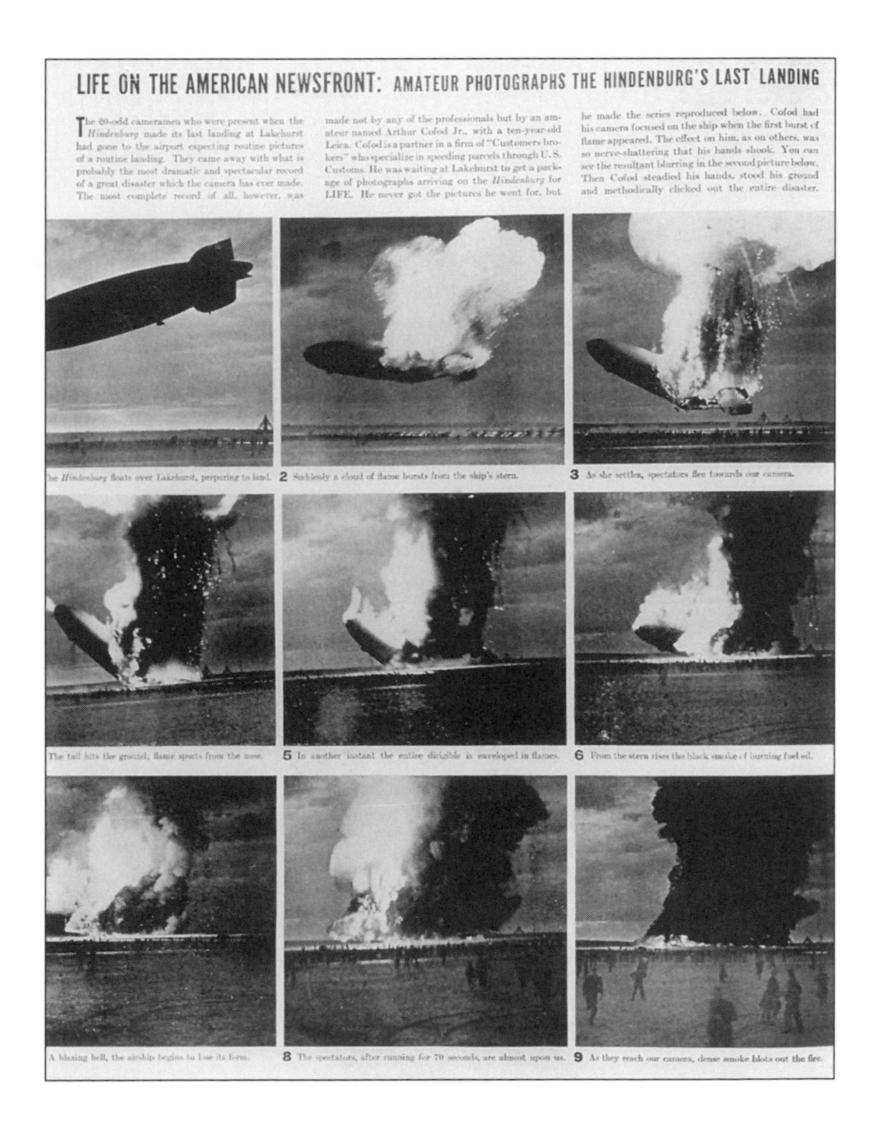

LIFE ON THE AMERICAN NEWSFRONT: AMATEUR PHOTOGRAPHS THE HINDENBURG'S LAST LANDING

The 20-odd cameramen who were present when the *Hindenburg* made its last landing at Lakehurst had gone to the airport expecting routine pictures of a routine landing. They came away with what is probably the most dramatic and spectacular record of a great disaster which the camera has ever made. The most complete record of all, however, was made not by any of the professionals but by an amateur named Arthur Cofod Jr., with a ten-year-old Leica. Cofod is a partner in a firm of "Customers brokers" who specialize in speeding parcels through U.S. Customs. He was waiting at Lakehurst to get a package of photographs arriving on the *Hindenburg* for LIFE. He never got the pictures he went for, but he made the series reproduced below. Cofod had his camera focused on the ship when the first burst of flame appeared. The effect on him, as on others, was so nerve-shattering that his hands shook. You can see the resultant blurring in the second picture below. Then Cofod steadied his hands, stood his ground and methodically clicked out the entire disaster.

he *Hindenburg* floats over Lakehurst, preparing to land.

2 Suddenly a cloud of flame bursts from the ship's stern.

3 As she settles, spectators flee towards our camera.

The tail hits the ground; flame spurts from the nose.

5 In another instant the entire dirigible is enveloped in flames.

6 From the stern rises the black smoke of burning fuel oil.

A blazing hell, the airship begins to lose its form.

8 The spectators, after running for 70 seconds, are almost upon us.

9 As they reach our camera, dense smoke blots out the fire.

SERIES OF PHOTOGRAPHS OF THE *HINDENBURG* MADE WITH A LEICA BY ARTHUR COFOD JR., AN AMATEUR, AND PUBLISHED IN *LIFE*. (LIFE MAGAZINE, COPYRIGHT 1937 TIME, INC. REPRINTED BY PERMISSION)

A NEWSSTAND IN OMAHA DISPLAYING *LIFE*, *LOOK*, AND OTHER LARGE-FORMAT PICTORIAL MAGAZINES THAT SO CAPTIVATED THE AMERICAN PUBLIC IN THE YEARS BEFORE TELEVISION. MADE IN NOVEMBER 1938 BY JOHN VACHON FOR THE FARM SECURITY ADMINISTRATION. (FARM SECURITY ADMINISTRATION COLLECTION, LIBRARY OF CONGRESS)

the others, Murry Becker had rushed toward the burning ship, snapping pictures until finally the heat drove him back. He remembered wandering over to a hangar after it was all over. "Then I just sat down on the ground with my back against the wall and cried. . . . Never had I seen such sudden, stark tragedy."[87]

*Life* magazine covered the story, of course, but the work of professionals shared space with a series of nine pictures made by an amateur armed with a small camera. Arthur Cofod Jr., a customs broker who was in Lakehurst to pick up a package of film for *Life*, used a Leica, and as the *Hindenburg* fell he "methodically clicked out the entire disaster."[88] The pictures made that day demonstrated the enormous power and appeal of news photographs, but they also presaged a new age of photojournalism, when picture stories made by photographers with small, unobtrusive 35-millimeter cameras would come to dominate the printed page. Cofod's photographs, all shot on a single roll of high-speed film, lack some of the brilliance and intricate detail of those made with Speed Graphics, but viewed together they provide an unbeatable sense of time and movement. In the new world of magazines, where the picture story reigned supreme, those were the qualities that counted.

# NOTES

## Introduction

1. Chas. D. Miller, "The Staff Photog," *Camera* 19, no. 5 (May 1915): 291.

2. J. Fortune Nott, "Photography and Illustrated Journalism," *Wilson's Photographic Magazine* 28, no. 395 (June 6, 1891): 321.

3. "The Journalistic Instinct," *Anthony's Photographic Magazine* 38, no. 532 (April 1901): 141.

4. "Experiences of a Newspaper Photographer," *Photographic Times* 37, nos. 2–7 (February–July 1905).

5. Miller, "Staff Photog," 295.

6. Gisele Freund, *Photography and Society* (Boston: David R. Godine, 1980), 113.

7. Wilson Hicks, *Words and Pictures: An Introduction to Photojournalism* (New York: Harper and Brothers Publishers, 1952), 108.

8. "'Happy' and the Happy Faces," *Time* 47, no. 9 (March 4, 1946): 68.

9. Alfred Stieglitz, "Four Happenings," *Twice A Year* 8 (spring–summer 1942): 121.

10. Lewis Wiley, "Photographers as News-Reporters," *Photo-Era Magazine* 61, no. 4 (October 1928): 182, 184.

11. Thomas Moorhead, "Defining Photojournalism," *PSA Journal* 62, no. 3 (March 1996): 17.

12. Brian Horton, *The Associated Press Photojournalism Style Book* (Reading, Mass.: Addison-Wesley, 1990), 16.

13. John Berger, "Appearances," in John Berger and Jean Mohr, *Another Way of Telling* (New York: Pantheon Books, 1982), 92.

14. Leo M. Solomon, *There's Money in Pictures* (New York: Funk and Wagnalls, 1951), 65.

15. "Photography and Truth," *Philadelphia Photographer* 13, no. 155 (November 1876): 323.

16. Jack Price, *News Pictures* (New York: Round Table Press, 1937), 38.

17. Vicki Goldberg, *The Power of Photography: How Photographs Changed Our Lives* (New York: Abbeville Press, 1991), 250.

18. Max Frankel, "Pixelography," *New York Times Magazine*, April 23, 1995, 28.

19. Paul Lester, *Photojournalism: An Ethical Approach* (Hillsdale, N.J.: Lawrence Erlbaum, 1991), 129.

20. Fred Richtin, *In Our Own Image: The Coming Revolution in Photography* (New York: Aperture, 1990), 4–5.

## CHAPTER ONE

## Photojournalism at the Turn of the Century

1. "Public Press-Points Pushed at Photography," *Wilson's Photographic Magazine* 30, no. 436 (April 1893): 177.

2. R. W. Amidon, Letter to the Editor, *New York Evening Post*, March 19, 1898, p. 7, col. 4.

3. "Newspaper Pictures," *Nation* 56, no. 1452 (April 27, 1893): 306.

4. William Gamble, "Pictorial Telegraphy: A Consideration of Various Methods of Transmitting Pictorial Records," *Penrose's Pictorial Annual* (1898), 2.

5. Frank Luther Mott, *American Journalism: A History, 1690–1960* (New York: Macmillan, 1962), 442. See also Simon Michael Bessie, *Jazz Journalism: The Story of the Tabloid Newspapers* (New York: E. P. Dutton, 1938), 38–41.

6. "Things Talked Of," *Harper's Weekly* 37 (April 22, 1893): 367.

7. Stephen H. Horgan, "Photography for the Newspapers," *Philadelphia Photographer* 23, no. 269 (March 6, 1886): 141.

8. Mott, *American Journalism*, 525–41.

9. Charlotte Perkins Gilman, "Newspapers and Democracy," *Forerunner* (December 1916): 315. For a discussion of Gilman's career, see Denise D. Knight, "Charlotte Perkins Gilman, William Randolph Hearst, and the Practice of Ethical Journalism," *American Journalism* 11, no. 4 (fall 1994): 336–47.

10. "Yellow Journalism Evils," *Editor and Publisher* 11, no. 8 (August 19, 1911): 8.

11. Editorial, *New York World*, February 21, 1884, p. 4.

12. "A Step Too Far," *Journalist*, no. 12 (June 7, 1884): 3.

13. Cited by W. A. Swanberg, *Citizen Hearst: A Biography of William Randolph Hearst* (New York: Collier Books, 1986), 36.

14. Kenneth Stewart and John Tebbel, *Makers of Modern Journalism* (New York: Prentice-Hall, 1952), 107.

15. Michael Schudson, *Discovering the News: A Social History of American Newspapers* (New York: Basic Books, 1978), 102.

16. Arthur Reid Kimball, "The Invasion of Journalism," *Atlantic Monthly* 86, no. 513 (July 1900): 120.

17. Carl Ackerman, *George Eastman* (Boston: Houghton Mifflin, 1930), 109, 270.

18. "Taking Pictures for Fun," *New York Times*, November 11, 1883, p. 6.

19. Ibid.

20. Cited in "The Latest Step in Photography," *Anthony's Photographic Bulletin* 16, no. 7 (April 11, 1885): 221.

21. Cited by Clarence Bloomfield Moore, "Women Experts in Photography," *Cosmopolitan*, 14, no. 5 (March 1893): 588.

22. See, e.g., "Horses in Motion," *New York Times*, February 27, 1885, p. 3; "Effect of Instantaneous Photography as a Means," *Wilson's Photographic Magazine* 26, no. 339 (February 2, 1889): 79–81; and "Mr. Muybridge's Photographs," *New York Times*, August 16, 1885, p. 5.

23. "Photographs on the Wing," *Anthony's Photographic Bulletin* 16, no. 19 (October 10, 1885): 604. See also "How the 'World' Expatiates on Photography," *Philadelphia Photographer* 22, no. 264 (December 1885): 388.

24. "The Camera Epidemic," *New York Times*, August 20, 1884, p. 4.

25. Cited in George Mortimer, "Could You Earn Your Living in More Than One Way?" *American Magazine* 91 (February 1921): 116.

26. Ackerman, *George Eastman*, 111.

27. *1894 Kodak Catalogue* (Rochester, N.Y.: Eastman Kodak, 1894; rpt., Norfolk, Conn.: John S. Craig, 1977).

28. George Eastman to Albert Jay, 1898. Cited by Elizabeth Brayer, *George Eastman: A Biography* (Baltimore: Johns Hopkins University Press, 1996), 163–64. See also Ackerman, *George Eastman*, 166–67.

29. Samuel D. Warren and Louis D. Brandeis, "The Right to Privacy," *Harvard Law Review* 4, no. 5 (December 15, 1890): 211, 215.

30. Emma Seckle Marshall, "The Camera and Its Work," *Traveler* 8, no. 4 (October 1896): 58.

31. Luke Sharp, "The Camera," *Detroit Free Press*, June 21, 1885, p. 16.

32. "A Lost Camera," *New York Times*, October 31, 1883, p. 16.

33. "Current Comment," *Illustrated American* 1, no. 1 (February 22, 1890): 3.

34. Arnold Genthe, *As I Remember* (New York: Reynal and Hitchcock, 1936), 45.

35. Gotthelf Pach, "You Cannot Bluff the Camera," *American Magazine* 89 (March 1920): 43.

36. George Gentile, "Progress of Photography," *Anthony's Photographic Bulletin* 16, no. 14 (July 25, 1885): 429.

37. Arthur H. Elliott, "Report on the Progress of Photography in America," *Philadelphia Photographer* 23, no. 278 (July 17, 1886): 421.

38. "Press Photography," *Amateur Photographer* 36, no. 944 (November 6, 1902): 368.

39. "Wreck of the 'Sea Wing,'" *Illustrated American* 3, no. 25 (August 9, 1890): 142–43.

40. Jack Wright, "The Story of Newspaper Photography," *American Annual of Photography* 56 (1942): 232. See also Arthur Goldsmith, *The Camera and Its Images* (New York: Ridge Press Books, 1979), 151.

41. *Harper's Weekly* 24, no. 1227 (July 3, 1880): 419.

42. "Actresses for the Camera," *New York Times,* November 5, 1882, p. 4.

43. "The Photographs Do Not Sell: Washington Letter to the *Philadelphia Telegraph*," *New York Times*, August 3, 1889, p. 3.

44. "Judge Parker and the Photographer," *Photographer* 1, no. 14 (July 23, 1904): 198.

45. "How a Presidential Candidate Should Be Photographed," *Photographer* 2, no. 28 (November 5, 1904): 21.

46. "Pachs Vobiscum," *New Yorker* 8, no. 50 (January 28, 1933): 9.

47. Cecil Carnes, *Jimmy Hare: News Photographer* (New York: Macmillan, 1940), 130.

48. "Photographing a Vice-Presidential Candidate," *Photographer* 1, no. 26 (October 22, 1904): 405.

49. Sally Stein, "Making Connections With the Camera: Photography and Social Mobility in the Career of Jacob Riis," *Afterimage* 10 (May 1983): 12.

50. R. Smith Schuneman, "Art or Photography: A Question for Newspaper Editors of the 1890s," *Journalism Quarterly* 42 (winter 1965): 52.

51. Stephen Horgan, "Photography for the Newspapers," 142.

52. H[arry] Jenkins, *A Manual of Photo-Engraving* (Chicago: Inland Printer, 1896), 8.

53. "The Development of Illustration," *Wilson's Photographic Magazine* 37, no. 521 (May 1900): 232.

54. Walter Sprange, "Facts Concerning Copyright and Reproduction, *Wilson's Photographic Magazine* 34, no. 482 (February 1897): 85.

55. Charles Watson Meade, "The American Newspaper: The City Editor," *Bookman* 20 (September 1904): 32.

56. Jack Price, *News Pictures* (New York: Round Table Press, 1937), 4.

57. Gilson Willets, "News-Photography," in *American Annual of Photography and Photographic Times Almanac*, ed. Walter E. Woodbury (New York: Scovill and Adams, 1900), 57,

58. Sammy Schulman, "*Where's Sammy?*", ed. Robert Considine (New York: Random House, 1943), 12.

59. Harry J. Coleman, *Give Us A Little Smile, Baby* (New York: E. P. Dutton, 1943), 75.

60. Will Irvin, "Yellow Journalism," in *Selected Readings in the History of American Journalism*, ed. Edwin H. Ford (Minneapolis: University of Minnesota Press, 1939), 412.

61. James C. Kincaid, *Press Photography* (Boston: American Photographic Publishing, 1936), 124.

62. "Press Photography," *Amateur Photographer* 34, no. 944 (November 6, 1904): 368.

63. Ellerslie Wallace, "Photographing Disasters," *The American Annual of Photography and Photographic Times Almanac*, ed. Walter Woodbury (New York: Scovill and Adams, 1883), 34.

64. Emma Little, "The Father of News Photography: George Grantham Bain," *Picturescope* 20 (1972): 125–32.

65. George Harris, "Time Exposure," *Rotarian Magazine* (April 1955): n.p.

66. Stephen J. Lynton, "Harris and Ewing Studio Closes After 72 Years," *Washington Post*, February 2, 1977, p. B7; Bryant Baker, "The Harris & Ewing Story," news release by the Harris & Ewing Photographic News Service, n.d., Harris & Ewing File, Prints and Photographs Division, National Portrait Gallery, Smithsonian Institution.

67. "Paul Thompson, 62, Early Cameraman," *New York Times*, November 28, 1940, p. 23.

68. William Welling, *Photography in America: The Formative Years, 1839–1900* (New York: Thomas Y. Crowell, 1978), 396.

69. William Culp Darrah, *The World of Stereographs* (Gettysburg, Pa.: Wm. C. Darrah, 1977), 49.

70. Frank Staff, *The Picture Postcard & Its Origins* (New York: Frederick A. Praeger, 1966), 68, 70.

71. Clyde Kelly, *United States Postal Policy* (New York: D. Appleton, 1931), 262; Paul J. Vanderwood and Frank N. Samponaro, *Border Fury: A Picture Postcard Record of Mexico's Revolution and U.S. War Preparedness, 1910–1917* (Albuquerque: University of New Mexico Press, 1988), 1; Staff, *Picture Postcard & Its Origins*, 44–46, 83–85.

72. Vanderwood and Samponaro, *Border Fury*, 6–7. See also Hal Morgan and Andreas Brown, *Prairie Fires and Paper Moons: The American Photographic Postcard, 1900–1920* (Boston: David R. Godine, 1981): xiv–xv, 115.

73. Kevin G. Barnhurst, *Seeing the Newspaper* (New York: St. Martin's Press, 1994), 40.

74. Thomas J. Schlereth, *Victorian America: Transformations in Everyday Life, 1876–1915* (New York: Harper/Perennial, 1991), 181.

75. W. D. Smithers, *Chronicles of the Big Bend: A Photographic Memoir of Life on the Border* (Austin, Texas: Madrona Press, 1976), 127.

76. Vanderwood and Samponaro, *Border Fury*, 63–74.

77. Walter H. Horne to Gertrude Horne, El Paso, Texas, September 24, 1911,

El Paso Public Library, W. H. Horne Letter File. Cited by Vanderwood and Samponaro, *Border Fury*, 65.

78. John Faber, *Great News Photos and the Stories Behind Them*, 2d rev. ed (New York: Dover Publications, 1978), 30–31.

79. "Letters to the Editor," *Camera* 19, no. 9 (September 1915): 569.

80. Kincaid, *Press Photography*, 142.

81. See, e.g., Stewart and Tebbel, *Makers of Modern Journalism*, 92; Charles R. McCabe, ed., *Damned Old Crank: A Self-Portrait of E. W. Scripps* (New York: Harper and Brothers, 1951), 146.

82. Cited in Dorothy Norman, *Alfred Stieglitz: An American Seer* (New York: Random House, 1973), 28.

83. "Experiences of a Newspaper Photographer. Part 2," *Photographic Times* 37, no. 3 (March 1905): 111.

84. Coleman, *Give Us A Little Smile*, 43–44.

85. Norman Alley, *I Witness* (New York: Wilfred Funk, 1941), 29.

86. Coleman, *Give Us A Little Smile*, 55–56.

87. Editorial, *New York Daily Graphic*, June 3, 1889, p. 2.

88. "Editorial Comment," *Pittsburgh Dispatch*, June 3, 1889, p. 4; Wallace, "Photographing Disasters," 34.

89. David McCullough, *The Johnstown Flood* (New York: Simon and Schuster, 1968), 217.

90. "Pictures Cause Suit," *Editor and Publisher* 2, no. 5 (July 29, 1911): 2.

91. "Not Entirely the Photographer's Fault," *Photo-Era Magazine* 27, no. 3 (September 1911): 138.

92. "Women's Place in Photography," *Photo-Era Magazine* 27, no. 1 (July 1911): 32.

93. Edward Bok, "Is the Newspaper Office the Place for a Girl?" *Ladies' Home Journal* 18, no. 3 (February 1901): 18.

94. Anne O'Hagan, "Women in Journalism," *Munsey's Magazine* 19, no. 4 (July 1898): 611.

95. "In Passing By," *Abel's Photographic Weekly* 19, no. 481 (March 17, 1917): 243.

96. "Taking Pictures for Fun," *New York Times*, November 11, 1883, p. 6.

97. Mildred Ring, "Kodaking the Indians," *Camera Craft* 31, no. 2 (February 1924): 74. See also "Woman's Place in Photography," *Photo-Era Magazine* 27, no. 1 (July 1911): 32.

98. Frances Benjamin Johnston, "What a Woman Can Do With a Camera," *Ladies' Home Journal* 15 (September 1897): 6.

99. Cited in Alexander Alland Sr., *Jessie Tarbox Beals: First Woman News Photographer* (New York: Camera/Graphic Press, 1978), 53, 56.

100. Ibid., 72.

101. [Henry W. Canfield], "The Opium Den Pictures—How They Were Taken," *Californian Magazine* 1, no. 5 (April 1892): 627.

102. "Aid for the San Francisco Photographers," *Photo-Beacon* 18, no. 6 (June 1906): 191.

103. See Faber, *Great News Photos*, 18; "Earthquake," *American Heritage* 34, no. 2 (February–March 1983): 36–45.

104. Genthe, *As I Remember*, 89–90, 94. See also, Naomi Rosenblum, *A World History of Photography* (New York: Abbeville Press, 1989), 461.

105. Coleman, *Give Us A Little Smile*, 143.

106. See, e.g., Louis J. Stellmann, *The Vanished Ruin Era: San Francisco's Classic Artistry of Ruin Depicted in Picture and Song* (San Francisco: Paul Elder, 1910); [S. Levy], *San Francisco: A City of Ruins* (Alameda: T.P.S. Publishing, 1906); and "Art and Business," *Philopolis* 1, no. 12 (September 25, 1907): 16.

107. James Boniface Schriever, ed., *Complete Self-Instructing Library of Practical Photography* 9: *Commercial, Press, Scientific Photography* (Scranton, Pa.: American School of Art and Photography, 1909), 17.

## CHAPTER TWO

## Covering War

1. "Outdoor Men and Women: Heroes of the Camera," *Outing Magazine* 46 (September 1905): 729.

2. Charles Belmont Davis, *Adventures and Letters of Richard Harding Davis* (New York: Charles Scribner's Sons, 1917), 232.

3. Ibid.

4. Richard Harding Davis, *The Cuban and Porto Rican Campaigns* (New York: Charles Scribner's Sons, 1898), 5.

5. James Creelman, *On the Great Highway* (Boston: Lathrop Publishing, 1901), 177–78. See also Allen B. Splete and Marilyn D. Splete, *Frederic Remington—Selected Letters* (New York: Abbeville Press, 1988), 190–91.

6. T. H. Cummings, "War Photography," *Photo Era* 1, no. 2 (June 1898): 25.

7. Editorial, *New York Times*, May 3, 1888, p. 4. See also Tony Hodges, *Historical Dictionary of Western Sahara* (Metuchen, N.J.: Scarecrow Press, 1982), 213–15.

8. James Burton, "Photographing Under Fire," *Harper's Weekly* 52, no. 2172 (August 6, 1898): 773–74.

9. Stephen Crane, "War Memories," *Anglo-Saxon Review* 3 (December 1899): 28. See also R. W. Stallman and E. R. Hagermann, eds., *The War Dispatches of Stephen Crane* (New York: New York University Press, 1964), 284.

10. W. D. Howells, "Arms and the Men," *Literature*, n.s. 19 (May 19, 1899): 433.

11. James F. Archibald, "The War Correspondent of To-Day," *Overland Monthly* 37 (1901): 791–92.

12. Richard Harding Davis, "The War Correspondent," *Collier's* 48, no. 3 (October 7, 1911): 30.

13. Ibid.

14. Davis, *Cuban and Porto Rican Campaigns*, 132.

15. Susan D. Moeller, *Shooting War: Photography and the American Experience of Combat* (New York: Basic Books, 1989), 48.

16. Frederic Remington, "With the Fifth Corps," *Harper's New Monthly Magazine* (November 1898): 968.

17. Ibid., 975.

18. Sargeant Noblet, "The Camera on the War-Path," *Wilson's Photographic Magazine* 36, no. 509 (May 1899): 231, 232.

19. Burton, "Photographing Under Fire," 774.

20. Albert Greaves, Lieut., U.S.N., "The Camera in War Time," in *The American Annual of Photography and Photographic Times Almanac for 1900*, ed. Walter Woodbury (New York: Scovill and Adams, 1900), 102.

21. Cummings, "War Photography," 25.

22. Greaves, "Camera in War Time," 101.

23. Arthur Brisbane, "Great Problems in Organization: The Modern Newspaper in War Time," *Cosmopolitan* (September 1898): 547–48.

24. "Prizes for War Pictures By Amateurs," *Frank Leslie's Illustrated Weekly* 86, no. 2227 (May 19, 1898): 310.

25. Greaves, "Camera in War Time," 101.

26. Cecil Carnes, *Jimmy Hare, News Photographer: Half a Century with a Camera* (New York: Macmillan, 1940), 257; Lewis L. Gould and Richard Greffe,

*Photojournalist: The Career of Jimmy Hare* (Austin: University of Texas Press, 1977), 11.

27. "Our Illustrations," *Illustrated American* 1, no. 1 (February 22, 1890): 3.

28. Carnes, *Jimmy Hare*, 290.

29. Ibid., 39.

30. Ibid., 39–40.

31. Ibid., 66–67.

32. John C. Hemment, *Cannon and Camera* (New York: D. Appleton, 1898), 199.

33. Pete Daniel and Raymond Smock, *A Talent for Detail: The Photographs of Miss Frances Benjamin Johnston* (New York: Harmony Books, 1974), 57–58; Amy S. Doherty, "Frances Benjamin Johnston 1864–1952," *History of Photography* 4, no. 2 (April 1980): 103.

34. Emma H. Little, "The Father of News Photography: George Grantham Bain," *Picturescope*, no. 3 (1972): 125–32.

35. Frances Benjamin Johnston, "What a Woman Can Do With a Camera," *Ladies' Home Journal* (September 1897): 6.

36. Daniel and Smock, *Talent for Detail*, 5; see also Osborne I. Yellott, "Miss Frances B. Johnston," *Photo-Era* 4, no. 4 (April 1900): 109, 114.

37. Estelle Jussim, "'The Tyranny of the Pictorial': American Photojournalism for 1880 to 1920," in *Eyes of Time: Photojournalism in America*, ed. Marianne Fulton (Boston: Little, Brown, 1988), 51.

38. Creelman, *On the Great Highway*, 336.

39. Winifred G. Helmes, *Notable Maryland Women* (Cambridge, Md.: Tidewater Publishers, 1977), 234–37.

40. Carnes, *Jimmy Hare*, 93–94; "A Council of War in Front of Santiago," *Collier's Weekly* 21, no. 20 (August 20, 1898): 12–13.

41. Jimmy Hare, "Foreword," in Carnes, *Jimmy Hare*, viii.

42. Joyce Milton, *The Yellow Kids: Foreign Correspondents in the Heyday of Yellow Journalism* (New York: Harper Perennial, 1990), 93–94.

43. Stephen Crane, "The Majestic Lie," in *Prose and Poetry* (New York: Library of America, 1984), 1134; cited in Milton, *Yellow Kids*, p. 285.

44. Charles H. Brown, *The Correspondents' War: Journalists in the Spanish-American War* (New York: Charles Scribner's Sons, 1967), 136.

45. Ray Stannard Baker, "How the News of the War Is Reported," *McClure's* 11, no. 5 (September 1898): 491, 494–95.

46. Cited by Susan Moeller, *Shooting War*, 49.

47. Walter Millis, *The Martial Spirit* (Cambridge, Mass.: Riverside Press, 1931), 163.

48. Archibald, "War Correspondents of To-Day," 802.

49. "The Heroes of Journalism," *Munsey's Magazine* 19, no. 6 (September 1898): 812–13.

50. William James, *McClure's Magazine* 35, no. 4 (August 1910): 464.

51. Milton, *Yellow Kids*, 359–61.

52. Hare, "Foreword," in Carnes, *Jimmy Hare*, viii.

53. *The Russo-Japanese War* (New York: P. F. Collier and Son, 1905), v, vi. See also James H. Hare, ed., *A Photographic Record of the Russo-Japanese War* (New York: P. F. Collier and Son, 1905), 7–8. The two books have nearly identical texts and run many of the same pictures.

54. Cited in Hare, ed., *Photographic Record*, 8.

55. "Bert Underwood, Photographer, 81," *New York Times*, December 29, 1943, p. 17; "Elmer Underwood Dead at Age 87," *New York Times*, August 19, 1947, p. 23.

56. "Outdoor Men and Women," *Outing Magazine* 46 (September 1905): 729; Christopher Lucas, ed., *James Ricalton's Photographic Travelogue of Imperial India* (Lewiston, Maine: Edwin Mellen Press, 1990), 35.

57. "Notes By the Way," *Photographer* 1, no. 2 (May 7, 1904): 28.

58. Peyton C. March Papers, Manuscript Division, Library of Congress; cited in Gould and Greffe, *Photojournalist*, 62.

59. Douglas MacArthur, *Reminiscences* (New York: McGraw-Hill, 1964), 30, 44–45.

60. Carnes, *Jimmy Hare*, 224.

61. "On Madero's Trail," *Editor and Publisher* 11, no. 4 (July 22, 1911): 7.

62. Carnes, *Jimmy Hare*, 227.

63. Walter Horne to Mrs. Henry Horne, El Paso, Texas, March 21, 1916; cited in Vanderwood and Samponaro, *Border Fury*, 68–69.

64. "War Photography," *Photographic Journal of America* 54, no. 12 (December 1917): 530.

65. Paul Fussell, *The Great War and Modern Memory* (New York: Oxford University Press, 1975), 178.

66. "Camera Men in Danger," *Photographic Journal of America* 52, no. 3 (March 1915): 163.

67. Charles Edward Montague, *Disenchantment* (London: Chatto and Windus, 1929), 98–99.

68. William G. Shepherd, *Confessions of a War Correspondent* (New York: Harper and Brothers, 1917), 64.

69. Archibald, "War-Correspondents of To-Day," 803.

70. "Army Heads Explain Press Censor Views," *New York Times*, July 7, 1916, p. 6.

71. Ibid. See also William Manchester, *American Caesar: Douglas MacArthur, 1880–1964* (Boston: Little, Brown, 1978), 76–77.

72. Moeller, *Shooting War*, 107.

73. Fussell, *Great War and Modern Memory*, 87.

74. Shepherd, *Confessions of a War Correspondent*, 110–11.

75. Oliver Gramling, *AP: The Story of News* (New York: Farrar and Rinehart, 1940), 241.

76. Cited in "Close Calls of American Cameramen," *Moving Picture World* 24 (October 1914): 498.

77. Cited in Raymond Fielding, *The American Newsreel, 1911–1967* (Norman: University of Oklahoma Press, 1972), 116–17. See also David H. Mould, *American Newsfilm, 1914–1919: The Underexposed War* (New York: Garland Publishing, 1983), 62–63; and Shepherd, *Confessions of a War Correspondent*, 106.

78. Francis J. Reynolds, ed., *Collier's New Photographic History of the World's War* (New York: P. F. Collier and Son, 1919), 3.

79. Shepherd, *Confessions of a War Correspondent*, 90.

80. Emmet Crozier, *American Reporters on the Western Front, 1914–1918* (New York: Oxford University Press, 1959), 16.

81. Cited by Shepherd, *Confessions of a War Correspondent*, 75.

82. "New Russian War Film," *New York Times*, December 10, 1917, p. 15.

83. Donald C. Thompson, *Donald Thompson in Russia* (New York: Century, 1918), vii.

84. E. Alexander Powell, *Fighting in Flanders* (New York: Grosset and Dunlap, 1915), 13–14.

85. Florence MacLeod Harper, "Introduction," in Donald C. Thompson, *From Czar to Kaiser: The Betrayal of Russia* (Garden City, N.Y.: Doubleday, Page, 1918), vi.

86. Mould, *American Newsfilm*, 100–131.

87. See, e.g., "Thompson Tells Tales of Battle," *Topeka Daily Capital*, December 30, 1915, p. 12; "How a Wise Photographer Fooled the Huns," *Abel's Photographic Weekly* 21, no. 527 (February 2, 1918): 82.

88. Shepherd, *Confessions of a War Correspondent*, 92–93.

89. Captain Ivor Castle, "With a Camera on the Somme," *Canada in Khaki* 1

(1917): 68; cited by Peter Robertson, "Canadian Photojournalism during the First World War," *History of Photography* 2, no. 1 (January 1978): 43.

90. Ibid. See also Jane Carmichael, *First World War Photographers* (London: Routledge, 1989), 50.

91. "United States Official War Photographers," *Photographic Journal of America* 54, no. 12 (December 1917): 529. See also "Fake War Movies," *Literary Digest* 51, no. 20 (November 13, 1915): 1079.

92. Montague, *Disenchantment*, 101.

93. "Army Heads Explain Press Censor Views," *New York Times*, July 7, 1916, p. 6.

94. George Creel, *Rebel at Large: Recollections of Fifty Crowded Years* (New York: G. P. Putnam's Sons, 1947), 156.

95. Committee on Public Information, "The Activities of the Committee on Public Information," War Information Series, no. 18 (February 1918): 5; "Creel Answers Some Pointed Questions," *Editor and Publisher* 50, no. 49 (May 18, 1918): 32.

96. George Creel, "Public Opinion in War Time," *Annals of the American Academy of Political and Social Science* 78 (July 1918): 187; Stephen Vaughn, *Holding Fast the Inner Lines* (Chapel Hill: University of North Carolina Press, 1980), 213; "Activities of the Committee on Public Information," p. 4.

97. Creel, "Public Opinion," 211. See also Moeller, *Shooting War*, 113.

98. *Information Concerning the Making and Distribution of Pictures that Show the Activities of the Army and Navy* (Washington, D.C.: Committee on Public Information, 1917), 4–5.

99. "Views and Reviews," *Photographic Journal of America* 54, no. 8 (August 1917): 344.

100. Deborah Willis-Thomas, *Black Photographers, 1840–1940: An Illustrated Bio-Biography* (New York: Garland Publishing, 1985), 14.

101. Catherine Tuggle, "Edward Steichen: War, History and Humanity," *History of Photography* 17, no. 4 (winter 1993): 364.

102. Edward Steichen, *A Life in Photography* (New York: Doubleday, 1963), n.p.

103. "Unique War Photography School," *Photographic Journal of America* 56, no. 4 (April 1919): 178.

104. Moeller, *Shooting War*, 125.

105. E. R. Trabold, "Couterattacking with a Camera: A Trip to the Front with a Signal Corps Unit," *Photographic Journal of America* 56, no. 9 (September 1919): 412.

106. Jussim, "Tyranny of the Pictorial," 64. See also Brian Coe and Paul Gates, *The Snapshot Photograph: The Rise of Popular Photography, 1888–1939* (London: Ash and Grant, 1977), 34.

## CHAPTER THREE

### Photojournalism, Documentary, and Reform

1. Jacob Riis, *The Making of an American* (New York: Macmillan, 1901), 177.

2. James W. Barrett, *The End of the World* (New York: Harper and Brothers, 1931), 27–28.

3. James W. Barrett, *The World, The Flesh, and Messrs. Pulitzer* (New York: Vanguard Press, 1931), 16.

4. "What It Means to Be 'Yellow,'" *New York Journal*, February 1, 1902, p. 16.

5. Charles R. McCabe, ed., *Damned Old Crank: A Self-Portrait of E. W. Scripps* (New York: Harper and Brothers, 1951), 146.

6. S. S. McClure, "Concerning Three Articles in This Number of McClure's, and a Coincidence that May Set Us Thinking," *McClure's* 20 (January 1903): 336.

See also S. S. McClure, *My Autobiography* (New York: Magazine Publishers, 1914), 237–46.

7. Ray Stannard Baker, *American Chronicle* (New York: Charles Scribner's Sons, 1945), 26.

8. Mott, *American Journalism*, 590. See also Theodore Bernard Peterson, *Magazines in the Twentieth Century* (Urbana: University of Illinois Press, 1964), 5, 15.

9. John Grierson, *Grierson on Documentary*, ed. Forsyth Hardy (New York: Harcourt, Brace, 1947), 99–100.

10. Ibid., 160, 101.

11. Beaumont Newhall, "Documentary Approach to Photography," *Parnassus* 10, no. 3 (March 1938): 5.

12. Cited by John Loengard, *Celebrating the Negative* (New York: Arcade Publishing, 1994), 22.

13. Erik Barnouw, *Documentary: A History of the Non-Fiction Film*, rev. ed. (New York: Oxford University Press, 1983), 313.

14. John Grierson, "Propaganda: A Problem for Educational Theory and for Cinema," *Sight and Sound* (winter 1933–34): 119; see also Richard Griffith, "The Film Faces Facts," *Survey Graphic* 27, no. 12 (December 1938): 596.

15. Maren Stange, *Symbols of Ideal Life: Social Documentary Photography in America, 1890–1950* (New York: Cambridge University Press, 1989), xiv.

16. Grierson, *Grierson on Documentary*, 100.

17. Ibid., 62.

18. Charles Loring Brace, *The Dangerous Classes of New York, and Twenty Years Work Among Them* (New York: Wynkoop and Hallenbeck, 1872), 282. See also Carol Shloss, *In Visible Light: Photography and the American Writer, 1840–1940* (New York: Oxford University Press, 1987), 121–22.

19. Riis, *Making of an American*, 173–74.

20. Ibid., 175. See also Alexander S. Alland Sr., *Jacob A. Riis. Photographer and Citizen* (New York: Aperture, 1993), 26–27.

21. *Chicago Times*, December 20, 1890; cited by Sally Stein, "Making Connections with the Camera: Photography and Social Mobility in the Career of Jacob Riis," *Afterimage* 10 (May 1983): 14.

22. Peter B. Hales, *Silver Cities: The Photography of American Urbanization, 1839–1915* (Philadelphia: Temple University Press, 1984), 180–81.

23. J. Thomson and Adolphe Smith, *Street Life in London* (London: Sampson Low, Marston, Searle and Rivington, c. 1877), n.p.

24. Jacob A. Riis, *The Battle with the Slum* (New York: Macmillan, 1902), 61.

25. Jacob A. Riis, *How the Other Half Lives: Studies Among the Tenements of New York* (Cambridge, Mass.: Belknap Press, 1970), 198, 6.

26. Jacob Riis, *Children of the Poor* (New York: Johnson Reprint, 1970), 288.

27. "Jacob Riis, Revivalist," *Survey* 24, no. 6 (May 7, 1910): 200.

28. "Flashes from the Slums," *New York Sun*, February 12, 1888, p. 10.

29. Riis, *Battle with the Slum*, 431.

30. Theodore Roosevelt, *An Autobiography* (New York: Macmillan, 1913), 187.

31. Louis Albert Banks, *White Slaves; or, The Oppression of the Worthy Poor* (Boston: Lee and Shepard, 1893), 18.

32. Henry W. Canfield, "How the Opium Fiends Were Fought with the Camera," *Wide World Magazine* 5, no. 26 (June 1900): 187. See also Peter E. Palmquist, "Photographing San Francisco's Opium Fiends," in Peter E. Palmquist, ed., *Photography in the West—2* (Manhattan, Kans.: Sunflower University Press, 1989), 113.

33. See Mason's obituary in the *New York Times*, March 17, 1921, p. 13.

34. Helen Campbell, *Darkness and Daylight; or, Lights and Shadows of New York Life* (Hartford, Conn.: Hartford Publishing, 1897), x, xi.

35. Ibid., 43.

36. Ibid., 168–69.

37. James Realf Jr., "Jolly Poverty in New York," *Illustrated American* 22, no. 407 (November 27, 1897): 681.

38. Edmond S. Meany, "Hunting Indians with a Camera," *World's Work* 15, no. 5 (March 1908): 10010.

39. Theodore Roosevelt, "Foreword," in Edward S. Curtis, *The North American Indian*, vol. 1 (Cambridge, Mass.: University Press, 1907; New York: Johnson Reprint, 1970), i.

40. The original images were made for the painter Walter Russell, who wanted to use them as models for his oil portraits of the children. The images were later published in the July 1905 issue of *McClure's Magazine*.

41. Barbara A. Davis, *Edward S. Curtis: The Life and Times of a Shadow Catcher* (New York: Chronicle Books, 1985), 65.

42. Edward S. Curtis, *In the Land of the Head-Hunters* (Yonkers-on-Hudson, N.Y.: World Book, 1915), vii. See also Barry Gifford, ed., *Selected Writings of Edward S. Curtis* (Berkeley, Calif.: Creative Arts Book Company, 1976), ii–iv.

43. George Bird Grinnell, "Portraits of Indian Types," *Scribner's Magazine* 37, no. 3 (March 1905): 273.

44. Ibid., [xiii].

45. See, e.g., Christopher M. Lyman, *The Vanishing Race and Other Illusions*, introduction by Vine Deloria Jr. (New York: Pantheon Books, 1982); James C. Faris, "The Navajo Photography of Edward S. Curtis, *History of Photography* 17, no. 4 (winter 1993): 377.

46. Paula Richardson Fleming and Judith Lynn Luskey, *Grand Endeavors of American Indian Photography* (Washington, D.C.: Smithsonian Institution Press, 1993), 107–17.

47. Mick Gidley, "Edward S. Curtis Speaks . . . ," *History of Photography* 2, no. 4 (October 1978): 349.

48. Pete Daniel and Raymond Smock, *A Talent for Detail: The Photographs of Frances Benjamin Johnston*, (New York: Harmony Books, 1974), 27.

49. Jeanne Moutoussamy-Ashe, *Viewfinders: Black Women Photographers* (New York: Dodd, Mead, 1986), 21–23.

50. Cited in Daniel and Smock, *Talent for Detail*, pp. 95–96. See also Amy S. Doherty, "Frances Benjamin Johnston 1864–1952," *History of Photography* 4, no. 2 (April 1980): 105.

51. Frances Benjamin Johnston, "Through the Coal Country with a Camera," *Demorest's Family Magazine* 28, no. 5 (March 1892): 265, 266.

52. Walter I. Trattner, *Crusade for the Children* (Chicago: Quadrangle Books, 1970), 41, 48. See also Ray Stannard Baker, "The Right to Work," *McClure's Magazine* 20, no. 3 (January 1903).

53. Elizabeth McCausland, "Portrait of a Photographer," *Survey Graphic* 27, no. 10 (October 1938): 502, 503.

54. "Workers and Employers," *New York Evening Post*, October 28, 1920, 9.

55. Hine to Elizabeth McCausland, October 25 [1938]; cited in Daile Kaplan, ed., *Photo Story: Selected Letters and Photographs of Lewis W. Hine* (Washington, D.C.: Smithsonian Institution Press, 1992), 128.

56. Hine to Paul Kellogg, April 8, 1924; cited by Naomi Rosenblum, Walter Rosenblum, and Alan Trachtenberg, *America and Lewis Hine* (New York: Aperture, 1977), 74.

57. Lewis Hine, "The Silhouette in Photography," *Photographic Times* 38, no. 11 (November 1906): 490; Hine to Florence Kellogg, February 17, 1933, in Daile Kaplan, ed., *Photo Story*, 49–50.

58. Edward W. Earle, "Halftone Effects: A Cultural Study of Photographs in Reproduction, 1895–1905," *CMP [California Museum of Photography] Bulletin* 8, no. 1 (1989): 1.

59. Daile Kaplan, *Lewis Hine in Europe: The Lost Photographs* (New York: Abbeville Press, 1988), 9.

60. Hine to "Old Oom" [Paul Kellogg], Jes' before Christmas [1923], Survey Associates Records, reel 3827, Archives of American Art, Smithsonian Institution, Washington, D.C..

61. Paul Kellogg to Lewis Hine, November 28, 1921, Survey Associates Records, Archives of American Art, Smithsonian Institution, Washington, D.C.

62. Rexford Guy Tugwell, Thomas Munro, and Roy E. Stryker, *American Economic Life and the Means of Its Improvement* (New York: Harcourt, Brace, 1925).

63. Lewis Wickes Hine to Roy Emerson Stryker, June 21, 1938; Stryker to Hine, November 14, 1935, in Daile Kaplan, ed., *Photo Story*, 109, 74.

64. Stryker to Mrs. Helen Hunt Miller, October, 11, 1960. Roy E. Stryker Papers, University of Louisville Photographic Archives, Ekstrom Library, Louisville, Kentucky (hereafter, RES Papers).

65. *Complete Report of the Chairman of the Committee on Public Information, 1917:1918:1919* (Washington, D.C.: Government Printing Office, 1920), 1. See also *Official U.S. Bulletin. Hearing Before the Joint Committee on Printing*. Sixty-sixth Congress, First Session (August 12, 1919): 53.

66. Stryker to Wallace Richards, November 7, 1949, RES Papers.

67. Stryker to Robert Doherty, August 9, 1962, RES Papers.

68. John Grierson, "The Documentary Idea," in *The Encyclopedia of Photography*, vol. 4, ed. Willard Morgan (New York: National Educational Alliance, 1949), 1376.

69. Dorothea Lange, *The Making of a Documentary Photographer: An Interview Conducted by Suzanne Riess* (Berkeley: Regional Oral History Office, University of California, 1968), 158.

70. Walker Evans, *Walker Evans at Work* (New York: Harper and Row, 1982), 112.

71. Walker Evans, "The Thing Itself Is Such a Secret and So Unapproachable," *Image* 17, no. 4 (December 1974): 14.

72. Henry A. Wallace, *America Must Choose* (New York: Foreign Policy Association, 1934), 3.

73. Irving Brant, "After 'Contagious Magic' Had Failed," *Editor and Publisher* 65, no. 45 (March 25, 1933): 7.

74. Cited by Anne Tucker, "The Photo League," *Modern Photography* (September 1979): 174.

75. Elizabeth McCausland, "Lecture delivered before the class of the documentary photography at the Photo League," *Photography Syllabus and Readings* (New York: Photo League, n.d.), 17; cited in Fiona M. Dejardin, "The Photo League: Left-wing Politics and the Popular Press," *History of Photography* 18, no. 2 (summer 1994): 161.

76. Dejardin, "Photo League," 159.

77. Stryker to Arthur Rothstein, May 23, 1936, RES Papers.

78. Stryker to Dorothea Lange, January 14, 1936, RES Papers.

79. Stryker to Lange, June 18, 1937, RES Papers.

80. Stryker to Russell Lee, May 22, 1941, RES Papers.

81. Lange, *Making of a Documentary Photographer*, 155–56.

## CHAPTER FOUR

## Tabloids, Magazines, and the Art of Photojournalism

1. A. J. Ezickson, *Get That Picture! The Story of the News Cameraman* (New York: National Library Press, 1938), 121.

2. Cited in Peter Marzio, *Men and Machines of American Journalism*, 123.

3. "Tabloid Poison," *Saturday Review of Literature* 3, no. 30 (February 19, 1927): 591.

4. Silas Bent, "Journalistic Jazz," *Nation* 122, no. 3169 (March 31, 1926): 341.

5. Simon Michael Bessie, *Jazz Journalism: The Story of the Tabloid Newspapers* (New York: Russell & Russell, 1969), 220–28; see also James E. Murphy, "Tabloids as Urban Response," in Catherine L. Covert and John D. Stevens, *Mass Media Between the Wars: Perceptions of Cultural Tension, 1918–1941* (Syracuse, N.Y.: Syracuse University Press, 1984), 62.

6. F. Scott Fitzgerald, "May Day," in *Babylon Revisited and Other Stories* (New York: Charles Scribner's Sons, 1960), 25.

7. Charles Stadler, "Photographing for Half-Tones," *Wilson's Photographic Magazine* 34, no. 485 (May 1897): 204.

8. Charles H. Caffin, *Photography as a Fine Art* (New York: Doubleday, Page, 1901; New York: American Photographic Book Publishing, 1972), 9–10.

9. Sidney Allan, "The Value of the Apparently Meaningless and Inaccurate," *Camera Work*, no. 3 (July 1903): 17, 18.

10. Judith Mara Gutman, "The Twin-Fired Engine: Photography's First 150 Years," *Gannett Center Journal* (winter 1990): 53.

11. Harold A. Williams, "A. Aubrey Bodine: The Man and the Colleague," in Kathleen M. H. Ewing, *A. Aubrey Bodine: Baltimore Pictorialist, 1906–1970* (Baltimore: Johns Hopkins University Press, 1985), 3.

12. H. Crowell Pepper, "The Eye That Sees," *Camera* 47, no. 4 (October 1933): 217.

13. Louis Wiley, "Photographers as News-Reporters," *Photo-Era* 61, no. 4 (October 1928): 183.

14. Bernarr Macfadden, *Vitality Supreme* (New York: Physical Culture Publishing, 1915), xi.

15. Manuscript, file "Muray, Nickolas," Prints and Photographs Division, National Portrait Gallery, Smithsonian Institution, Washington, D.C.

16. Emile Gauvreau, *My Last Million Readers* (New York: E. P. Dutton, 1941), 111.

17. John Dos Passos, *The Big Money* (New York: Houghton Mifflin, 1946; rpt., New York: Penguin Books, 1979), 208.

18. "Valentino and Yellow Journalism," *Nation* 123, no. 3192 (September 8, 1926): 207.

19. Emile Gauvreau, "To the Reader," in *Hot News* (New York: Macaulay, 1931), vii.

20. Lester Cohen, *The New York Graphic: The World's Zaniest Newspaper* (Philadelphia: Chilton Books, 1964), 100–101.

21. "Rhinelander's Bride Goes on Trip Abroad," *New York Times*, July 24, 1926, p. 11.

22. "Hits Press and Readers," *New York Times*, December 7, 1925, p. 24. See also "Criticizes the Press on Rhinelander Case," *New York Times*, November 25, 1925, p. 24.

23. *Editor and Publisher* 62, no. 15 (August 31, 1929): 5.

24. "Graphic Publisher Is Hauled to Court," *New York Times*, February 25, 1927, p. 17. See also Gauvreau, *My Last Million Readers*, 111.

25. John D. Stevens, *Sensationalism and the New York Press* (New York: Columbia University Press, 1991), 142–43. See also John L. Spivak, "The Rise and Fall of a Tabloid," *American Mercury* 32, no. 127 (July 1934): 306–14.

26. "The Ways and Wiles of the Camera Man," *Camera* 19, no. 2 (February 1915): 102.

27. Ezickson, *Get That Picture!*, 132.

28. Laura Vitray, John Mills Jr., and Roscoe Ellard, *Pictorial Journalism* (New York: McGraw-Hill, 1939), 260.

29. "'Buck' May Remembers When," in *White House News Photographers Annual Awards, 1969* (Washington, D.C.: White House News Photographers Association, 1969), 17.

30. Dickey Chapelle, *What's a Woman Doing Here? A Reporter's Report on Herself* (New York: William Morrow, 1962), 49.

31. Weegee, *Naked City* (New York: DaCapo Press, 1975), 240; see also Marianne Fulton, "Bearing Witness," in Marianne Fulton, ed., *Eyes of Time: Photojournalism in America* (Boston: Little, Brown, 1988), 115.

32. John Chapman, *Tell It to Sweeney: An Informal History of the Daily News* (Garden City, N.Y.: Doubleday, 1961), 93.

33. Cited in Price, *News Pictures*, 90.

34. Ibid., 33. See also Vitray, Mills, and Ellard, *Pictorial Journalism*, 118–19.

35. Marlin Pew, "Shop Talk at Thirty," *Editor and Publisher* 65, no. 51 (May 6, 1933): 40.

36. Leo Solomon, *There's Money in Pictures* (New York: Funk and Wagnalls, 1951), 177–78.

37. See, e.g., Fulton, *Eyes of Time*, 106–24; Ken Kobre, *Photojournalism: The Professionals' Approach* (Somerville, Mass.: Curtin & London, 1980), 19–24.

38. James Boniface Schriever, ed., *Complete Self-Instructing Library of Practical Photography*, vol. 1: Elementary Photography (Scranton, Pa.: American School of Art and Photography, 1909), 346–47, 352.

39. Claude Cookman, *A Voice Is Born* (Durham, N.C.: National Press Photographers Association, 1985), 4; Jack Wright, "The Story of Newspaper Photography," in Frank Fraprie and Franklin I. Jordan, eds., *The American Annual of Photography 1942* (Boston: American Photographic Publishing, 1941), 235.

40. "Show," *Time* 19 (June 27, 1932): 44.

41. Weegee, *Naked City*, 239.

42. Schulman, *Where's Sammy?*, 47.

43. Ibid., 55–60. See also Neal Gabler, *Winchell: Gossip, Power and the Culture of Celebrity* (New York: Alfred A. Knopf, 1995), 171–72.

44. "Gaynor's Picture," *Editor and Publisher* 10, no. 7 (August 13, 1910): 7; Faber, *Great News Photos*, 24–25.

45. Silas Bent, *Ballyhoo: The Voice of the Press* (New York: Horace and Liveright, 1927), 68.

46. Gordon Belmont, "Speed Tele-Photographs," *American Annual of Photography* 28 (1914): 226, 228.

47. Coleman, *Give Us a Little Smile*, 46.

48. Thomas Phillips, "Press-Photography and Newspaper Reporting," *Photo-Era Magazine* 62, no. 6 (June 1929): 312.

49. Charles A. Lindbergh, *Autobiography of Values* (New York: Harcourt Brace Jovanovich, 1977), 73, 75.

50. Cited in Schulman, *Where's Sammy?*, 79.

51. Ibid., 85.

52. "Scoop: News Photographers Take Baby Jon Lindbergh's Picture," *News-Week* 4, no. 23 (December 8, 1934): 37.

53. "Fourth Estate. Flemington: 11,500,000 Words, Words, Words, Words, Words," *News-Week* 5, no. 7 (February 16, 1935): 36.

54. Dr. Paul Wolff, *My First Ten Years with the Leica*, trans. by H. W. Zieler (New York: B. Westermann, 1935): 25, 37.

55. Schulman, *Where's Sammy?*, 50.

56. Cited in Tim N. Gidal, *Modern Photojournalism: Origin and Evolution, 1910–1933* (New York: Macmillan, 1973), 17.

57. Faber, *Great News Photos,* 52.

58. Ibid., 65.

59. Frank J. Scherschel and Stanley E. Kalish, "News and Press Photography," in *Graphic Graflex Photography,* ed. Willard D. Morgan and Henry M. Lester (New York: Morgan and Lester Publishers, 1940), 261.

60. Cited in Jack Hurley, *Portrait of a Decade* (Baton Rouge: Louisiana State University Press, 1972), 42, 44.

61. John Szarkowski, *From the Picture Press* (New York: Museum of Modern Art, 1973), 5.

62. "Be a News Photographer," *Time* 20 (November 14, 1932): 20.

63. John Szarkowski, *Photography Until Now* (New York: Museum of Modern Art, 1989), 212.

64. Gramling, *AP: The Story of News,* 334. See also Ezickson, *Get That Picture!*, 28; Vitray, Mills, Ellard, *Pictorial Journalism,* 19; Mott, *American Journalism,* 684.

65. Bent, *Ballyhoo,* xv–xvi.

66. "Veteran Chicago Cameraman Dies," *National Press Photographer* 3, no. 11 (November 1948): 14; Faber, *Great News Photos,* 36–37.

67. Faber, *Great News Photos,* 46–47.

68. Advertisement in *Camera* 48, no. 4 (April 1934): [292].

69. "New Books," *Camera* 43, no. 1 (July 1931): 75.

70. "Questions and Answers," *Camera* 19, no. 12 (December 1915): 749; Jane Livingston with Frances Fralin and Declan Haun, *Odyssey: The Art of Photography at National Geographic* (Charlottesville, Va.: Thomasson-Grant, 1988), 25, 27.

71. "National Geographic Society," *National Geographic* 21, no. 12 (December 1910): 1074.

72. *Mid-Week Pictorial,* December 26, 1918, p. 24.

73. Keith Kenney, "*Mid-Week Pictorial*: Pioneer American Photojournalism Magazine," paper presented to the Visual Communication Division of the Association for Education in Journalism and Mass Communication Conference, Norman, Oklahoma, August 1986, 7–8.

74. Robert T. Elson, *Time Inc.: The Intimate History of a Publishing Enterprise, 1923–1941* (New York: Atheneum, 1968), 7–8.

75. Cited in Hicks, *Words and Pictures,* 37.

76. Daniel Longwell, office memorandum to Ralph Ingersoll, January 14, 1936. Time, Inc. Archive, Time-Life Building, New York, New York. Cited in C. Zoe Smith, "Germany's Kurt Korff: An Emigré's Influence on Early *Life*," *Journalism Quarterly* 65, no. 2 (summer 1988).

77. Margaret Bourke-White, *Portrait of Myself* (New York: Simon and Schuster, 1963), 62.

78. Ibid., 63–64, 68. See also Vicki Goldberg, *Margaret Bourke-White: A Biography* (Reading, Mass.: Addison-Wesley Publishing, 1987), 101–3.

79. Gidal, *Modern Photojournalism,* 28.

80. Smith, "Germany's Kurt Korff," 417–18.

81. Kurt Korff, letter of resignation to Henry Luce, July 31, 1936. Time, Inc. Archive, Time-Life Building, New York, New York. Cited by Smith, "Germany's Kurt Korff," 419.

82. Gardner Cowles, *Mike Looks Back* (New York: Gardner Cowles, 1985), 44.

83. Ibid., 59.

84. Robert E. Girvin, "Photography as Social Documentation," *Journalism Quarterly* 24, no. 3 (September 1947): 213.

85. Ezickson, *Get That Picture!*, 41.

86. Schulman, *Where's Sammy?*, 103–4.

87. Cited in Dan Perkes, *Eyewitness to Disaster* (New York: Gallery Books, 1985), 63.

88. "Life on the American Newsfront: The *Hindenburg* Makes Her Last Landing at Lakehurst," and "Amateur Photographs the *Hindenburg*'s Last Landing," *Life* 2, no. 20 (May 17, 1937): 26–28.

# SELECTED BIBLIOGRAPHY


Ackerman, Carl W. *George Eastman*. Boston: Houghton Mifflin, 1930.

Alland, Alexander, Sr. *Jacob A. Riis: Photographer and Citizen*. Preface by Ansel Adams. New York: Aperture, 1993.

———. *Jessie Tarbox Beals: First Woman News Photographer*. New York: Camera/Graphic Press, 1978.

Baker, Ray Stannard. *American Chronicle*. New York: Charles Scribner's Sons, 1945.

Barsam, Richard Meran. *Non-Fiction Film: A Critical History*. Foreword by Richard Dyer MacCann. New York: E. P. Dutton, 1973.

Bendavid-Val, Leah. *National Geographic: The Photographs*. Foreword by Gilbert M. Grosvenor. Washington, D.C.: National Geographic Society, 1994.

Bent, Silas. *Ballyhoo: The Voice of the Press*. New York: Horace and Liveright, 1927.

Bessie, Simon Michael. *Jazz Journalism: The Story of the Tabloid Newspapers*. New York: E. P. Dutton, 1938.

Bourke-White, Margaret. *Portrait of Myself*. New York: Simon and Schuster, 1963.

Brayer, Elizabeth. *George Eastman: A Biography*. Baltimore: Johns Hopkins University Press, 1996.

Carmichael, Jane. *First World War Photographers*. London: Routledge, 1989.

Carnes, Cecil. *Jimmy Hare, News Photographer: Half a Century with a Camera*. New York: Macmillan, 1940.

Chapelle, Dickey. *What's a Woman Doing Here? A Reporter's Report on Herself*. New York: William Morrow, 1962.

Clendenen, Clarence C. *The United States and Pancho Villa: A Study in Unconventional Diplomacy*. Ithaca, N.Y.: Cornell University Press, 1961.

Coe, Brian, and Paul Gates. *The Snapshot Photograph: The Rise of Popular Photography, 1888–1939*. London: Ash and Grant, 1977.

Cohen, Lester. *The New York Graphic: The World's Zaniest Newspaper*. Philadelphia: Chilton Books, 1964.

Coleman, Harry J. *Give Us a Little Smile, Baby*. New York: E. P. Dutton, 1943.

Cookman, Claude. *A Voice Is Born*. Durham, N.C.: National Press Photographers Association, 1985.

Cowles, Gardner. *Mike Looks Back*. New York: Gardner Cowles, 1985.

Creel, George. *Rebel at Large: Recollections of Fifty Crowded Years*. New York: G. P. Putnam's Sons, 1947.

Crozier, Emmet. *American Reporters on the Western Front*. New York: Oxford University Press, 1959.

Davis, Barbara A. *Edward S. Curtis: The Life and Times of a Shadow Catcher*. New York: Chronicle Books, 1985.

Doherty, R. J. *Social-Documentary Photography in the USA*. Garden City, N.Y.: American Photographic Book Publishing 1976.

Ellis, John. *Eye-Deep in Hell: Trench Warfare in World War I*. Baltimore: Johns Hopkins University Press, 1976.

Ezickson, Aaron Jacob. *Get That Picture! The Story of the News Cameraman*. New York: National Library Press, 1938.

Faber, John. *Great News Photos and the Stories Behind Them*. 2d rev. ed. New York: Dover Publications, 1978.

Fielding, Raymond. *The American Newsreel, 1911–1967*. Norman: University of Oklahoma Press, 1972.

Fleming, Paula Richardson, and Judith Lynn Luskey. *Grand Endeavors of American Indian Photography*. Washington, D.C.: Smithsonian Institution Press, 1993.

Ford, Edwin H., ed. *Selected Readings in the History of American Journalism*. Minneapolis: University of Minnesota Press, 1939.

Freund, Giselle. *Photography and Society*. Boston: David R. Godine, 1980.

Fulton, Marianne, ed. *Eyes of Time: Photojournalism in America*. Boston: Little, Brown, 1988.

Fussell, Paul. *The Great War and Modern Memory*. New York: Oxford University Press, 1975.

Galassi, Peter, and Susan Kismaric. *Pictures of the Times: A Century of Photography from The New York Times*. New York: Museum of Modern Art, 1996.

Genthe, Arnold. *As I Remember*. New York: Reynal and Hitchcock, 1936.

Gidal, Tim N. *Modern Photojournalism: Origin and Evolution, 1910–1933*. New York: Macmillan, 1973.

Gilbert, Martin. *The First World War: A Complete History*. New York: Henry Holt, 1994.

Goldberg, Vicki. *Margaret Bourke-White: A Biography*. Foreword by Phyllis Rose. Reading, Mass.: Addison-Wesley, 1987.

———. *The Power of Photography: How Photographs Changed Our Lives*. New York: Abbeville Press, 1991.

Goldsmith, Arthur. *The Camera and Its Images*. New York: Ridge Press, 1979.

Gramling, Oliver. *AP: The Story of News*. New York: Farrar and Rinehart, 1940.

Hales, Peter B. *Silver Cities: The Photography of American Urbanization, 1839–1915*. Philadelphia: Temple University Press, 1984.

Ham, Deborah Newman, ed. *The African-American Mosaic*. Washington, D.C.: Library of Congress, 1993.

Hare, James H. *A Photographic Record of the Russo-Japanese War*. New York: P. F. Collier and Son, 1905.

Heller, Jonathan, ed. *War and Conflict: Selected Images from the National Archives, 1765–1970*. Washington, D.C.: National Archives and Records Administration, 1990.

Hicks, Wilson. *Words and Pictures: An Introduction to Photojournalism*. New York: Harper and Brothers, 1952.

Hurley, Jack. *Portrait of a Decade*. Baton Rouge: Louisiana State University Press, 1972.

*Images of Our Times: Sixty Years of Photography from the Los Angeles Times*. Commentary by William F. Thomas, Jim Wilson, and Iris Schneider. New York: Harry N. Abrams, 1987.

Jackall, Robert, ed. *Propaganda*. New York: New York University Press, 1995.

[Johnston, Frances Benjamin.] *The Hampton Album*. Introduction and notes by Lincoln Kirstein. New York: Museum of Modern Art, 1966.

Kaplan, Daile. *Lewis Hine in Europe: The Lost Photographs*. New York: Abbeville Press, 1988.

———, ed. *Photo Story: Selected Letters and Photographs of Lewis W. Hine*. Foreword by Berenice Abbott. Washington, D.C.: Smithsonian Institution Press, 1992.

Kincaid, James C. *Press Photography*. Boston: American Photographic Book Publishing, 1936.

Kobre, Ken. *Photojournalism: The Professionals' Approach*. Somerville, Mass.: Curtin & London, 1980.

Kobre, Sidney. *The Yellow Press and Gilded Age Journalism*. Tallahassee: Florida State University Press, 1971.

Kozol, Wendy. *Life's America: Family and Nation in Post-war Photojournalism*. Philadelphia: Temple University Press, 1994.

Lester, Paul. *Photojournalism: An Ethical Approach*. Hillsdale, N.J.: Lawrence Erlbaum Associates, 1991.

*LIFE: The First Decade, 1936–1945*. Boston: New York Graphic Society, 1980.

Livingston, Jane, with Frances Fralin and Declan Haun. *Odyssey: The Art of Photography at National Geographic*. Charlottesville, Va.: Thomasson-Grant, 1988.

Lyman, Christopher. *The Vanishing Race and Other Illusions: Photographs of Indians by Edward S. Curtis*. New York: Pantheon Books, 1982.

McCabe, Charles R., ed. *Damned Old Crank: A Self-Portrait of E. W. Scripps*. New York: Harper and Brothers, 1951.

Miller, Francis Trevelyan. *Lindbergh: His Story in Pictures*. New York: G. P. Putnam's Sons, 1929.

Montague, Charles Edward. *Disenchantment*. London: Chatto and Windus, 1929.

Morgan, Willard D. and Lester, Henry M. *Graphic Graflex Photography*. New York: Morgan and Lester Publishers, 1940.

Mott, Frank Luther. *A History of American Magazines*. Vols. 4 (1885–1905), 5 (1905–1930). Cambridge, Mass.: Harvard University Press, 1957.

———. *American Journalism. A History: 1690–1960*. New York: Macmillan, 1962.

Mould, David H. *American Newsfilm 1914–1919. The Underexposed War*. New York: Garland Publishing, 1983.

Mydans, Carl. *More Than Meets the Eye*. New York: Harper and Brothers, 1959; Westport, Conn.: Greenwood Press, 1974.

———. *Carl Mydans, Photojournalist*. New York: Harry N. Abrams, 1985.

Powell, E. Alexander. *Fighting in Flanders*. New York: Grosset and Dunlop, 1915.

*Press Photography: Minnesota Since 1930*. Minneapolis: Walker Art Center, 1977.

Price, Jack. *News Pictures*. New York: Round Table Press, 1937.

Reynolds, Francis J., ed. *Collier's New Photographic History of the World's War*. New York: P. F. Collier and Son, 1919.

Riis, Jacob A. *The Battle With the Slum*. New York: Macmillan, 1902.

———. *The Children of the Poor*. Introduction by Rudolph J. Vecoli. New York: Johnson Reprint Corporation, 1970.

———. *The Making of an American*. New York: Macmillan, 1901.

Rosenblum, Naomi, Walter Rosenblum, and Alan Trachtenberg. *America and Lewis Hine*. New York: Aperture, 1977.

Scherman, David E., ed. *The Best of LIFE*. New York: Time-Life Books, 1973.

Schudson, Michael. *Discovering the News: A Social History of American Newspapers*. New York: Basic Books, 1978.

Schulman, Sammy. *Where's Sammy?*. Robert Considine, ed. New York: Random House, 1943.

Schuneman, R. Smith. *Photographic Communication. Principles, Problems and Challenges of Photojournalism*. New York: Hastings House, 1972.

Shepherd, William G. *Confessions of a War Correspondent*. New York: Harper and Brothers, 1917.

Stallings, Laurence, ed. *The First World War. A Photographic History*. New York: Simon and Schuster, 1933.

Stange, Maren. *Symbols of Ideal Life: Social Documentary Photography in America. 1890–1950*. Cambridge and New York: Cambridge University Press, 1989.

Steichen, Edward. *A Life in Photography*. New York: Doubleday, 1963.

Stevens, John D. *Sensationalism and the New York Press*. New York: Columbia University Press, 1991.

Stott, William. *Documentary Expression and Thirties America*. New York: Oxford University Press, 1973.

Swanberg, W. A. *Luce and His Empire*. New York: Charles Scribner's Sons, 1972.

Szarkowski, John, ed. *From the Picture Press*. New York: Museum of Modern Art, 1973.

Tebbel, John. *An American Dynasty. The Story of the McCormicks, Medills and Pattersons*. Garden City, NY: Doubleday, 1947.

Thomson, J[ohn] and Smith, Adolphe. *Street Life in London*. London: Sampson Low, Marston, Searle and Rivington, c. 1877; reprint ed., New York: Benjamin Blom, 1969.

Thompson, Donald C. *From Czar to Kaiser. The Betrayal of Russia*. New York: Doubleday, Page, 1918.

———. *The Crime of the Twentieth Century*. New York: Leslie-Judge, 1918.

Trachtenberg, Alan. *The Incorporation of America: Culture and Society in the Gilded Age*. New York: Hill and Wang, 1982.

Vanderwood, Paul J. and Samponaro, Frank N. *Border Fury: A Picture Postcard Record of Mexico's Revolution and U.S. War Preparedness, 1910–1917*. Albuquerque: University of New Mexico Press, 1988.

Vaughn, Stephen. *Holding Fast the Inner Lines: Democracy, Nationalism, and the Committee on Public Information*. Chapel Hill: University of North Carolina Press, 1980.

Weegee. *Naked City*. New York: E. P. Dutton, 1945; Da Capo Press, 1985.

———. *The Village*. New York: Da Capo Press, 1989.

Welling, William. *Photography in America: The Formative Years, 1839–1900*. New York: Thomas Y. Crowell, 1978.

Willis-Thomas, Deborah. *Black Photographers, 1840–1940: An Illustrated Bio-Bibliography*. New York: Garland Publishing, 1985.

Wolff, Dr. Paul. *My First Ten Years with the Leica*. New York: B. Westermann, n.d.

# INDEX

# P



# R



# S



# T



# U

## W

TYPESET IN BODONI BOOK WITH
COPPERPLATE DISPLAY BY
BLUE HERON, INC., LAWRENCE, KANSAS.

ALL VERSIONS OF BODONI ARE BASED ON
THE WORKS OF GIAMBATTISTA BODONI, A
MASTER PRINTER FROM 18TH CENTURY
ITALY. THE MOST POPULAR FACES OF
BODONI WERE DRAWN BY MORRIS F. BENTON
FOR AMERICAN TYPE FOUNDERS COMPANY
(ATF) OF ELIZABETH, NEW JERSEY, OR THEY
WERE LATER ADAPTED FROM BENTON'S
WORK BY OTHER MANUFACTURERS.
COPPERPLATE GOTHIC HEAVY WAS DESIGNED
BY FREDERIC W. GOUDY IN 1903.
ADDITIONAL WEIGHTS AND WIDTHS WERE
LATER DRAWN BY CLARENCE C. MARDER
FOR ATF.
AMERICAN TYPE FOUNDERS COMPANY WAS
FORMED IN 1892 WHEN TWENTY-THREE TYPE
FOUNDERS MERGED. MANY WORKS BY ATF
WERE ACQUIRED BY THE SMITHSONIAN
INSTITUTION IN 1970.

PRINTED ON 80 LB. FORTUNE MATTE BY
THOMSON-SHORE, INC., DEXTER, MICHIGAN.

DESIGNED BY LISA BUCK VANN.